THE INFORMED INVESTOR

A HYPE-FREE GUIDE TO CONSTRUCTING A SOUND FINANCIAL PORTFOLIO

Frank Armstrong III

AMACOM

American Management Association

New York • Atlanta • Brussels • Chicago • Mexico City • San Francisco
Shanghai • Tokyo • Toronto • Washington, D. C.

This publication is designed to provide accurate and authoritative
information in regard to the subject matter covered. It is sold
with the understanding that the publisher is not engaged in
rendering legal, accounting, or other professional service. If
legal advice or other expert assistance is required, the services of
a competent professional person should be sought.

Many of the illustrations contained in this book are reprinted or
adapted from *Stocks, Bonds, Bills & Inflation® 2001 Yearbook* © Ibbotson
Associates, Inc. Based on copyrighted works by Ibbotson and
Sinquefield. All rights reserved. Used with permission.

Library of Congress Cataloging-in-Publication Data

Armstrong, Frank III.
        The informed investor : a hype-free guide to constructing a sound financial
portfolio /
    Frank Armstrong III.
        p. cm.
    Includes bibliographical references and index.
    ISBN 0-8144-7250-8 (pbk.)
    1. Investments. 2. Portfolio management. I. Title.

HG4521.A72 2004
332.6—dc22

                                                                          2003020936

Printing number
10 9 8 7 6 5 4 3 2

For my parents:

Frank Armstrong, Jr.—
A good man gone too soon, but we never forget

Lois M. Armstrong—
Larger than life, an indomitable spirit, and a
lesson in courage

CONTENTS

LIST OF FIGURES

PREFACE TO THE PAPERBACK EDITION

The world has changed a great deal since the initial edition of *The Informed Investor* was "put to bed," so to speak. Basic financial economics has not. The message remains the same, although the audience may be more inclined to listen today. The last three years have devastated many investors. The carnage has been immense. The utter futility of "Voodoo Finance" has been laid bare for all to see.

Investors grope for better answers. Yet those better answers are available to anyone who cares to seek them out. Financial economists have learned a great deal about how markets work and how individuals can harness effectively those markets to achieve their goals with minimum cost and risk, and the highest probability of success. The timeless investment principals, strategies, and tactics I outline have been validated during some of the most dramatic events and worst market downturns since the Great Depression.

We all know the recent history: The tragedy of 9/11 followed by wars in Afghanistan and Iraq; financial scandals and the collapse of major international corporations; a slowing economy; a falling dollar; the tech stock/dot-com debacle. The list goes on and on. Some of these events are external, and we could not have foreseen them in our worst nightmares. It is clear that the world and its markets are risky places. Rather than react after the fact, you must design your investment strategy to anticipate randomness and to be hedged against adverse events.

Properly designed portfolios endured recent market shocks with minimal distress. Widely diversified, properly balanced strategies, while not flourishing, preserved capital while others hemorrhaged. Such portfolios are well positioned to profit from the inevitable recovery (which may be underway today). It goes without saying that your strategy should accept no more risk than you can afford financially and are comfortable with emotionally.

Many investors feel shocked, betrayed, brutalized, and bewildered. There's been damage aplenty: fortunes lost, retirements delayed, college funds squandered, and dreams destroyed. Such debacles were almost entirely avoidable. To a very large extent, burned investors have only themselves to blame. Informed investors who (1) knew the rules and (2) followed them escaped virtually unscathed.

That's right, Mother Market has rules! And if you don't follow them, she will administer some tough love sooner or later. Mother Market is a generous and benevolent force. She has issued a few basic commandments that, if followed, will lead to a successful investment experience and the attainment of your financial goals.

Being the basic free market capitalist that she is, Mother Market allows her children to exercise free choice. She will give you enough rope to hang yourself. Violate the rules and, eventually, she'll pull you up short. After being ignored for a decade, Mother Market made her point—decisively. The results are not pretty. She unleashed an almost perfect three-year market storm upon her wayward children.

Mother Market's rules are not difficult. Anyone with a high school diploma can easily grasp them. She doesn't accept ignorance as an excuse. Mother Market demands both knowledge and compliance. Fortunately, readers of *The Informed Investor* know the rules. If they took them to heart and applied them with discipline, the recent carnage was almost a nonevent.

So, just how did Mother Market's other wayward children get into so much trouble? How did so many get it so wrong? We could review a whole laundry list of investor faux pas, but that's all water over the dam now. Instead, start today to get it right. What better time to learn how the world's markets work, review your situation, and plan a strategy that will meet your exact needs while standing the test of time?

The mission of *The Informed Investor* is to do just that. I promise you a painless review of modern investment finance and a complete roadmap to develop and implement your own tailored asset allocation strategy that is as economical, effective, and sophisticated as any large institution can offer.

My mantra is: low cost, low risk, low tax cost, and effective strategies that offer the highest probability of success.

Your investments are your future. For good or for evil, today's investment policy will dictate tomorrow's reality. *The Informed Investor* can show you how to be financially successful, educate your children, and enjoy a safe retirement.

ACKNOWLEDGMENTS

Robert Carroll and Cebra Graves encouraged me in my early efforts to inform investors. Without their support, backing, and enthusiasm, I never would have had the courage to tackle writing.

Cathy Pareto labored cheerfully to proofread, prepare graphs, tables, and illustrations, through numerous revisions and updates. Without her determination and assistance, the project never would have succeeded.

Ray O'Connell and Mike Sivilli of AMACOM helped bring order out of chaos. Their patience and kindness with a neophyte author was remarkable.

Danette Brogno performed miracles by converting my numerous sloppy mistakes into the King's English.

Any remaining errors are all my fault.

ONE

INTRODUCTION

The *Informed Investor* will help you to make better investment decisions. Examining the best academic research, real-world experience, and institutional practices reveals better investment practices. Better investment decisions lead to lower costs, more predictable returns, lower risk, and lower taxes. They yield the highest possible opportunity to actually meet your financial goals.

The enemy of the informed investor is voodoo investing. Voodoo investing's witch doctors, shamans, and charlatans dominate popular discussion and mind-set. The voodoo investors are everywhere. They are loud and persistent. By comparison, the voices of informed investing have done a very poor job of getting our message out. Fortunately, we have right and reason on our side, but it will still be an uphill battle against the forces of darkness.

We are at the beginning of a powerful revolution in financial thought and practice. We have far better theory, technology, and products than our fathers could have dreamed of. Harnessing the power of this revolution will yield great benefits to you and your family.

To harness the power of modern finance, you must be prepared to abandon ideas and practices that are outmoded, counterproductive, and self-defeating. This is hard, I admit. Shedding a lifetime of preconceived ideas and ingrained prejudices requires some discipline. The temptation to backslide will be ever-present. You can, however, resist the lure of the dark side. Just as you once abandoned the tooth fairy, you can avoid voodoo finance. It is far better to deal with the world as it really is than to cling to superstition, alchemy, and magic formulas for success.

My job as your mentor and teacher is to make the journey to informed investing as painless, entertaining, and profitable as possible. We can have fun, avoid all those vexing textbook hieroglyphic formulas, and develop strategies and tactics that will economically and effectively meet your investment objectives.

DUMPING THE PERFORMANCE FAIRY

One of the chief obstacles to becoming an informed investor is the belief in a performance fairy. Unlike Tinkerbell, who flew around doing nice things, the performance fairy robs investors of their rightful gains. Performance fairies are really gremlins in disguise. By convincing unsuspecting people that it is easy to beat Mother Market, they induce investors to do all kinds of crazy things. Unfortunately, the damage that they do is far from trivial.

Because performance fairies are part of the official religion of Wall Street, most investors believe in one form or another of these gremlins. There are several well-known variations of performance fairy, and investors may shift allegiance from one to another at various times. These belief shifts most often occur when a well-known performance fairy appears to have lost his magic, or when another one demonstrates a miraculous burst of juju power.

If you believe in performance fairies, you are convinced that somewhere out there is one that can "beat the market." You might even believe that you yourself are a performance fairy. You persist in this delusion against all the available evidence, but remember, it is extraordinarily difficult to beat Mother Market. Few actually do it over the long haul, but many a fool continues to confuse pure, dumb luck with skill.

I admit that Mother Market is often capricious and nobody really understands her. That's the nature of complex systems. However, while she is a little quirky, Mother Market provides for her children through the miracle of capitalism. That's all you really have to believe. If you embrace Mother Market you will find her benign, benevolent, and bountiful.

The central fallacy, and core belief, of all performance fairies is that Mother Market does not do her job properly. That's what we refer to as market inefficiencies. Furthermore, performance fairies claim to predict the future. Some believe that they can divine the intent of Mother Market. Others believe that they can tell which of Mother Market's children will thrive and which will fail. Although this has never worked before, they stubbornly cling to their pagan beliefs.

You must begin to realize that the performance fairy isn't coming. Get over it. The performance fairy never delivered, and you are far better off without him. Informed investors know that making decisions in an atmosphere of uncertainty is difficult. They don't demand miracles. They don't rely on magic. They don't need to. There is a huge body of academic theory and real-world experience that will help you make better investment decisions without resorting to voodoo finance. The enormous revolution in finance brings to us better theory, better products, and lower costs. Once you give up on the impossible, you can focus effectively on the possible. Markets work pretty well, at least in the long run. You can make far more progress by riding that wave rather than fighting it.

You can get better returns, control risk, lower costs, lower taxes, and design investment plans with the highest probability of actually meeting your goals. You don't need an advanced degree. You don't need any inside information or friends on the trading floor. You can apply the very latest financial research to your investment portfolio and ape the practices of leading-edge institutions.

We will soon find out there is no free lunch. You must do your part. That means learning the basics about how markets actually work, exercising discipline, and changing your self-destructive behavior. That's not too much effort, is it? And there's a big upside: You can turn off all that noise and get a life.

Like any other superstition, belief in performance fairies lacks any shred of credible evidence. Nevertheless, the various voodoo priests, shamans, witch doctors, false profits, and charlatans are so loud, persistent, and prominent that most investors simply accept them. The dark side is strong. Misguided people tend to stay misguided. All they ever get for their delusions is higher costs, higher risks, and lower performance than Mother Market would have given them. However, before condemning average investors, let's stop to consider that the popular media reinforces their delusions at every turn. One example is the wide acceptance of the fallacy that data and information are the keys to generating excess returns.

DROWNING IN DATA

It is relentless and remorseless. The stately drip, drip of financial information a few years ago has turned into a torrent of data that spews out of every faucet. Around the clock, around the world, twenty-four hours a day, 365 days a year, somewhere a market is trading. There is no trade too obscure, no market too small to escape attention and analysis.

During any lulls in the action, instant replays provide a thorough postmortem of yesterday's battle. Little lines of information scroll and dance across television screens telling their own chronicle of events. We have plenty of chances to get a jump on tomorrow's trading. There is no end of opinion about the likely tone at opening bell.

Information comes at you from all directions: e-mail, television, the Internet, radio, newspapers, pagers, and magazines. The demand for—and supply of—financial information is insatiable. There are hundreds of magazines, newsletters, newspapers, television networks, radio stations, billboards, and Web sites dedicated to filling this demand. All of them clamor for attention and compete for market share, influence, advertisers, and revenue.

Unfortunately, it's all a waste of time. The sum total value of all that information, data, spin, opinion, commentary, and just plain, old-fashioned bull is far less than zero. You can listen your entire life to this "advice" without ever improving your investment returns. None of it will help you to understand how markets work or how to make them work for you. It's all just noise, and it will lead you in just the wrong direction. Instead of providing enlightenment, all this drivel reinforces belief in the performance fairy.

If up-to-date financial data and information improved results, then we should all expect above-average market returns with reduced risk. Clearly that's not happening. For all the attention lavished on financial news, for all the hype and the time investors spend digesting the data, they are still getting lousy returns. In fact, over their lifetimes most investors obtain only a small fraction of the results that they should expect. So, it's not working. The answer to this problem isn't more of the same. Beating that old, dead horse is not going to improve it.

The information deluge is symptomatic of a larger problem. Investors are poorly educated about the financial system. Their chances of obtaining meaningful insight from the traditional sources are remote. Schools rarely teach financial economics, thereby overlooking a critical survival skill for modern man. Most of the popular press is focused on selling advertising space, papers, or airtime rather than providing fundamental guidance. Wall Street maximizes its own profits so that any positive returns enjoyed by retail investors are simply a happy coincidence. A commission-based distribution system so badly taints the advice process that investors stand little chance of receiving objective guidance from most brokers, financial planners, and other financial institution representatives. In this jungle investors wander at their peril.

The bottom line for investors is that they must take responsibility for their own education. Starting here. Starting now. *The Informed Investor* will help you make that journey. In the first part of our expedition, we will examine the major findings of financial economics over the last thirty years and explain the practical applications for individuals. Then we will show you how to economically and effectively build a portfolio, tailored to your exact needs, that's as good as any major institution's.

Along the way we are going to have a little fun. This stuff is easy, once you get over the idea that you will have to relearn some of the stuff you think you already know. True, the performance fairy has got to go, but you will be far better served to place your faith in Mother Market. She delivers.

At any point before, during, or after your reading *The Informed Investor*, feel free to visit my Web site at www.InvestorSolutions.com. You will find hundreds of current articles on investing and financial planning. While you are there, take the opportunity to sign up for our free newsletter: *The Enlightened Investor*. Direct comments, questions, and flames to frank@InvestorSolutions.com. I will look forward to hearing from you.

GATHERING INTELLIGENCE

A good general gathers intelligence about the enemy prior to forming a strategy. A good investor gathers information about his friend, the market, before he forms his investment strategies. Fortunately for investors, gigabytes of useful market data are readily available for analysis.

Let's start at the beginning—rates of return. As we shall see, rates of return are directly linked to the amount of risk that we are willing to assume. We make returns because we are willing to assume risk, not in spite of risk. Rates of return vary in different markets because we have different levels of risk. By examining long-term returns, we smooth out the short-term fluctuations that can be so confusing. Long-term returns establish the range of reasonableness that should anchor our expectations for investment.

The original process of gathering this information on rates of return was a Herculean task. The laborers have never been properly recognized. We are all deeply in debt to researchers like Ibbotson and Sinqfield, organizations like the Center for Research in Securities Prices (CRISP), and hundreds of other individuals who worked in obscurity. The data they assembled is enormously valuable to us. Armed with it, we can begin to see clearly what is going on in the marketplace. With a clean database and a modern computer, researchers can sift, sort, analyze, and test their hypotheses. The forest, previously hidden by all those pesky leaves and trees, becomes visible.

Today we take this information for granted, but our grandfathers didn't have anything like it. It wasn't until the mid-1960s that a researcher was able to show that stocks outperformed bonds. Similarly, we take our computers for granted. They weren't always there, either. The first primitive PCs were introduced about twenty years ago. Today, the average 386 computer has more capacity than the United States had at its disposal during the entire Korean War. Astoundingly, in 1969, NASA put a man on the moon with far less computing capacity than is available on my "old" 486 computer.

Now, all this information is instantly available worldwide. Investors no longer need to be in financial capitals. You or I can track trades at the same time that a trader in Hong Kong or New York does. We have access to the same databases and research that Wall Street's barons have. Our grandfathers couldn't have even dreamed about these powerful tools. It's up to us to adapt this new information and the insights we glean from it as we construct our investment strategies for the twenty-first century.

RATES OF RETURN

Investing is a multidimensional process. Of course, the first dimension is rate of return. The basic economic dilemma is this: Should we consume now or later? Given that our wants and needs are almost infinite, we have a strong preference for immediate consumption. Instant gratification isn't a concept developed by the yuppies. If we are going to delay gratification, then most of us demand a reasonable prospect of payback and profit. Otherwise, we might as well enjoy it now.

A person seeking profit can choose from a number of markets. Cash, stocks, and bonds are the traditional liquid markets which most of us first consider. There are also options, currencies, futures, commodities, and other more exotic derivatives that are freely traded and totally liquid. Or an investor might want to consider real estate, fine artwork, baseball cards, stamps, coins, or other valuable tangibles.

We shall see that each market can be broken down into smaller and smaller submarkets. Furthermore, each submarket, or segment, may have distinct properties that an informed investor will want to understand before placing any funds. I will restrict my discussions to examining the traditional cash, stocks, and bonds and how we can form them into portfolios that will meet our needs.

The different markets have produced greatly different average rates of return over a long period of time. In the short term, on a fairly regular basis, markets will vary around the averages. These short-term variations are aberrations when viewed from the long-term perspective. Short periods of over- or underperformance are sooner or later reversed as the markets regress to the mean. Looking at the long-term data gives us a fair platform for evaluating markets. It provides us with a powerful tool to estimate the "ranges of reasonableness" when we build or evaluate our portfolios. Investors ignore this data at their peril.

We all know that if it sounds too good to be true, it probably is. Long-term data gives us the yardstick to measure whether something is too good to be true. You will buy a lot less pie in the sky if you keep this in mind.

Later we will see that individual investors are often their own worst enemies. Investor behavior can be extraordinarily shortsighted. Foolish investors insist on making their long-term decisions based on very recent experience. Lemming-like, they run from gloom and doom to euphoria. In the process, basic discipline flies out the window, and bad things happen to their investment results. Remembering long-term results can keep individual investors from shooting themselves in the foot. A long-term outlook will stiffen resolve to stick with a well-thought-out investment plan.

DEFINITIONS

A few basic definitions are in order here before we go on to discuss rates of return:

- ■ *The Consumer Price Index (CPI).* The consumer price index is a commonly used measure of inflation. Inflation is the erosion of buying power over time, if dollars are used as a store of value. Investment returns must be adjusted by the inflation index in order for us to evaluate "real" returns. In other words, our returns must jump this hurdle in order to provide meaningful increases in value.

- *Treasury Bills (T-Bills).* T-bills are short-term obligations issued by the U.S. government. Because the government guarantees them and the government can always print more dollars, they carry no credit risk. Treasury bills are considered "zero risk" instruments in many academic discussions. We shall see that that is not always the case. T-bills are a good proxy for many savings plans and they track certificate of deposit (CD) rates reasonably close.

- *Treasury Bonds.* Treasury bonds are longer-term obligations issued by the government. They also carry no credit risk, but there is a substantial capital risk as interest rates change prior to redemption. An existing bond's value changes inversely as interest rates change in the economy. We will discuss these bonds later in more detail.

- *Commercial Bonds.* These bonds represent long-term debts issued by corporations. They carry both a default or credit risk and a capital risk as interest rates change. They are usually issued with a fixed interest rate (coupon) payable every six months. Bonds are also generally issued with a maturity date, at which time they are redeemed for the face amount of the bond. While a commercial bond may default and become worthless, it can never be worth more than the face amount at maturity. The corporation has no other obligation other than to pay the interest and principal upon maturity. Bondholders usually have no say in the operation of the corporation unless the interest payment is in default. Bonds may be issued with specific assets of the corporation to back up the corporate debt, or as a general obligation of the firm. Treasury bills, treasury bonds, commercial bonds, cash, savings accounts, and CDs are all debt instruments.

- *Stocks.* Stocks represent ownership or equity in a corporation. Stocks may or may not pay a dividend. If a stock pays a dividend, it may change in amount from time to time and the dividend is not guaranteed to continue. Like bonds, stocks may become worthless if a company fails. Unlike bonds, if the company prospers there is no theoretical limit to the increase in value and no redemption date. As owners of the corporation, stockholders are entitled to vote on the board of directors and may influence the operation of the company.

- *Large Company Stocks.* Domestic companies equal in size to those in the top half of the New York Stock Exchange (NYSE).

- *Small Cap Stocks.* Small cap stocks (as I'll be referring to them) are equal in size to the smallest 20 percent of the NYSE-traded firms. (Small is a relative term. If a firm is traded on the NYSE, it has already reached a respectable size.)

The foregoing definitions are generalizations. My aim is to keep things simple and not get bogged down in terminology. Of course, there are hybrid investment instruments such as convertible bonds and preferred stocks. These securities have some properties of both stocks and bonds. If you want to know more about them, there are plenty of good finance books available that you can use in your research of these securities. You will find some of them listed on my bookshelf in the archives. However, for now, let us move on.

A LOOK AT THE LONG-TERM DATA

The following figures show performance data from 1926 to 2002. What can we learn from all this? Plenty!

First, let's look at compound rates of return since 1926 in the broad domestic markets we just defined (see Figure 2-1). Then let's look at Figure 2-2 to see how a dollar grew from 1926 to 2002. Due to the magic of compounding, what seems like a relatively small difference in rate of return will compound to giant differences in total accumulation. Look at the difference over time when we move from the large company stocks to small company stocks.

THE RANGE OF REASONABLENESS

Long-term data gives us some very useful yardsticks. The 1980s and early 1990s were especially good for both stocks and bonds. However, in the late 1960s and early 1970s bad things happened to America. The Vietnam War divided the country as an entire generation watched senseless and violent death on national television over dinner each evening. Protesters took to the streets and grew violent themselves. Groups like the Symbionese Liberation Army (SLA) and the Weathermen conducted campaigns of

Figure 2-1. Average return 1926-2002.

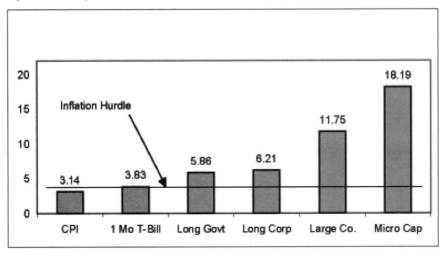

Figure 2-2. Real returns 1926-2002.

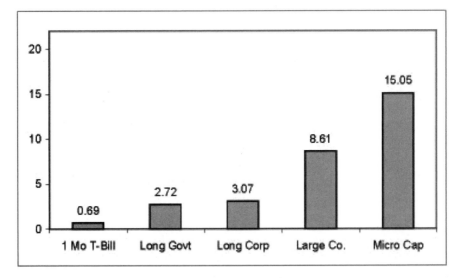

terror with bombings, kidnappings, robberies, and murder. The government became increasingly paranoid. The Nixon administration and J. Edgar Hoover's FBI systematically violated our constitutional rights. The National Guard shot peaceful protesters on their college campus at Kent State University. Both a president and vice president resigned in disgrace from office and narrowly missed jail sentences. Nixon administration

Figure 2-3. Growth of $1, 1926-2002.

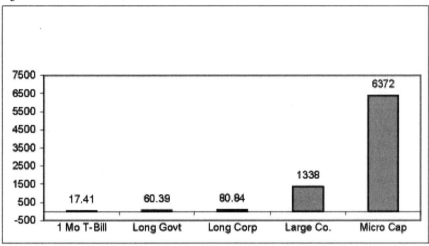

Figure 2-4. Real growth of $1, 1926-2002.

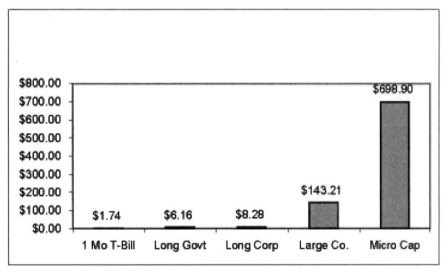

henchmen marched off one by one to prison. The public's belief in government was sorely tried.

On the economic front, things were just as bad. We charged the costs of the Vietnam War and Lyndon Johnson's Great Society. When the bill came due, OPEC cut off the oil. The government deficit mushroomed. Inflation soared, and interest rates climbed to unheard-of heights.

American industry became bloated and could not compete effectively on the international markets. The stock market accurately reflected the economic turmoil. In the 1970s investments on returns on investments could, at best, be called dismal. During 1973–1974 the large company stocks dropped 50 percent. Rising interest rates brutalized bond investors.

The 1980s saw some financial recovery. Over twenty years of concerted government policy steadily brought down inflation and interest rates. American industry painfully modernized and became competitive. Bondholders were rewarded by falling interest rates and reaped rewards far in excess of coupon rates. Stock market returns rebounded after the previous lost decade. Even after two short "crashes" in 1986 and 1989, investors realized fantasy gains. Some of those gains evaporated as economic realism set in during 2000–2002, but the past decades's returns remain above average.

As a result, investors have come to expect rates of return that are greatly higher than the historical averages. I view these recent returns as an aberration. There is no data to indicate that either rates of return or risk premium have changed in any fundamental way. We are not all entitled to returns in the high teens or low twenties as a birthright. In any event, it seems foolish to project these rates on into the indefinite future. Investors who do use 1980s returns to predict skyrocket rates do themselves serious financial injuries. These "poor" investors are often guilty of following three unsound practices:

1. *They set themselves up to endlessly chase rainbows.* As they fail to attain unrealistic goals, they often move from advisor to advisor or scheme to scheme to their detriment. In the process, they inadvertently churn their own accounts. Wall Street is only too eager to help. The brokerage community is ever ready to promise far more than they can ever deliver to get the business. Investors who achieve, or advisors who deliver only solid realistic results, are at a distinct disadvantage in an atmosphere of hype and perfect twenty-twenty hindsight.

2. *They often place faith in an accumulation plan based on a higher-than-realistic rate of return projection.* Thus, they may be setting aside far too little to meet their long-term goals.

3. *They may also be living off their nest eggs.* Many establish withdrawal plans based on rates of return they cannot achieve in order to finance lifestyles they can no longer afford. They run the very

real risk of causing their capital to implode, and they will become destitute in their old age.

SAVINGS VS. INVESTMENT

Many academics might quibble, but I find it useful to distinguish between savings and investment. Savings might include all the debt instruments, cash, T-bills, bonds, CDs, and annuities. Investments (equity) offer a long-term return sufficient to overcome inflation. Because investments are traded each day, they fluctuate in value. If you don't have long-term return both above inflation and fluctuation, you have a savings plan. (Fluctuation is a nice, nonthreatening way to say that sometimes prices will go down! We really shouldn't sugarcoat this little fact—it's built right into the system. Later, we will discuss fluctuation in more detail.)

Notice that the little boxes on the left of all the charts in this chapter represent debt or savings, while the tall boxes on the right represent equity. A saver who put a dollar into T-bills in 1926, and who faithfully reinvested the proceeds for seventy-seven years, saw his savings only grow to $1.18 on an after-tax, after-inflation basis! In other words, the dollar you put away in 1926, together with all the earnings on it, won't buy as many Cokes or ice cream cones today.

The data shows that savers must abandon hope of achieving an after-tax, after-inflation rate of return. Think of CD as standing for constantly diminishing. The stability of CDs does not translate into long-term security. Viewed from this perspective, the government-guaranteed savings plans are not wise, conservative, or responsible. They are actually almost guaranteed to shrink in value. Even when interest rates are high, savings are a bankrupt investment policy. Many savers fondly look back over the last twenty years of high interest rates. But even if all interest was reinvested, the after-tax, after-inflation rate of return on CDs from 1975 to 2002 was only 2.15 percent. Interest rates are high during periods of inflation. A progressive tax eats away more at the higher nominal rates of return. Later we will examine how inflation ravages a fixed return over time. If a saver attempts to live off the interest on his nest egg, the results are catastrophic over time. He better hope not to live very long.

Zero-risk rates of return are very closely tied to inflation rates. So if you just want to keep up with inflation, you can accomplish that limited objective with debt instruments, but not much more. Most of us want an inflation hedge, growth, and the ability to make withdrawals. Debt instruments haven't been able to support that. Savings are a unique and treacherous form of capital punishment. Every day, millions of well-meaning savers unnecessarily punish their capital and prevent it from growing and thriving.

Another way to look at the data is to say that equity has returned about inflation plus 6 percent to 8 percent rate of return. Many advisors set the real rate of return as a long-term target. Anyone who builds his financial empire on a required rate of return of higher than 8 percent is skating on very thin ice indeed.

Long-term data provides us with the information to conduct a vital reality check on savings and investment. Prudence and realism dictate use of the more conservative data for planning. And, no matter how you look at it, equity returns swamp anything available in debt. Only equity offers investors the prospect of real rates of return. So why isn't everybody investing in equity? We'll examine the answer to this question in Chapter 3, which deals with the investor's four-letter word: risk.

THREE

ASSESSING THE RISK

isk is the investor's four-letter word. Everybody is risk-averse. We all would prefer a certain, or riskless, result. It's rational and normal to be concerned about investment risk. Yet at some point, normal concern becomes irrational fear. That exaggerated fear keeps too many Americans from making appropriate investment choices. Understanding the nature of risks and how they can be managed and mitigated will help you to be a more successful and confident investor.

Investment risk can be an extraordinary stress for many people. I have seen investors throw up when the value of their portfolio drops by 5 percent. Others worry themselves sick over a long period of time. Perhaps that shouldn't surprise us. After all, we live in a society that judges happiness, security, power, and prestige by the number of zeros in a bank account. Money takes on a sacred aura, so any threat to wealth, even a temporary one, seems life-threatening.

Risk aversion is not a matter of personal courage. I know combat-tested fighter pilots, infantry officers, and tank commanders who cannot make themselves leave their comfortable, "safe" CDs. I believe in many cases that risk aversion is a fear of the unknown, a feeling of being out of control or of not knowing how bad things might get. Without solid information on the threat, risk becomes a twelve-foot-tall bogeyman!

The conventional image of the stock market as something that's treacherous and dangerous certainly contributes to the problem. As we have seen, the conventional viewpoint is often wrong. In fact, stocks have been a highly reliable engine of wealth for long-term investors. In this chapter we will demonstrate that market risk is almost exclusively a short-term phenomenon that decreases and falls over time and that not participating in the market may be one of the biggest risks of all.

Even investors who are comfortable with risk will benefit from a better understanding of what it is, where it comes from, how it is measured, and how it can be managed. Later we will use this information to construct efficient portfolios to meet your individual needs. Efficient means that either we will obtain the maximum amount of return for any level of risk we choose to bear, or meet our rate-of-return objective with the least amount of risk

A WORLD WITHOUT RISK

Just for a second, let's try to imagine an investment world where there was only one dimension: rate of return. In that environment, investment choices might look like Figure 3-1.

Figure 3-1. One-dimension investment: rate of return.

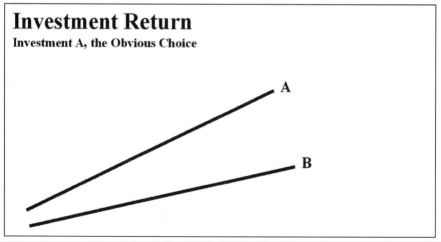

Investment Return

Investment A, the Obvious Choice

A

B

All returns are certain. Investors would, of course, decide that more is better. So everyone would want investment A. No one would consider investment B. Investment B would cease to exist as a choice for lack of takers. Everyone would get the same investment result and no one could aspire to a higher rate of return.

Risk Offers the Chance for Higher Returns

Now let's imagine a second dimension. Investment choices might look like Figure 3-2.

Figure 3-2. Investment returns with variable results based on risk.

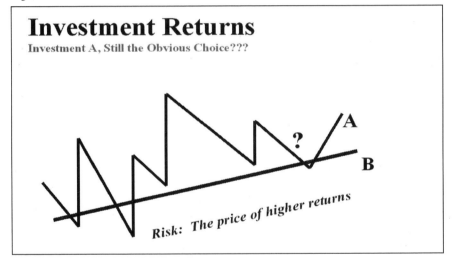

Investment B offers a known outcome. Investment A introduces an amount of uncertainty. The results are variable.

The Investor's Dilemma

True choice now exists. Investors face a dilemma. They prefer a certain result. However, they also want the higher returns offered by investment A. They are trapped between wanting a certain result and wanting more. Some investors will opt for the known result, and some will decide to go for the higher rate of return.

Risk is, of course, the primary concern of investors. Acceptance of risk is what separates our savings from investments. Successful investors must come to terms with the implications of accepting risk. They know they cannot have it both ways. They cannot hope for higher returns without accepting the fluctuation, and they must realize that all fluctuations are not positive. Not every day will be uniformly wonderful. Successful investors must be honest about their tolerance for risk and resist the temptation to second-guess their strategy when the inevitable bad day arrives. Bad days are built right into the investment strategy. As we shall see, there should be many more good days than bad, and we will make more during the good days than we will lose during the bad. However, it makes no sense to pretend that bad days aren't going to come.

Investors who pretend that they are somehow exempt from risk set themselves up for disaster. One of the very worst things an investor can do is accept a risk with the expectation that his investments will only go straight up. Markets do not work that way. And investors who don't understand that will fall prey to the buy high, sell low, vicious downward spiral syndrome. The time to fully understand your risk tolerance and the risks in your investment portfolio is before you make your investments.

In economic theory we all have many different combinations of risk and reward that we find equally attractive. If we were to plot all those combinations, the resulting line would be called our indifference curve. We have to examine the concept of indifference curves once more in relation to Modern Portfolio Theory (MPT). Since I have never found a real, live investor who has plotted this indifference curve, we won't spend too much time on it. I have to confess that I have no idea what mine would look like.

The amount of additional return, which must be offered to an investor in order to pry him away from his known result, is called the risk premium. The belief that investors often change their risk premiums as a result of recent events goes a long way toward explaining market excesses and the lemming-like behavior of investors.

REEXAMINING RISK

Some words have such a strong emotional impact that, once they come up in conversation, normal dialogue may be impossible. Words like that are sometimes referred to as loaded. Risk is a loaded word. When the subject of risk comes up, investors often become visibly uncomfortable. The conversation can become quickly strained. I've often wondered why risk has a bad rap.

As an investment counselor, one of my concerns is to convince investors to take at least enough risk to meet their objectives. However, many investors have a mental equation that says:

$$\text{RISK} \rightarrow \text{LOSS} \rightarrow \text{RUIN}$$

I look at the problem a little differently. My equation is:

$$\text{RISK} \rightarrow \text{GAIN} \rightarrow \text{RICHES!}$$

In studying both equations, I'm reminded of the guard in *Cool Hand Luke* who said to Paul Newman: "What we have here is a failure to communicate." I wonder how to get potential clients out of their CDs while they wonder if I haven't been flying a little too high without my oxygen mask.

Investing Is Not Gambling

Investors often lump all risks together and equate them with gambling as something bad. Of course, you have every reason to expect to win. As in every other part of life, there are both good and bad risks, and it's pretty easy to tell which is which.

Not All Risks Are Created Equal

Good Risks	Bad Risks
Compensated	Uncompensated
Highly confident of winning	Highly confident of losing
The odds are stacked in your favor.	The odds are stacked against you.
The longer you play, the more certain you are to win.	The longer you play, the more certain you are to be wiped out.
Rational	Irrational
Positive sum	Negative or zero sum
Smart	Dumb

High-probability shot	Long shot
Shrewd investment	Sucker's bet
Winner's game	Loser's game

The keyword for investors is "compensation." Investors should demand compensation for taking risks, and they should avoid any uncompensated risks.

A large part of investment success depends on staying away from sucker's bets or uncompensated risks. An investor who asks: "How certain am I that I will be compensated for taking this risk?" has gone a long way to solve investment problems.

As we shall see, uncompensated risks are hiding everywhere. One of our primary objectives will be to identify them and then ruthlessly eliminate them from our portfolios.

THE CASINO

It's important not to confuse investing with gambling. Gamblers should expect to lose; investors should expect to win. If you think that investing is gambling, you may not play at all. That would be a terrible mistake. You must understand the fundamental differences between the two.

First, let's admit that both investing and gambling possess a degree of uncertainty. Gamblers should wonder how long it will be before they are wiped out. Long-term investors wonder how much they will earn.

Walk through any casino. The first thing you must understand is that you will not see an even and fair game anywhere. Every game in the casino is stacked against you. The only remote exception is blackjack. Here, if you can keep track of the cards in six decks, you may be able to win. However, your reward will be short-lived. You will be photographed and have your picture circulated to other casinos. Then, you will be firmly asked to leave. If you persist and insist on staying, you will find management becomes distinctly unfriendly. The casino is dedicated to making sure suckers never get an even break.

Of course, somewhere in the casino someone is always on a roll. Even in a stacked game, the suckers have to get a few rewards to keep them coming back. A great deal of attention will be lavished on the few temporary winners. At the slots, bells will ring, lights flash, and a girl in a short skirt will deliver your winnings. It's important to keep up the illusion of winning but, you can rest assured, you will never get a fair bet.

The house has a great investment. The only real risk it faces is that not enough gullible people will show up to play. With the law of large numbers operating in their favor, the variations in earnings from gambling operations will be slight indeed.

The gambler may console himself with a discount meal, a fancy show, a little excitement, and a cheap room. But, make no mistake about it, gambling is a loser's game. The house wins every time. The gambler encounters a classic lose-lose situation, a classic negative sum game.

Gamblers justify their losing ways by mindlessly repeating: "High risk, high reward." They miss the point. Losers are addicted to high, uncompensated risk. Hoping to get lucky in a game stacked against you is a one-way ticket to disaster.

THE WALL STREET CASINO

Wall Street's casino is an entirely different animal. While there are plenty of sucker's bets being offered, there are also games so strongly rigged in the investor's favor that it requires superior skill and cunning in order to lose. Lots of investors lose, but the fault doesn't lie with the game. It rests with the total ineptness of the player.

Temptations to do something really stupid abound. There are lots of win-lose, negative-sum games being offered. You can expect to be carefully trained and continuously encouraged to act against your own interests.

The good news is that it is now very simple to sort out the opportunities. We can easily recognize risks for which we will be compensated, plot a strategy to maximize our benefits, and systematically whittle down the chances of being wrong. We can do this in an effective and economical manner. And, you don't have to have megabucks to participate. Investors of very modest means can design and implement strategies as sophisticated and effective as those of billion-dollar institutions.

While there is never a guarantee, long-term investors should expect to win. They should expect to win consistently. They should be highly confident that they will win. This wasn't always the case. But today the financial revolution offers us powerful insights and information that were not previously available, plus economical implementation, and high-tech solutions to simplify execution and monitoring of investments.

"Pure luck" doesn't dominate the investment process; rather, who wins and loses is determined by knowledge, strategy, and discipline.

So, get it out of your head that investing equals gambling and that all risks are created equal. In fact, there are a wide variety of risks that have always compensated long-term investors. Some investments have always compensated investors more than others. There is strong economic reason to expect that pattern to continue. It's reasonably easy to tell which is which. And finally, you can use this information to plot a successful financial and investment strategy.

DECISION MAKING IN AN ATMOSPHERE OF UNCERTAINTY

Nobody can predict the future. There is a certain amount of uncertainty in everything. As adults, we have to understand that there are no guarantees, ever. We must get used to the idea of planning in an atmosphere of uncertainty. But, uncertainty is not the same thing as chaos. We can adopt strategies with high probabilities of success.

We can't avoid risk. But we can use it effectively, manage it, and reduce it to its lowest possible level.

THE PROFESSIONAL'S VIEW

Stock market returns can be described as random distributions with a strong upward bias. Over a long period of time, returns in a market, or a particular part of a market, remain fairly constant. Periods of over- and undertrend performance are often followed by a regression to the mean.

Distributions around the average line fall in a rather predictable bell-shaped curve. Investment managers describe investment risk as deviation around the expected rate of return. They measure it with standard deviations. One standard deviation will contain about 68 percent of the expected future returns (see Figure 3-3). A small standard deviation will indicate a closer grouping around the average and less risk.

Figure 3-3. Standard deviations on investment return.

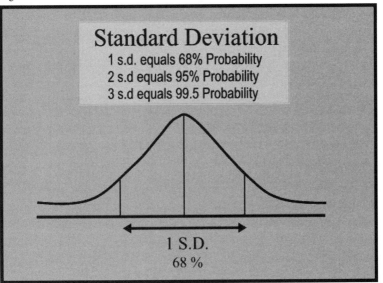

Since most of us don't think about standard deviations very much, there may be a more visual and intuitive way to look at it. The S&P 500 has an average rate of return of about 10 percent, as shown in Figure 3-4.

Figure 3-4. Average rate of return on the large company stocks.

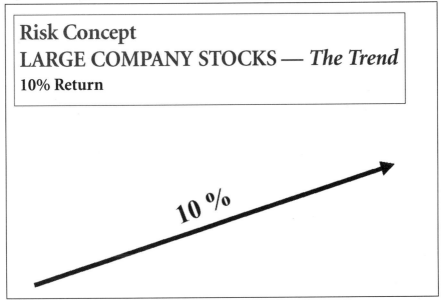

The standard deviation of the large company stocks is about 20 percent (see Figure 3-5). Sixty-eight percent of the time, results should fall between -10 percent and +30 percent. So we might call a return falling inside this range an average result.

Figure 3-5. Standard deviation of the large company stocks.

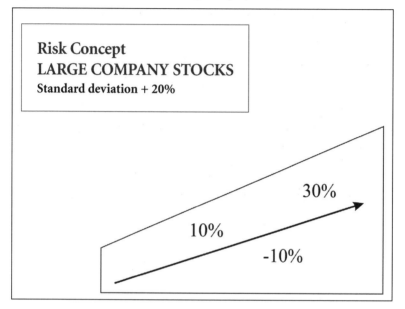

Risk Concept
LARGE COMPANY STOCKS
Standard deviation + 20%

30%

10%

-10%

Yet about 32 percent of the time, returns will fall outside of the range, as shown in Figure 3-6.

Thus, a result may fall outside of one standard deviation, but within two standard deviations (-30 percent to +50 percent). We might say that these are unusual returns. Returns will stay within two standard deviations about 95 percent of the time, or nineteen out of twenty years.

Returns may go outside the two standard deviation range. The three standard deviation range is from -50 percent to +70 percent. Results will fall within three standard deviations 99.5 percent of the time, or 199 out of 200 years. In layman's terms, we might describe a result over two standard deviations as very weird.

The smaller the variation around the expected result, the smaller the standard deviation and the smaller the risk. It's important to understand that risk doesn't necessarily mean loss. All investments vary a little from year to year, even savings accounts, so they have a measurable risk. But, in the case of savings accounts, we would never expect to have a loss.

Figure 3-6. Returns outside the standard deviation of the large company stocks.

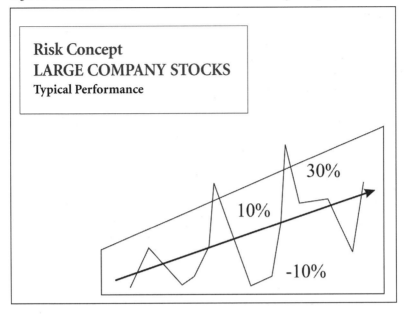

Various markets will have different rates of return and different standard deviations. Using standard deviation as a measurement for risk is a very good starting point. However, as we shall see later on, using it by itself doesn't explain all the dimensions of risk or how investments are priced in the marketplace.

SOURCES OF RISK

Risk comes from several sources. Most finance books break it down this way:

- *Business Risk.* A company may fail, leaving the stocks or bonds you hold worthless. Business risk is uncompensated. It can and should be diversified away.

- *Market Risk.* Even if you have a strong company, a declining market may carry your stock down with it. Market risk is compensated. Markets with higher risks carry higher returns.

- *Interest Rate Risk.* The value of bonds varies inversely with interest rates. Stocks and other property are also affected by general interest rates.

- *Inflation Risk.* Your investment may not keep place with inflation, resulting in a decrease in wealth or buying power.

- *Currency Risk.* Foreign holdings may change in value as the value of currency changes.

- *Political Risk.* The government may do something to harm the economic climate. This can vary from raising taxes, revolution, war, and confiscation of property to imposing a minimum wage. There is clear evidence that political risk is compensated by higher returns to investors. To a large extent political risk can be diversified away.

- *Investor Behavior.* Investor behavior presents the biggest risk of all. This risk not defined in college textbooks. It is the risk that the investor will be so inept that he blows a game he should easily win. While there are exceptions, economists are constantly amazed at the ability of individual investors to obtain poor results. In an efficient market, individuals should not be able to do as poorly as they do. In fact, an entire branch of economics has devoted itself to trying to explain investor behavior and how it affects their results and the markets, and we will have lots more to say about it later. The investor's behavior is a chief uncompensated risk. The market does not reward you for being irrational.

- *Management Risk.* Another risk that we don't find in traditional finance books is the very real risk that an investment management decision in either market timing or individual security selection may be wrong. Active investment management always adds additional cost, may not produce an additional return sufficient to cover the cost, and may introduce additional risk into the portfolio. All these risks are uncompensated. The debate over active versus passive investment style is one of the hottest in finance. (For an entertaining and enlightened discussion of this subject, I recommend *A Random Walk Down Wall Street* by Burton Gordon Malkiel.)

RISK IS PART OF THE INVESTMENT PROCESS

Risk never goes away. It is part of life and part of the investment process. Any investor who thinks he has banished risk is just fooling himself. Usually he has traded one risk he understands for another he doesn't. In another scenario, investors simply choose to ignore some risks, often underestimating or ignoring the devastation that inflation can cause on fixed income. Inflation is like a slow-growing cancer. At first you may not notice it, but eventually it will kill you.

Each risk can be mitigated and managed using well-defined techniques. The trick is to manage your portfolio to achieve the maximum level of return at any level of risk you are willing to accept, achieve your goals with the least risk possible, and develop a strategy that has the highest possible probability of success.

You can take much more risk than what we advocate here. However, our discussion is intended for the vast majority of Americans looking for a sensible college fund, retirement plan, or a general wealth-accumulation strategy. We will confine ourselves to the traditional liquid markets and avoid more risky speculations.

FACTORS THAT MULTIPLY RISK

Of course, there are some factors that multiply risk. These include:

■ *Concentration of Investments.* An investor who holds only Pan American, Eastern Airlines, or Kodak suffers by violating the fundamental investment principle of diversification. Remember, you are never compensated for assuming concentrated risks.

■ *Leverage or Margin.* We will see how leverage magnifies risk. Buying a stock on margin, or any other form of financial leverage, vastly increases risk.

■ *Options, Futures, or Commodities.* Speculation in all of these markets utilizes extraordinary amounts of leverage and carries the appropriate amount of risk. Most speculators are rather quickly wiped out. Ironically, these markets exist to allow businesses or investors to hedge risk and insure themselves against an adverse market move. Used in this manner, hedgers can usually accomplish their goal at a nominal cost.

AN INVESTOR'S VIEW OF RISK

In the real world, investors define risk in a variety of ways. Mention risk, and many will begin to imagine total, irrevocable, gone-forever loss of their principal. Fluctuation is not loss of principal. It is just fluctuation. Here's an example that should make the difference clear. Let's say you decided that your backyard contains oil. After a million dollars spent drilling, it turns out that there is no oil. No matter what you do, no matter how long you look at the well, no matter what happens to the price of oil, your money is gone. You have had an irrevocable loss of capital.

Let's say that you took the same million dollars and bought a diversified stock market portfolio. You then have an unusually bad result the first year, and lose 20 percent of your investment. Well, you have had an interesting fluctuation, but have not had a capital loss if you can refrain from doing the very worst possible thing and selling while the market is down. Markets have always recovered in the past. History indicates that all you must do to recover and go on to acceptable profits is to hang tight. While an individual stock can certainly go to zero value, entire markets don't. Except for war or revolution, I am unaware of any market that has gone down without recovering. As long as we expect the value of the world's economy to continue to grow, the value of the securities markets will reflect that growth. Equity investors will profit and be rewarded handsomely for enduring the aggravation that risk entails.

VISUALIZING RISK

Standard deviations may be a very precise and technically correct way to describe risk, but I don't find this method very intuitive. If we look at the pattern of returns in individual markets, we can perhaps get a better sense for risk and reward. For instance:

■ *Treasury Bills.* T-bills have low returns and little risk. As you already know, they have never had a loss, but don't earn enough to provide meaningful real returns (see Figure 3-7).

Figure 3-7. Annual returns on one-month T-bills 1926-2002.

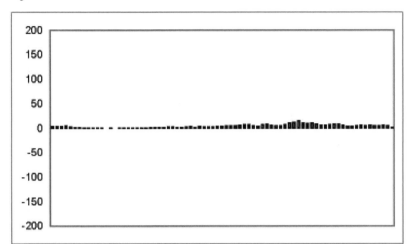

■ *Long-Term Treasury Bonds.* These treasury bonds have displayed a surprising amount of volatility as interest rates change. Many investors with "safe" government bonds or high-grade corporate bonds have been shocked to see how much their capital account varies as interest rates change (see Figure 3-8).

Figure 3-8. Annual returns on long-term government bonds 1926-2002.

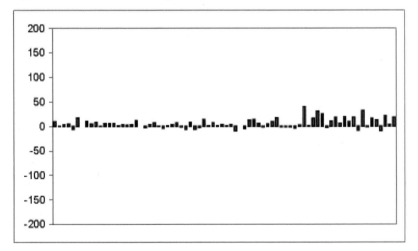

■ Commercial Bonds. Commercial bonds show some increased risk, but they still have disappointing returns, as shown in Figure 3-9.

Figure 3-9. Annual returns long-term corporate bonds 1926-2002.

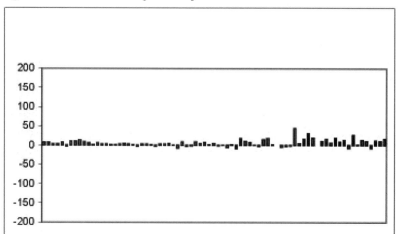

■   *Stocks.* Turning to stocks, the large company stocks shows an increased amount of risk, but has generated meaningful real returns (illustrated in Figure 3-10). Small company stocks have even higher returns, but also the highest amount of variation. This variation can be seen in Figure 3-11. Not all investors want to endure this much fluctuation in their accounts. As you can see, it can be a wild ride.

The relationship between annual (i.e., short-term) rates of return and risk becomes pretty clear when you examine the previous series of graphs.

Figure 3-10. Annual returns, large company, 1926-2002.

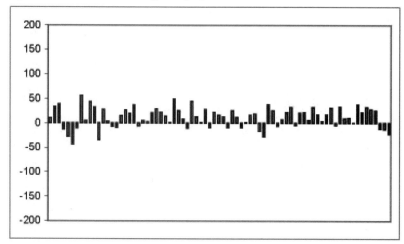

Figure 3-11. Annual returns, microcaps, 1926-2002.

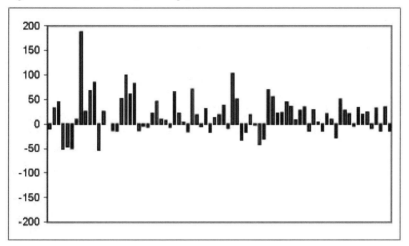

MARKET RISK IS SHORT-TERM RISK

Short-term results aren't the whole story. If that's all you focus on, you will miss the boat. Successful investors know that market risk is a short-term risk that dramatically decreases over time. The longer we hold a risky asset, the more risk decreases. Again, let's look at the S&P 500. The longer we hold the asset, the lower chance there is of loss. In fact, there has never been a loss during any single fifteen-year period since 1926.

RISK FALLS OVER TIME

Look how the pattern of returns changes as we go from one- to five-, ten-, fifteen-, and twenty-year holding periods (Figures 3-12, 3-13, 3-14, 3-15, and 3-16, respectively). You can see that there is much less variation during longer holding periods. While the chance of loss is reasonably high (30 percent) in any one year, it falls rapidly. Even during the Depression and in the 1970s, there has never been a loss while holding the S&P 500 for fifteen or more years.

Figure 3-12. Annual returns, large company, 1926-2002.

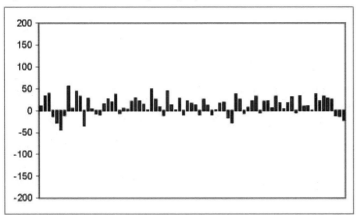

Figure 3-13. Five-year rolling returns, large company, 1926-2002.

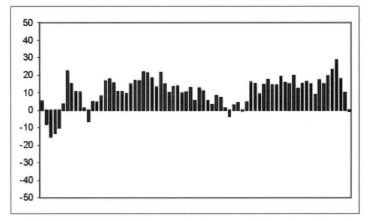

Figure 3-14. Ten-year rolling returns, large company, 1926-2002.

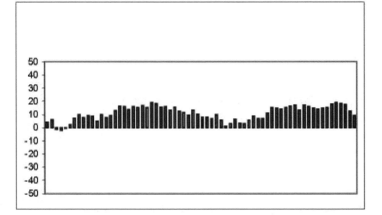

Figure 3-15. Fifteen-year rolling returns, large company, 1926-2002.

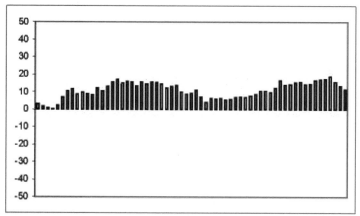

Figure 3-16. Twenty-year rolling returns, large company, 1926-2002.

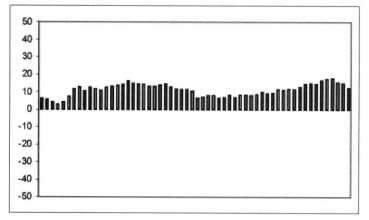

HOW OFTEN CAN YOU EXPECT LOSSES?

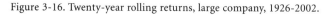

Here is another way to look at risk. In any one-year period there is a 23 percent chance that you may not make money. An optimist, like me, would say that means there is a 77 percent chance of gain. Now, I will deny until my dying breath that stock market investing in any way resembles gambling. But, if it *were* gambling, the odds would be stacked heavily in your favor. A racetrack couldn't last an afternoon with odds like that! And look how quickly the odds improve as time passes (Figure 3-17):

Figure 3-17. Chance of loss, 1926 to 2002, large company stocks.

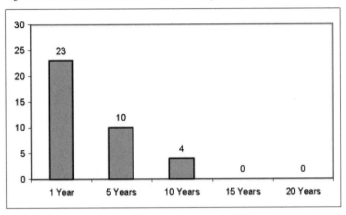

HOW BAD/GOOD CAN IT GET?

Investors often are concerned with a worst-case analysis. They ask themselves: "What's the worst thing that can happen to me?" As we have seen, in a one-year period or shorter, results can vary dramatically. Over time, a different pattern emerges. Here is a best-case, worst-case, and an average result analysis for the markets we have looked at for all twenty-year periods in the last sixty years. Notice in Figure 3-18 that the worst-case result for equities almost equals the average results for T-bills (a good proxy for most savings instruments), and the average result for equities exceeds the best case for any debt instrument.

Figure 3-18. Best, worst, and average returns 1926-2002.

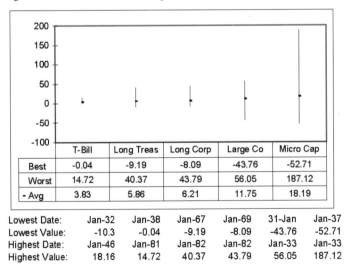

	T-Bill	Long Treas	Long Corp	Large Co	Micro Cap
Best	-0.04	-9.19	-8.09	-43.76	-52.71
Worst	14.72	40.37	43.79	56.05	187.12
- Avg	3.83	5.86	6.21	11.75	18.19

Lowest Date:	Jan-32	Jan-38	Jan-67	Jan-69	31-Jan	Jan-37
Lowest Value:	-10.3	-0.04	-9.19	-8.09	-43.76	-52.71
Highest Date:	Jan-46	Jan-81	Jan-82	Jan-82	Jan-33	Jan-33
Highest Value:	18.16	14.72	40.37	43.79	56.05	187.12

How Often Will You Beat Inflation?

Some investors may view risk as the chance of not beating inflation, the failure to obtain real rates of return, or the conservation of buying power. Here again, stocks perform very well for long-term investors. The chance of beating inflation starts out better with stocks and rises to certainty at twenty years. No one who held S&P 500 stock for any twenty-year period since 1926 has ever failed to beat inflation. The chance of beating inflation with bonds is lower than with stocks in early years and falls sharply over time (see Figure 3-19).

Figure 3-19. Summary beat-inflation chart, large company vs. long government bonds, 1926-2002.

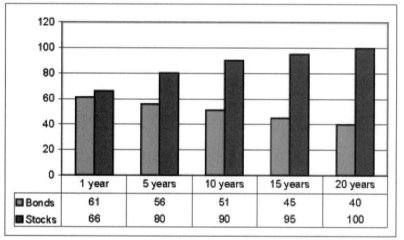

	1 year	5 years	10 years	15 years	20 years
Bonds	61	56	51	45	40
Stocks	66	80	90	95	100

The Risk-Reward Line

Each asset class that we have examined has both a rate of return and a risk associated with it, as shown in Figure 3-20. And, if we plot the risk against the reward, we come up with the risk-reward line we all know intuitively exists (see Figure 3-21).

The markets are far too efficient to allow higher rates of return without increased levels of risk. As they are so fond of saying at the University of Chicago, "There ain't no such thing as a free lunch." An investment proposal in violation of the free lunch rule is an early warning indication of a con job. Investment results far from the risk-reward line are just not going to happen. There is never a high return without high risk. If investors kept that rule in mind, most of the boiler room operations would be out of business overnight, and many of the horror stories we have heard would never have happened.

Figure 3-20. Risk and return statistics, 1926-2002.

Asset Class	Std. Deviation	Avg. Return
T-Bills	3.15	3.83
Long Govt. Bond	9.41	5.86
Long Corp Bond	8.75	6.21
Large Co. Stock	20.15	11.75
Micro Cap Stock	39.32	18.19

Figure 3-21. Asset class risk and reward, 1926-2002.

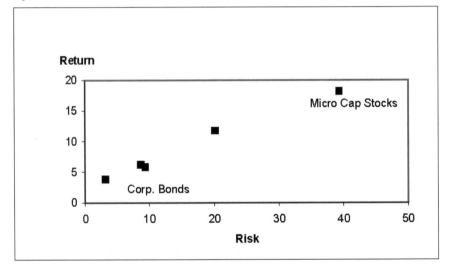

Risky Business

As we have seen, there are several ways investors may view risk. Investors might want to consider if the real risk they face is the failure to meet their goals. If so, they will want to construct portfolios that have the highest probability of meeting them. The paradox investors must deal with is that what appears risky in the short term turns out to be very conservative in the long view. The longer your time horizon, the more certain you are that stocks will outperform alternative markets. Given the higher rates of returns associated with stocks, and the high probability of attaining those superior returns, what long-term investor in his right mind would want to be protected against that?

An appreciation of risk makes you a better investor. Hopefully, we have cast some light on the dimension of risk. Risk is real, and it is built right into the investment process. However, it may not be as great as many Americans think. It's not a bogeyman. Risk shouldn't prevent you from making rational investment choices.

Most of you have probably realized by now that with risk in equities so closely related to holding period, time must be a very important dimension of the investment problem. We will need to pay close attention to time horizon as we design portfolios to meet your specific needs.

No one can eliminate investment risk, but there are effective techniques to manage and mitigate each type of risk. We will deal with the classic risk management techniques in the next chapter. Later we will explore modern portfolio theory, a great advancement in reducing risk by properly balancing and structuring your holdings.

FOUR

❖❖❖❖❖❖❖

TAMING THE BEAST

We have already identified risk as the central problem in the investment process. Specific techniques allow investors to mitigate the effects of each type of risk. At best, these techniques offer limited relief. In other words, you can get a lot of help alleviating the effects of risk, but there is no miracle cure for it.

Don't forget that we get paid to assume risk. Managing risk is a process of maximizing return per unit of risk and matching our total portfolio risk against our time horizon and objectives. Assume what risk you must to accomplish your objectives, but balance your appetite for risk with your need for safety and security.

Most investors will find that they should hold both risky (equity or stock) and nonrisky (bond) assets to meet their unique needs. As we discuss each of the classic risk classes in turn, remember that while none of us can entirely avoid risks, we can pick and choose the risks we wish to bear. Also keep in mind that we should expect to be compensated for risk. Without risk, no one can expect rewards above the zero-risk rate of return. Having said that, please understand that we are not advocating excessive risks. Investors should carefully evaluate which risks they will bear, and chart a strategy with the highest probability of maximizing their rewards.

Don't take this discussion to an illogical extreme. Recently the airwaves have sprouted infomercials advocating everything from penny stocks to speculations in home heating oil or soybean futures. And, of course, there is the day trading frenzy. Normally sane and sensible individuals are quitting their jobs to enjoy the easy riches that day trading firms advertise. Big mistake!

Each of these quick return schemes carefully explains that there are risks, but also opportunities for huge rewards. Don't fall for this. Invariably, these schemes are sucker traps, almost sure disasters. In fact, a government report on day trading activity concluded that only about 11 percent of day traders had the basic skills to hope to make a profit, and that 70 percent of them promptly lost their entire investment.

Keep a healthy level of skepticism, and remember that there are con artists out there. There is a basic difference between investments in which you should expect to make a profit over time, zero-sum games in which you should expect eventually to get wiped out (gambling, options, and futures), and fraud where you never have a chance (penny stocks). Always remember, if something sounds too good to be true, it probably is.

BUSINESS RISK

Business risk is the risk most investors first consider. Many fearful investors see their investments being wiped out by a business failure. A business need not fail to cause your holdings to be unprofitable. It can come on hard times that will severely affect the value of its securities.

Even large, established institutions can disappear suddenly and without a trace. Miami residents lost three major international airlines, their largest bank, and their largest savings and loan in just about two years. Equity investors in those businesses received nothing.

Entire industries can decline and fade as their products become obsolete. There are few remaining buggy whip manufacturers, and we can assume that equity investors in that once thriving industry are dissatisfied today.

Other industries find themselves unable to compete in a shifting global economy. America no longer manufactures a single color television.

Our shoe industry has almost vanished. Again investors in poorly diversified or concentrated portfolios have suffered.

Disasters can strike at any time from strange and unexpected directions. Utility investors suddenly found themselves evaluating their atomic exposure after Three Mile Island. Orange County bondholders endured a different type of business risk when they found that an obscure bureaucrat had put one of the richest counties in the country into bankruptcy. Texaco, one of the world's largest oil companies, found itself in bankruptcy after it interfered in an acquisition by a relatively tiny competitor. We live in an age where what should never happen does!

Of course, investors have every right to find this distressing. Fortunately, this type of risk can be reduced to insignificance. Diversification is the basic investor protection strategy. Diversification offers the only free lunch in the investment business. If an investor owns a single stock and that company goes broke, the investor has lost his entire portfolio. If the company that went broke is only one-tenth of one percent of the investor's portfolio, the investor will hardly notice. Single companies often go broke, entire markets do not.

As the number of investments held increases, business risk falls very rapidly. Statisticians often claim that as few as ten to fifteen stocks will offer adequate diversification. After that, further risk reduction reaches a point of diminishing returns. As a practical matter, investors of very modest means can own diversified portfolios of thousands of stocks by using no-load mutual funds or other pooled investments. Business risk is then effectively removed as a serious concern.

It's very important for investors to understand that expected rate of return does not fall as a result of diversification. Only the variation around the expected rate of return falls. Variation is risk.

Investors are never compensated for a risk that they could have diversified away. Securities are priced with the assumption that investors hold diversified portfolios. Almost any basic finance textbook will explain the math, and no one with an IQ over room temperature will dispute the benefits of diversification. You may assume that this is a fundamental and undisputed truth.

Here's another fact of life: For every undisputed truth, eventually someone will devise a ridiculous distortion. Diversification has been used as a rationale for some pretty dumb investment schemes. Everything from collectible plates and dolls to oil wells, gold, diamonds, oil paintings, futures, commodities, and even more blatant scams have been palmed off on unwitting investors by slick salesmen in the name of diversification. While diversification is the best thing an investor can do to reduce his portfolio risk, a dumb investment is still a dumb investment.

The informed investor considers the merits of each investment before he includes it in his portfolio. The first key question the informed investor asks is: "How sure am I that I will get compensated for taking this risk?" Investments that add a diversification benefit to the portfolio should have attractive risk-reward characteristics as well. We will come back to the effect of diversification when we discuss modern portfolio theory.

MARKET RISK

No matter how many issues we hold in a market, there still remains a risk that won't go away—market risk. Market risk is often called nondiversifiable risk. No matter how well an individual company performs, its price may be affected by broad market trends. Any neophyte on Wall Street will quickly tell you: "A rising tide will carry all boats." Few stocks can swim against the tide.

Earlier we made the argument that market risk was primarily a short-term problem. As a result, equity investments are not suitable for short-term obligations. I use this rule of thumb: Any known obligation coming due within the next five years (seven is better) should never be covered by variable assets (stocks or long-term bonds). In addition, all insurance needs and a healthy cash reserve should be taken care of before an investor begins a long-term investment plan. Don't put yourself in the position of having to liquidate stocks at a loss to cover expenses you should have anticipated.

Markets don't move in the same direction at the same time. A properly diversified portfolio has assets in several markets or segments of markets. In most years, this will offer significant relief from market risk. However, investors who violate the previous five-year rule of thumb do so at their peril. The proper allocation to markets to obtain the maximum benefit from this effect is the subject of a chapter on modern portfolio theory.

Interest Rate Risk

Interest rates affect investments in several ways. As interest rates rise, the value of existing bonds falls. Consider a bond issued at par with a 7 percent coupon rate. One month later, interest rates have increased to 8 percent, and the company issues new bonds at the 8 percent coupon rate. You are an investor with a sum of money considering both bonds. Would you rather have a 7 percent or 8 percent rate? Of course, you would like the higher coupon being offered. So, in order to induce you to purchase a 7 percent bond, the holder has to cut the price of the bond below par. At some price below par, the 7 percent coupon, plus the appreciation between the discounted price and par, will make the bonds equally attractive to you. However, the original owner of the 7 percent bond has had to sacrifice principal value in order to unload his bond. Of course, if interest rates fall, bondholders will enjoy capital appreciation. The rise and fall of capital values introduces a serious risk in what many consider a safe investment.

The longer the remaining life of the bond, the more the bond is affected by changes in interest rates. A bond with one week until maturity will be virtually unaffected by even large changes in prevailing interest rates. Yet the holder of an identical bond with thirty years until maturity will be whipsawed by even small changes.

Because of this increased capital risk, longer-term bonds must provide a higher return than shorter maturities. If we were to graph the yield to maturity of a bond at different maturity lengths, we would usually see an upward slope. This upward slope is called a positive yield curve. At times during the economic cycle, long-term rates may not offer any enhanced yield to maturity over short-term rates. This is called a flat or inverted yield curve.

Bond managers spend a lot of time studying yield curves in order to define the optimum point of yield to risk. Conservative investors will prefer to accept a small decrease in yield in order to have a large decrease in risk. More aggressive investors will prefer the opportunity of capital gains in long-term bonds if they forecast falling interest rates.

Bond traders also spend a lot of time trying to forecast future interest rates. Such forecasts are notoriously inaccurate, and anyone with a success rate of over 40 percent is entitled to consider himself an expert.

In general terms, longer durations are not well compensated. Risk goes up a lot, yield goes up a little, and the chance of consistently and suc-

cessfully forecasting rate changes is not high. Individuals should generally stick to short-term bonds, that is, bonds that mature within a one-to
five-year period, with the average maturity hovering at about two years or
less.

Bonds of high credit quality are less volatile than lower-rated issues.
Of course, these lower-rated bonds must provide a higher yield to maturity to compensate investors for the additional default risk they carry.
Again, quality risk is not well-compensated. Stick to high-quality liquid
bonds.

Bond managers, convinced that interest rates are going to rise, short-
en the average length of their portfolios and seek higher-quality bonds. If
they are right, this preserves principal. However, the record of bond managers actually adding value through such predictions is pretty dismal.

MATURITY VS. DURATION

Recently a great issue has been made of the difference between maturity
and duration. Maturity means just what it implies: the date the bond will
mature and receive the principal back. Duration is linked to the length of
time a bond requires to pay off the principal at its coupon rate. Because
the largest part of the value of a bond is the stream of coupon payments,
bonds with higher coupons should carry less capital risk. The price at
which a bond is purchased also affects its duration. Bonds purchased at
discount have a shorter duration than bonds purchased at a premium
price because principal will be repaid faster due to the lower-cost basis.
Many mutual funds report both average maturity and duration to assist
investors in evaluating the risk of the portfolio.

DOES CAPITAL FLUCTUATION MATTER?

Investors who plan to hold a bond to maturity may be less concerned with
capital fluctuations along the way. They reason that they will receive their
principal at the agreed date and have the agreed income. However, the
capital account accurately reflects the investor's position. For instance,
let's examine the case of an investor who invested $100,000 at 7 percent
interest and then found the interest rate environment changed to 8 percent. The capital account is down. Had the investor kept the $100,000 in
cash, a great deal more income could be bought for the same price. The
reverse is also true. Had interest rates fallen in the previous example, our
investor would have a capital appreciation and more income to purchase

with the cash. Capital fluctuation does matter, and only a foolish investor will ignore the risk.

REINVESTMENT OR ROLLOVER RISK

Interest rate risk also refers to the risk of not being able to reinvest your principal at the same rate when your bond or CD reaches maturity. In times of high interest rates, many investors believe they can avoid market risk by holding CDs or bonds. This is a big mistake. Retirees and other investors can be devastated by the assumption that high rates will persist indefinitely.

Here is a real-world example: If we examine the variation in income from CDs, we find that it is very high. From 1981 to 2002 CD rates fell from 17.27 percent to1.78 percent. In other words, income fell by 90 percent. On an after-inflation basis the results were even more disastrous. Retirees that had bet the farm on high rates were cruelly punished.

Had these investors purchased a diversified portfolio including stocks, foreign equities, bonds, and CDs, they would be wealthy today. Their failure to anticipate and understand reinvestment risk prevented them from making that decision.

OTHER INTEREST RATE EFFECTS

Investors must be aware that the level of interest rates in the economy has a major influence on all other capital goods. Stocks become less attractive to investors during times of high interest rates. Even if risk premiums don't change, the zero-risk rate goes up with high interest rates. The resulting higher return requirements cause stock prices to contract. High interest rates are often associated with inflation expectations, generally a sign that the economy is not healthy. Interest costs impact some businesses much more than others. Financial institutions and highly leveraged companies often suffer. Higher costs to finance real estate have a major impact on that market.

Some stocks act very much like bonds during the interest rate cycle. For instance, utilities and real estate investment trusts (REITs) are often purchased for their dividends by yield-hungry investors. Rising interest rates tend to depress these stocks in particular.

CURRENCY RISK

International investors quickly discover currency risk. Of course wherever we live, most of us consider the local currency as the real money. Everyone else's money is funny money. We have a natural reluctance to trust foreign currencies. But, even if we choose not to invest in foreign markets, none of us can avoid currency risk. If the value of our local currency falls, we become poorer because many things we purchase from other countries will cost more. International diversification gives investors an opportunity to diversify their currency exposure, as well as their equities. On balance, the diversification benefit swamps the currency risk in equities. Exposure to currency risk in foreign equity investing provides a valuable benefit over the long haul.

International equity and bondholders are affected in different manner. If you hold stock in a foreign brewery and the currency devalues, the effect on beer sales may not be very great. The value of the business may not be horribly impacted, and for long-term investors the net result may not be very noticeable. However, if you hold a bond, you may experience a more dramatic effect. You have had a real loss that may not be soon made up. (The reverse is also true. You can benefit from an upward valuation.) On balance, bond investors are not compensated enough to endure currency risk. They should either invest only in their local currency or only in hedged bonds.

THE THEORY OF ONE PRICE

There is good economic reason why bonds are more directly affected by currency risk. The T-bill is a zero-risk investment for Americans. A short-term investment in German government paper would be a zero-risk investment for a German. There is no particular reason why two zero-risk investments should sell at far different rates in different markets except for currency risk. If there were no currency risk, normal arbitrage would eliminate the difference in returns. So, most economists believe that differences in real interest rates are almost exclusively a reflection of currency risk expectations.

TO HEDGE OR NOT TO HEDGE? THAT IS THE QUESTION!

In the short term, currency risk can be rather distressing. Local market gains may be offset by losses in currency. Worse, local market losses could be compounded by currency losses. So every international investor must decide whether he wishes to hedge against the currency fluctuations. Most developed markets and some emerging markets can be easily hedged for currency risk, but there is a high price to pay in performance. For instance, a perfectly hedged, foreign bond portfolio would perform exactly like a T-bill minus the transaction costs of the hedges. (This again demonstrates that without risk, there is no prospect for higher returns.)

Portfolio managers are sharply divided on the subject of hedging. Some take the position that currency risk will work itself out in the long run, and the price of hedging isn't worth it. These same managers might argue that attempting to forecast currency swings and structure the portfolio accordingly could add another element of risk if the predictions are wrong. After all, forecasting is always difficult, especially if it concerns the future. Other portfolio managers believe they can properly forecast currency swings and add value while reducing risk. The weight of the evidence seems to favor the unhedged approach.

OTHER CURRENCY EFFECTS AND PROBLEMS

As with any other trend, there are winners and losers. Portfolio managers try to develop strategies based on the relative impact on various areas and industries of currency shifts. Everyone knows that exports are made more attractive and tourism is bolstered by a falling currency. Imports become less affordable. Foreign vacations less attractive. But beyond these elementary effects, many interesting trends develop that cause either problems or opportunities for portfolio managers.

Currency changes can have serious effects on the local economy. Mexico provides a recent and almost a worst-case example. After their currency devaluation in late 1994, major economic contractions, very high interest rates, business failures, and inflation were expected. Predictably, the market tanked. (Of course, there is a chicken and egg problem here. The economic problems probably caused the currency changes.) The same situation occurred in Thailand and other Asian countries where currency crises triggered an economic meltdown in 1997.

Many foreign governments have tied their currencies to the U.S. dollar. As our dollar falls, their exports also become more affordable, and the trend contributes to their economic development.

Most commodities still are quoted and traded in U.S. dollars. Companies, industries, and countries that are heavy commodity users benefit from a falling dollar. For instance, if the dollar is weak against the German mark and a German company consumes large amounts of oil, their price of oil will decrease even if the nominal price of oil remains flat. That company will experience lower costs and have higher profits as well. These profits increase the share value of the firm.

American investors who hold foreign stocks will profit, or at least off-set some of their losses in domestic holdings. The long-term dollar weakness has been a distinct advantage to America's international investors. As with most market trends, there are occasional periods of reversal. But, the average American's fear of currency risk would appear unjustified in light of other benefits of foreign investing.

POLITICAL RISK

For good or evil, governments at all levels have a tremendous impact on the investment climate. We often equate political risk with international or emerging market investing. Our own markets are just as sensitive. You don't have to have an insurrection to experience political risk. Political risks include tax, trade, regulation, education, and social policies. A government's attitude on capital and business sets the stage for either the success or failure of their economy.

Political risk is not always negative. If we can find a country where political risk is falling, we might expect earnings in the economy to increase as the economy expands. We also might expect that price-to-earnings ratios (P/Es) will expand as a result. Investors will demand less risk premium. To put it another way, the cost of capital will fall. One of the highest-profile international investment advisors seeks out countries where political risk is very high but improving. (Of course, all the problems of forecasting still remain.) America in the 1980s, the United Kingdom under Margaret Thatcher, and many emerging markets benefited by enlightened governments who created optimum conditions for capital and markets to thrive.

There is ample evidence that investors willing to bear political risks in emerging markets or high-growth economies are amply compensated. Because what happens in Poland bears little relationship to what happens in South America or the countries of the Pacific rim, it's easy to diversify away much of the political risk associated with emerging markets.

A Bite out of the Old Free Lunch

As we have seen, portfolio managers have a full menu of techniques to reduce risk. Many rely on forecasts, and then the result is only as good as the forecast. Some managers rely on hedging, which adds cost or reduces returns. The only free lunch we have discovered so far is diversification. Now diversification has one more dimension that we must explore: modern portfolio theory. Modern portfolio theory adds a new level of risk control that has revolutionized how many large institutions view the investment process. Investors of more modest means can also benefit from this theory; Chapter 5 will show you how.

FIVE

A NIBBLE FROM THE FREE LUNCH

Spend a little time wandering around the University of Chicago, and you are likely to spot joggers with some unusual T-shirts. The shirts appear to have handwriting and scribbles all over them. If you inquire about the shirt, you will be told that the signatures on the shirt are those of all the faculty members who have won Nobel prizes! The University of Chicago is a world-class institution in many ways. It dominates the fields of finance and economics. No other university is even close.

On the university campus you may also spot T-shirts emblazoned with TANSTAAFL (There ain't no such thing as a free lunch). TANSTAAFL is more than a neat saying on a T-shirt at the University of Chicago. Free lunches are identified and rooted out with the same passion and conviction that heresy was at the Inquisition. A true Chicago graduate will deny to the death that there ever has been, or ever can be, a free lunch. At this institution it is great sport to debate the implications of tax-deductible lunches, or tax-subsidized school lunches. Investors everywhere would be well advised to adopt TANSTAAFL as their personal credo. Beware of the salesman offering free lunches.

THE BEGINNING OF MODERN PORTFOLIO THEORY

Harry Markowitz is a very bright star in the University of Chicago's galaxy of superstars. His Ph.D. thesis laid the groundwork for Modern Portfolio Theory, a theory that revolutionized finance. Legend has it that Markowitz wrote the paper in a single afternoon in the University of Chicago library in 1952. The paper was later edited, expanded, and published as *Portfolio Selection*. In 1990 Markowitz's contribution earned him a Nobel prize in economics.

Ironically, Markowitz's paper almost didn't earn him his Ph.D. The review committee had grave doubts about whether it was pure economics! That story, and many more about the founders of modern finance and their contributions, is told in *Capital Ideas* by Peter Bernstein.

MPT is the watershed theory of modern finance. Every investor can apply modern portfolio theory to substantially reduce total portfolio risk without necessarily giving up expected return. In fact, in some cases it's possible to reduce risk and increase expected returns at the same time. That's as close to a free lunch as investors are ever likely to see.

Markowitz demonstrates that diversification benefits transcend the simple business risk elimination previously described in Chapter 4 and shows that some types of diversification are better than others!

WHAT IS MODERN PORTFOLIO THEORY?

What follows is a simplified description of modern portfolio theory. My aim is not to turn you into economists, but to demonstrate how investors can use MPT to control risk. Read the original work. The book is very readable, even for those of us who are mathematically challenged. Markowitz does us all a great favor by alternating the chapters of text with the math. I highly recommend the book for anyone with an interest in finance.

Markowitz began by assuming that we are all risk-averse. He defined risk as the standard deviation of expected returns. However, instead of measuring risk at the individual security level, he believed it should be measured at the portfolio level. Each individual investment should be examined not on its individual risk, but on the contribution it makes to the entire portfolio.

Now comes the great leap forward: In addition to the two dimensions of investment, risk and return, Markowitz considered the degree that investments can be expected to move together. This third dimension is the correlation of investments to one another (or covariation). While Markowitz considered the impact of individual securities in a portfolio, today many advisors use MPT techniques with asset classes in lieu of individual stocks to construct globally diversified portfolios.

Correlation is a very simple concept. If investments always move together in lockstep, they have perfect correlation, and that is assigned a value of plus one. If they always move in opposite directions, they have perfect negative correlation, and that value is minus one. If you can tell nothing about the movement of one investment by observing another, they have no correlation, and that is assigned a value of zero. Of course, two investments can fall anywhere on the spectrum between plus one to minus one in relation to one another.

Here is where it gets interesting. If diverse investments always moved together, there would be no diversification benefit. On the other hand, if they never moved together, there would be no risk. For example, many factors affect all airlines at once. Interest rates, cost of labor, the confidence of flyers, landing fees, regulation costs, and the cost of fuel are very much the same for American, Delta, and United airlines. We would expect that the price of their stocks would tend to move together throughout the market cycle. In fact, the price of the stocks often move together. They are strongly correlated.

Often factors that are good for one industry are bad for another. Let's look at oil companies and airlines. Fuel is a large expense for airlines. If the price of fuel goes up, we would expect that oil companies will profit and airlines will suffer. As a result, the price of their stocks should move in opposite directions. They often do. They have a low or negative correlation.

So, how can we use this? Imagine that somewhere in the world we can find one high-risk, high-return investment. As it goes through the market cycle it would have a positive return, but strong variations. It might look like Figure 5-1.

Figure 5-1. Scenario one: a high-risk, high-return investment with strong variations.

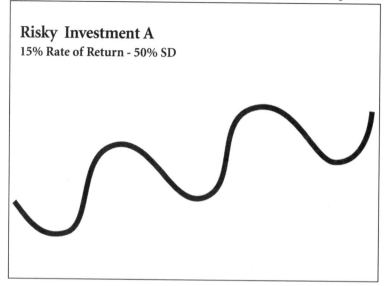

Let's also imagine another high-risk, high-return investment some-where else. This second investment has perfect negative correlation with the first. Every time the first goes up, the second goes down, and vice versa. We combine them into a portfolio, and the two of them might look like Figure 5-2 as they go through time.

Figure 5-2. Scenario two: two high-risk, high-return investments with perfect negative correlation.

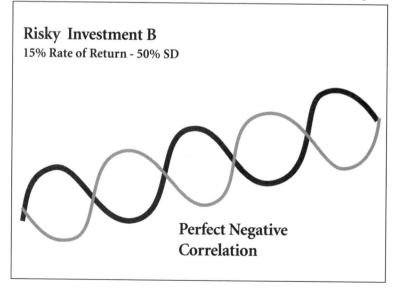

If we combine them together in a portfolio, the combined portfolio will have high return and zero risk. Short-term gains in one holding are exactly offset by losses in the other, but because the underlying trend in both investments is high return, the combination has a high return (see Figure 5-3).

Figure 5-3. Scenario three: two high-risk, high-return investments in perfect negative correlation equal a zero-risk portfolio.

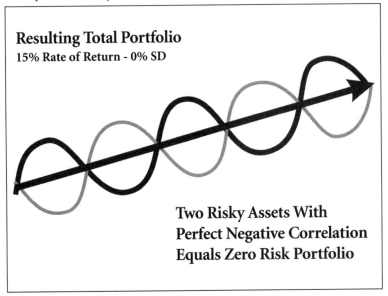

Resulting Total Portfolio
15% Rate of Return - 0% SD

**Two Risky Assets With
Perfect Negative Correlation
Equals Zero Risk Portfolio**

Now is the time for a little reality check. In the real world, we never find two holdings with perfect negative correlation. The good news is that we don't need to. Any correlation with less than perfect positive correlation will reduce the risk in the portfolio. Risk has not been removed, but it has been reduced. Remember that there's no such thing as a free lunch. But, perhaps, MPT offers investors a discounted lunch. Or maybe it's a free nibble!

The implications of modern portfolio theory are staggering. For the first time, investors can construct portfolios free of the old risk-reward line. In mathematical terms, the portfolio has a rate of return equal to the weighted average rate of return of the holdings, but the risk may fall below the weighted average of the portfolio.

We have come to the point where we must conclude that where most diversification is good, some is better than others. We get a better diversification benefit by including an airline and an oil company in our portfolio than by holding two airlines. Classic diversification reduces business risk. Diversification in the sense that MPT uses it can actually serve to reduce market risk. Ideally we want investments that combine attractive risk-reward characteristics with low correlation to our other investments.

I must be clear here: I am not looking for an opportunity that simply offers the chance to lose money while everything else is making money. That's just another dumb investment to me. Each investment in my client portfolios must contribute to expected return. There is another (perhaps even rational and reasonable) point of view. Many practitioners include an asset like gold purely for its low correlation with other asset classes. This may be a purer point of view. And, perhaps this approach leads to a lower portfolio risk. However, I look at gold's twenty-year low rate of return combined with its high fluctuation (risk) and decide not to waste a percentage of my portfolio on that asset. In my opinion, investors have been poorly compensated for bearing risk in precious metals markets.

The math is very heavy-duty because for each investment we must have an expected rate of return, a risk, and the correlation to every other investment we are considering. So, the required data grows exponentially as we increase the number of possible holdings. Even worse, we must consider an infinite number of possible portfolios for just two assets. We all know that we cannot have more than an infinite number of portfolios. So I will leave it to the mathematicians to decide what happens when the potential number of assets in our portfolio grows over two. These types of puzzles always made my head hurt. The answer to them may be closer to Zen than to math. In any event, the math cannot be done without some heavy-duty computer power.

Markowitz laid out the math in his 1952 paper. Most people thought he had it nailed. Nevertheless, Markowitz had to wait more than twenty years, until the mid-1970s, to get his hands on a mainframe computer to prove that he had it right. Markowitz confessed that that day was the happiest one of his life, not the day he won the Nobel prize. At the time, a single run of the optimization problem on a mainframe cost as much as a brand new car. Today, the definition of heavy-duty computer power has changed. You can do the same example on an old 8088 PC in a heartbeat.

THE EFFICIENT FRONTIER

In a portfolio of a certain number of holdings, only one possible combination will result in the maximum possible return for each amount of risk we might assume. Markowitz called this optimum combination of holdings "efficient." Any other combination of holdings results in a lower return at that same level of risk. These inferior combinations are less efficient. If we graph the efficient portfolios against the various levels of risk, the resulting line of best possible combinations is called the "efficient frontier." Happily, the efficient frontier falls above the old risk-reward line (see Figure 5-4).

Figure 5-4. Markowitz's optimum combination of holdings: the efficient frontier.

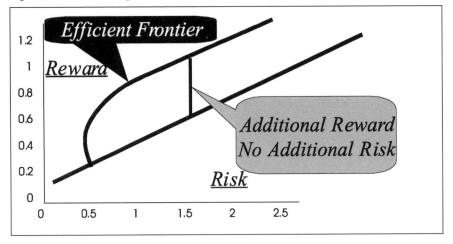

Every point on the efficient frontier offers the investor the highest return for a particular level of risk, but the investor is still faced with an infinite number of efficient portfolios, and must decide how much risk to take. The theoretical answer is that the investor should select the portfolio on the efficient frontier that is tangent to his indifference curve. I personally think that answers like this give economists a bad name. Later, I will outline some ways investors might reach a more real-world conclusion to this question. In the meantime, if you should meet an investor who knows where his indifference curve touches the efficient frontier, please have him contact me. I would like to meet him—I think.

The MPT optimization process allows the investor to approach the investment decision from two perspectives. Begin by deciding how much risk is comfortable and then seek the optimum level of return at that point. An investor might frame the problem like this: I want to be 95 percent certain (two standard deviations) that I endure no more than a 10 percent decline in value during any one year. An advisor can then construct a portfolio that has the highest possible expected return within that risk criteria. Or, the investor can frame the problem like this: I need to achieve a 12 percent rate of return and want a portfolio to do that at the least possible risk.

Modern portfolio theory shifts the emphasis away from individual security selection to the portfolio level. No longer do we look at a single stock or bond in isolation. Instead, we look at the effect of adding that individual security to the portfolio. If a new asset adds return and/or reduces risk at the portfolio level, it should be considered for inclusion no matter what its individual characteristics.

Is MPT a free lunch? No, but it is an incredibly powerful tool to manage risk and construct portfolios to meet various constraints. More than any other person, Markowitz has dragged portfolio management out of the dark ages. As we shall see, modern portfolio theory has substantial limitations, and it isn't a cure for risk. Today financial management is still somewhere between art and science, but we have come a long way from alchemy. Investors who wish to achieve anything close to an optimum performance must not ignore MPT. The investment problem is multidimensional. The days when you could solve it by wandering into your nearest brokerage and letting the friendly salesman select a few good stocks are long gone. If your advisor isn't using MPT, find one who does.

If this sounds a little theoretical at this point, hold on. We are about to look at some simple but powerful applications of MPT. In Chapter 6 we will examine just how far the MPT revolution has spread in today's finance, look at some of its practical limitations, and consider two examples that demonstrate concrete benefits for investors. All of the portfolios we build in later examples of this book will utilize MPT as a primary risk-control method.

TRAVELS ON
THE EFFICIENT
FRONTIER

L et's look at how Modern Portfolio Theory might be applied in the real world with two very simple examples. We are going to illustrate how risk can be managed by simply diversifying into dissimilar assets.

As Harry Markowitz defended his dissertation in the early 1950s, it's doubtful that anyone present had any inkling of the tremendous impact his paper would have on modern finance. But the revolution didn't exactly spread like wildfire. It took a long time for the impact to be felt. Academics labored away in obscurity, steadily building a wealth of knowledge until the world was ready for it.

For the most part, Wall Street ignored the academics. The old ways were good enough, and change would have imperiled many of the Street's most sacred myths. During the early 1980s a few academics infiltrated into the large financial houses and institutions, but they were considered slightly unusual. More than any other event, the crash of 1987 focused Wall Street's attention on the need to better understand the world's markets. Wall Street was ready to listen, at least at the institutional level. Now financial economics has come into vogue, and academics are widely consulted and sought after by large money managers.

Even the law is rapidly changing to incorporate elements of the new financial theory and practice. Fiduciaries run substantial personal risk if they fail to follow MPT basics. The old legal list of approved investments is long gone, replaced by an "expanded federal prudent man rule" for fiduciaries. Risk is required to be measured at the portfolio level, and no single asset is deemed too risky for a prudent portfolio. Instead the impact of the asset on the portfolio as a whole is deemed the appropriate test. Pension trustees and other fiduciaries are now required to properly diversify, follow a written investment policy, consider possibilities for profit as well as risk of loss, and build asset allocation plans with appropriate attention to expected rate of return, risk, and correlation of investments.

What practical benefits does modern portfolio theory have for investors? How can you apply this to your needs? Let's look at a couple of real-world, simple applications.

IMPROVING AN ALL-BOND PORTFOLIO

First, let's look at the case of a retiree living on the income of his portfolio, as illustrated in Figure 6-1. The primary concern is safety of principal and income. The present portfolio is comprised exclusively of government bonds. Recently the retiree has noticed that income isn't going as far as it used to. In addition, the gyrations of her principal value have been disconcerting. The retiree doesn't want to do anything risky, but is curious about how to improve the situation.

Our retiree finds herself stuck on the old risk-reward line. Let's examine her portfolio of 100 percent long-term government bonds (portfolio A in Figure 6-1). By itself, it isn't a very efficient portfolio. Risk is high compared to the meager total return. The expected return is 5.73 percent with a standard deviation (risk measurement) of 9.43 percent.

Before the advent of MPT, the traditional answer to increasing her yield would have been to creep ever further out the risk spectrum with bonds. Start first with high-grade corporate bonds, then junk bonds. Each bond has a growing risk. MPT, however, expands the list of options.

From the retiree's start position, any movement either upward (more return) or to the left (reduced risk) improves her position. (Note that every investment manager longs to be in the northwest quadrant of the risk-reward chart.) If we add different combinations of cash and stocks, it is possible either to substantially improve returns without increasing risk (portfolio B) or dramatically reduce risk without sacrificing returns (portfolio C). Paradoxically, the addition of a more risky asset can actually reduce the risk in the total portfolio. This occurs because cash, bonds, and stocks often move in different directions during market cycles (low correlation). MPT proves that the risk level of the portfolio as a whole should be considered paramount rather than any separate component.

Figure 6-1. Enhancing returns on an all-bond portfolio.

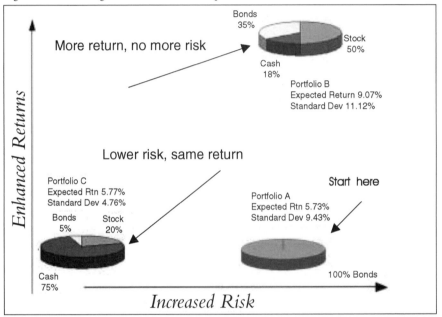

Historical returns from 1926 to 2000, courtesy of Dimensional Fund Advisors (DFA) and Ibbotson and Associates. Cash based on thirty-day treasury bills, bonds, and stocks based on the S&P 500 index. Historical returns are no guarantee of future performance.

Portfolio B contains 50 percent stocks, 35 percent bonds, and 15 percent cash. The expected rate of return has increased to 9.07 percent while standard deviation is 11.12 percent (much higher return, minimal increase in risk).

Portfolio C contains 20 percent stocks, 5 percent bonds, and 75 percent cash. This combination achieves 5.77 percent expected return while lowering the risk to 4.76 percent standard deviation (approximately the same return but with less than half the risk).

INTERNATIONAL INVESTING AND MODERN PORTFOLIO THEORY

Here's another example of the practical benefits of MPT: An investor who holds a portfolio of large domestic stocks would like to see if international investing would improve his position. He is comfortable with equity risk, but would like to improve his returns, or lower his risk.

Here are various mixes of domestic large stocks, represented by our large company index, and foreign large stocks of developed nations, represented by Morgan Stanley's Europe, Australia, and Far East (EAFE) index. The foreign stocks have both a higher return and a higher risk than our domestic market. You would expect that, as we mixed the two together, the resulting portfolio combinations would fall on a line connecting them. But you can see in Figure 6-2 that as we add foreign stocks to a domestic portfolio, return increases (moves up) and risk decreases (moves left) until we reach an optimum position at about a 60/40 ratio of domestic to foreign stocks. The combination of lower risk and higher returns is why we feel so strongly that global diversification is essential for all investment portfolios.

Figure 6-2. Global diversification: an essential element for investment portfolios.

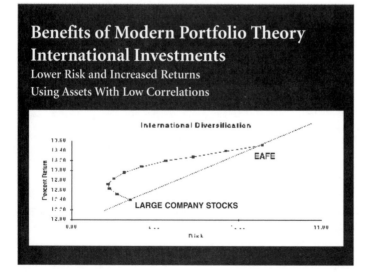

International investing has two key benefits for American investors: higher returns and a strong diversification effect. International markets have a very low correlation with our domestic markets. This diversification effect will lower risk at the portfolio level, which is one of the chief advantages offered by modern portfolio theory. (This is a very simple two–asset class illustration. We are pretending here that the investor has no other choices. In the real world, our investor should also consider the impact of small cap stocks, emerging markets, value investing, real estate, hard assets, and other asset classes as he builds his program.)

Modern portfolio theory is certainly a great leap forward in our ability to construct rational investment plans. But, like any good tool, it must be used with judgment. And, like any good idea, there will always be someone who will take it to an illogical extreme.

MODERN PORTFOLIO THEORY AS A RISK MANAGEMENT TOOL

First, we must understand, MPT is not a risk elimination process. It is a risk management tool. It allows us to build more rational investment plans, control risk, and get "the most bang for the buck" of risk. It is not a substitute for judgment, and in fact requires great judgment for its proper application. There are severe limitations that, if not properly understood, can lead to very strange and counterproductive results. When dealing with investment tools we must always remember that none of them work every day, every quarter, or every year. An optimized portfolio is not a substitute for CDs. Patience and discipline are still required if the process is to bear fruit.

MPT is based on an examination of past results. We can say that some things happen more often than not, but there is no guarantee that tomorrow will always be just like today. Short-term returns will always remain random and variable.

We can take a great deal of comfort that none of the three variables appear to be changing in any fundamental way. In particular, there doesn't seem to be any fundamental change in the correlation between the world's markets. While we may be moving toward a global economy, individual economies and markets still respond to local conditions and politics.

There are a number of optimization programs readily available to financial planners and portfolio managers that will quickly and easily solve the math problems associated with MPT. However, like any computer program, if we put garbage in, we will get garbage out. Many of us put far too much value on the output of a computer program without considering the input and programming problems. Beware of the black box approach to solving life's little problems.

The MPT process and math is particularly vulnerable to data-input distortions. For each asset or asset class, we must enter the expected rate of return, risk, and correlation to every other asset class. This leads to two problems. First, the data changes every day. Next, a tiny change in an input of any of the three factors will have giant impacts on the suggested allocation. Even if we assume that all the data going in is totally accurate, we still have problems.

Left to its own devices, the optimizer will identify the one most efficient asset and suggest that you put all your resources in that asset. Of course, this leads to a gross violation of the diversification principal. In practice, most advisors restrain the program to reasonable asset allocations. Blindly following the black box will lead to putting all your assets into one stock or one market.

I attended a meeting in 1994 where Bill Sharpe, who shared the Nobel prize with Markowitz for his work on the implications of MPT for capital markets, spoke on the problem of optimizers. According to Dr. Sharpe, optimizers will readily identify input errors and recommend that you put 100 percent of your assets in the wrong asset. Sharpe developed the capital asset pricing model and other refinements to MPT. I believe he speaks with some authority on the problem.

If the computer inputs are updated frequently, another strange abnormality creeps into the process. Because assets that are underperforming recently will show lower rates of return and higher risk, the optimization program will decide that they are no longer efficient. The program then recommends sale of the asset. Blindly following the black box will, consequently, lead to buying high and selling low. In the real world, tax and transaction costs are high. Frequent updates and the resulting frequent trading will increase transaction costs far beyond the benefits that MPT can offer. Most of us don't need that kind of advice. How often to update the data and what time frames to use becomes a matter of judgment. The computer can't solve that for you.

For instance, if we examine monthly or quarterly data on foreign investing, we will get different results than if we use annual data in our series. In a like manner, if we look at ten-year time periods, we will get different results than if we use three-year or five-year time periods. There is always some effect, and it is almost always better to have a diversified portfolio. However, the optimum ratio of foreign to domestic will change with each different set of data observations.

Two very clear examples come to mind in illustrating the problem of blindly following the black box. During the preparation for Desert Storm, foreign markets performed miserably. All the optimization software I saw recommended selling foreign stocks. Those investors and advisors who sold locked in their losses and were not invested when the inevitable turn came.

During 1993 emerging markets exploded upward. Mutual fund companies rushed new emerging market funds through registration. Their representatives touted an asset allocation of up to 40 percent in emerging markets and used optimization results to add to the hype. Of course, they downplayed the very short-term data that they were using as input to the process. The very short-term data indicated that emerging markets had high expected rates of return and almost no risk. Investors who rushed out to load up on emerging markets were left with egg on their faces and had all of 1994 to wonder what went wrong.

The cycle repeated itself in 1998 when the Pacific economic crisis affectionately remembered as the "Asian Flu" struck after the Thai currency collapsed. Longer-term data would have showed a very high rate of return, very high risk, very low correlation, and an optimum portfolio with a low percentage of assets in emerging markets.

Most advisors use past data for expected rates of return and risk inputs. However, some advisors may forecast based on their research or feelings. In my not very humble opinion, this adds another layer of risk and complication to the process.

A better approach, and one that I have used successfully in my practice for years, is to use long-term data to structure a portfolio that makes sense and then test the results with the optimizer. Rather than sell assets that are underperforming in the short term, as the optimizer programs might suggest, we use reallocation to increase positions in down markets and decrease positions in markets that have had strong short-term results. This can be emotionally painful and requires discipline. I can't honestly say that I enjoy selling winners to buy losers. It causes some client distress, and I get to explain it to concerned clients rather often. It goes against the grain. But this discipline will lead to more consistent results and lower risk. It reverses the buy-high/sell-low problem.

The terrible truth is that financial management remains an art much more than a science. Forecasts are notoriously difficult and unreliable, and judgment is always required. We must recognize that nothing works every day, quarter, or year. Discipline is difficult in the face of intense media speculation and hype, but discipline leads to acceptable long-term investment results. As long as the world's economy continues to grow, patient investors will profit.

For all its limitations, modern portfolio theory offers one of the strongest tools available to the rational investor. Used properly (that is, with judgment, patience, and understanding), it will go a long way toward smoothing out the often-bumpy investment process.

In Chapter 7, I will discuss a closely related area: the impact of asset allocation on investment results.

SEVEN

THE ASSET ALLOCATION DECISION

I n this chapter we will consider the merits of the investor's obsession with individual stock selection and market timing. Just how much do these two elements of the investment process contribute to overall success or failure? Is there a better way to think about investing? It turns out that we have been putting all the emphasis in just the wrong places. We have been concentrating on details that are virtually insignificant and over which we have little control, while ignoring the critical areas where we could have a much higher impact.

From personal experience, I can tell you that it is very difficult to unlearn something you have always known. We tend to cling to old, familiar, and comfortable ways of thinking in most unreasonable ways. Change is difficult and painful. We resist it. We rationalize our aversion to it. We fight for the old ideas every step of the way. We practically have to be hit over the head with a better idea before we will consider it. We want to ignore the idea and discredit the person who calls it to our attention. Most of us are neither as flexible nor rational as we would like to think we are.

Like most of my clients, I grew up believing in the performance fairy. I had some preconceived ideas about investing firmly planted in my head. These ideas seemed so sensible that they were almost considered by me to be universal truths. Everyone I knew seemed to believe the same things. There didn't seem much point in checking the facts.

In general terms, these were my basic understandings in the past:

- Knowing which stocks to buy and when to be in the market is the key to investment success.

- A good investor can predict which way the market is going and which stocks will make the most profit. This power is held by only a chosen few. The chosen few will readily share their power with you, for a nominal cost. This minor cost will be repaid many times over by enhanced investment performance. However, one must always avoid the charlatans who give false advice. A member of the chosen few is defined as someone whose stocks go up, and a charlatan is someone whose stocks go down.

- Knowing when the market will fall is a prime concern to the successful investor. One should leave the market when it is about to go down in order to preserve principal.

- Successful investors trade often and dart in and out of the market, or a particular stock, with uncanny skill. Their portfolios benefit from a hands-on approach.

- It is rather easy to spot good companies through an examination of financial data, and to determine what the stock in those companies should be worth.

- An astute investor can apply superior insight, to make big killings on mispriced stocks. Using his superior insight, he will be able to take action long before other investors catch on.

- Studying past price movements is an aid to predicting future price movements. This skill can be applied to both individual stocks, and the movement of the market as a whole.

- Economic predictions are reliable and form another strong foundation for success.

- It is reasonably easy to select good advisors and managers because their past track records are reliable indicators to future success and skill.

Given all of the above-mentioned statements, we tend to assess the investment process in the following terms:

- What stocks should I buy?
- Should I be in or out of the market now?
- When should I sell my stocks?
- Which manager should I hire?
- What mutual fund should I buy?

Unfortunately, almost all of this "conventional wisdom" is dead wrong! It doesn't do us any good to think of investing in these terms. In fact, it contributes to the problems with investing and keeps us from enjoying the fruits of a game strongly tilted in our favor.

A GROUNDBREAKING STUDY

In the landmark study "Determinants of Portfolio Performance," published in the July–August 1986 issue of the *Financial Analysts Journal,* Gary P. Brinson, L. Randolph Hood, and Gilbert Beebower (BHB) examined the investment results of ninety-one very large pension funds to determine how and why their results differed. The pension plans, which ranged in size from $100 million to well over $3 billion, were studied for a ten-year period ending in 1983. Very complete and extensive data was made available on each of the plans from the SEI performance database.

Even the smallest of these pensions is a very large investment pool. We can assume that they can command the very best talent available. Each is the valued client of one or more of the largest and most prestigious investment managers in the world. As such, they automatically receive the best research and information. In other words, they certainly had the resources available to beat the market.

The team did a very simple but powerful and elegant analysis. They reasoned that only four elements could contribute to investment results: investment policy, individual security selection, market timing, and costs. By using a rather straightforward regression analysis, they were able to attribute the contribution (or lack of it) to each of these four elements.

Investment policy was defined as the average base commitment to three asset classes: stocks, bonds, and cash. For instance, a pension plan might have a mix of 60 percent stocks, 30 percent bonds, and 10 percent cash. (Most investment advisors use the term asset allocation rather than investment policy.)

Market timing was then determined by variations around the base commitments. If the pension plan changed their commitment to the three asset classes over time, it was assumed to be an attempt to profit from market timing.

The conclusions were remarkable. Brinson, Hood, and Beebower were able to explain 93.6 percent of the performance of a pension plan by just knowing the investment policy. (The study used market index returns for the three asset classes, large company stocks for stocks, Shearson Lehman Government/Corporate Bond Index for bonds, and thirty-day treasury bills for cash.) The biggest single factor explaining plan performance was simply the investment policy (asset allocation) decision: deciding how much the plan should hold in stocks, bonds, or cash.

Figure 7-1. Asset allocation (investment policy) can explain about 94 percent of pension plan performance.

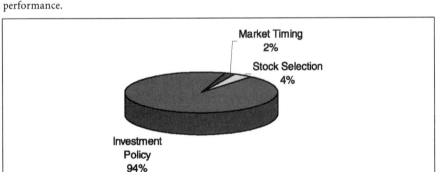

Source: Brinson, Hood, and Beebower, 1986, 1991.

That left less than 6 percent of the difference in results attributable to all other causes. The other factors contributed to the differences in total return, but not necessarily in a positive way. Attempts at market timing almost always resulted in a reduction of return. Individual stock selection on average also resulted in a reduction to the plan's returns. There was a wider variation in individual stock selection impact than in market timing, and a few managers were able to affect performance during the time period in a positive manner. Cost and execution differences for these very large investment plans were not an important factor. (But you can believe they are very important factors for you!)

Continuing the analysis, the study concluded that, on average, attempts to actively manage the portfolios actually cost the average plan 1.10 percent reduction in net returns per year when compared to just buying and holding the appropriate indexes. The best and the brightest managers that Wall Street offered couldn't reliably deliver the goods.

WALL STREET CALLS FOUL

The Brinson, Hood, and Beebower study touched off a major war within the industry and between Wall Street and the academics. After all, Wall Street's entire business is built around the idea that they can contribute value to the investment process by insight into individual security selection or market timing. Each brokerage house or investment manager wants the public to believe that somewhere in the back office is a genius who can make you rich. (Our research/contacts/methods/insights/forecasts/gurus are better/smarter/more effective than the other guy's.)

Suddenly there was a great cry through the Street. Suppose investors suddenly got the idea that Wall Street's vaunted research was garbage, and that massive, active trading didn't add value? What if investors started to believe that Wall Street's advice was worth less than zero? What would happen to fees and commissions? The idea was unthinkable. Huge fortunes and giant egos were on the line.

When faced with a study whose conclusions you don't like, one of the first lines of defense is to attack the data. If the data is published for all to see and is indisputable, all is still not lost. You can always claim that the other side "mined the data." (These are serious fighting words in academia.) Mining the data means that the entire study is flawed because the data is so limited that the results cannot be projected to other areas. In other words, the conclusion only applies in this single, obscure, and unimportant case. Although interesting and amusing in an academic sense, the study is, at best, trivial.

When someone is accused of mining the data, the first defense is to go and find new data and get similar results. The more sets of data that you can find with similar results, the stronger your claim. Consequently, Brinson, Hood, and Beebower redid their study and generated almost identical results.

Today the issue is reasonably considered settled. No one with an IQ of higher than room temperature disputes the impact of asset allocation on investment results. Large institutions and sophisticated investors are increasingly turning to asset class investing. Studies such as the BHB one have contributed to the diversion of over $500 billion in assets away from active management and into passive or index funds during the period following their introduction in 1970 until 1990. The trend is accelerating as more investors catch on to the advantages of asset class investing: more reliable performance, lower cost, and lower risk.

More recently the BHB papers have been attacked again on the basis of statistical methodology. However, there is no putting the cat back into the bag. The role of asset allocation as a key component determining investment results has been firmly established. The BHB study broke a mental logjam on Wall Street. Active management would henceforth be on the defensive.

ASSET ALLOCATION: THE LESSONS FOR INVESTORS

Asset class investing, that is, investing and making commitments to whole markets rather than to individual securities, is a fundamental shift in emphasis from what most of us grew up with. Rather than pondering over whether to purchase GM or Ford, we should be deciding how much of our assets to commit to large, U.S. company stocks. Rather than wondering whether to buy now or later, we should be thinking in terms of long-term commitments to our chosen asset classes.

Is there a lesson here for us? If the vast majority of investment returns can be attributed to an asset allocation decision, shouldn't we concentrate our efforts where it will have the most impact? The impact of asset allocation or investment policy swamps the other decisions. Putting the asset classes together to form a portfolio that meets your goals is where the bulk of the heavy work should be done.

Asset allocation offers more control, lower risk, and a more consistent, disciplined approach to the entire problem of making decisions in an atmosphere of uncertainty.

EIGHT

THE EFFICIENT MARKET DEBATE

A sset allocation investing opens up a whole new bag of worms to deal with. What role should investment managers play? Can traditional managers add value to the process? Are they worth their costs? Can they beat the market? Most financial economists believe that markets work far too well (too efficiently) to allow investors to consistently earn excess returns.

If you believe markets are efficient, then the traditional stock-picking, market-timing, active managers have a tough case to prove that they add value. The logical conclusion of the efficient markets debate is to fire your traditional manager and buy index funds. Notwithstanding the overwhelming evidence that supports efficient markets, you can understand that this approach finds little favor on Wall Street, where management fees are considered both a sacred right and an entitlement program. But, if markets are efficient, then investors are wasting billions on management fees each year in a futile attempt to outperform. A lot is at stake here. It's not an academic debate.

THE INFORMATION AGE

You know how quickly information can spread worldwide. And you are aware how thoroughly our lives are being changed as a result. We can all plug into almost unimaginable wells of information, much of it updated in real time as we watch. If we choose to, many of us can work effectively from home, or on an ice flow in the South Pacific. Our clients and associates may neither know nor care where we are located. I'm no longer surprised to see prominent Miami attorneys negotiating deals and settlements on their cell phones, faxing copies of contracts and pleadings back and forth, setting their court calendars, or checking for e-mail messages— all from the backs of their sport fisherman while trolling for giant tuna off Bimini. Anybody, anywhere can be plugged into almost anything.

How quickly and effectively information spreads is at the heart of the debate over just how efficient our markets are. The question, far from being of only academic interest, directly impacts every investor. Even if the term "efficient market" is unknown to them, investors form their strategies and view their alternatives based on their opinions on the efficiency of the various markets.

MARKET FUNDAMENTALS

For markets to operate properly, to set prices and values, two conditions are necessary: There must be willing buyers and sellers (under no particular pressure to buy or sell), and these buyers and sellers should both possess perfect knowledge. (Should one side possess more information than the other, then we must expect that that side has a tremendous advantage. We must then expect the holder of this additional knowledge to use it to extract undeserved profits or economic rents.)

Markets are the very heart and soul of the capitalistic system. The invisible hand sets prices, determines how goods and services are distributed, and encourages further growth of the system with benefits for all. For markets to work at all, there must be a general feeling that they are fair.

In organized markets, governments and regulators go to a great deal of trouble to ensure that both sides operate on a level playing field. Ideally no one should have an advantage. So government requires mountains of disclosure, sets accounting and financial reporting standards, licenses brokerages, dealers, representatives, investment advisors, salespeople, and even the markets themselves. The government monitors for compliance, prohibits certain insider trading, and acts as the policeman to create an equal opportunity environment.

In a Perfect World

Let's look at a perfect market: lots of buyers and sellers, homogenous product, perfect knowledge, and instantaneous spread of new information. Prices are determined by the independent judgment of thousands of buyers and sellers. New information reaches buyers and sellers instantly, prices adjust instantly, and neither side can expect an advantage, or anticipate economic rents. The market is perfectly efficient.

Prices in an Efficient Market

In this perfect market, no amount of additional research will improve the investor's position. All that can be known is already known about each security and the economic prospects. Prices settle into equilibrium at a level that reflects both the market rate of return and the additional risk that each security carries. All that is necessary for an individual investor to attain the appropriate rate of return is to buy and hold a diversified portfolio. The individual investor need not exhibit either superior skill or cunning to match the most sophisticated institution. Furthermore, the individual cannot possibly underperform no matter how brain-dead he is. The market has set the appropriate price for each security.

Pricing Models

How the market accomplishes the miracle of setting the proper price for each security is still the subject of lively debate. Various models have been proposed that should lead to appropriate pricing. Buyers and sellers are attempting to discount all the future benefits of owning a security to a present value that is equal to the price.

Buyers and sellers must also assess the risk in a particular asset, and compare that risk to the market as a whole in arriving at the price that will clear the market. Asset pricing and expected returns are directly related. Risky assets have lower costs and higher expected returns than less risky assets. In a later chapter, we will discuss some improvements to the theory of asset pricing that can assist you in plotting your own investment strategy.

No market is perfectly efficient, but our securities markets are pretty darned efficient. Today, as we have all observed, information spreads worldwide with the speed of light. Millions of people have access to the same information at the same time. Millions of traders constantly monitor for pricing aberrations around the world. Where such pricing discrepancies exist, they are almost instantly closed by normal arbitrage. Thousands of computers continuously screen prices against multiple criteria, formulas, and models to detect mispricing. Hundreds of analysts may follow a single stock. Secrets are very few.

With all this activity going on, investors must ask themselves what the chances are that they will be able to develop a single investment idea that hundreds or thousands of others haven't already considered. If others have already considered and acted on our idea, then their knowledge must be factored into the price of the stock. Is it ever possible to get an edge, and, if so, can we get it reliably enough to make a difference? In the real world, research, transaction, and tax costs are high. We would have to be right a rather daunting percent of the time to overcome our trading costs.

In a real way, the very skill, quality, access, and number of the people doing research limits the value of the process. If nobody did research, then giant market discrepancies would occur. Simple research should lead to giant gains. But with so many players, the point of diminishing returns may be far behind us. The hundreds of thousands of often brilliant researchers and analysts make the market efficient. Notice that we are not saying that you can never win, only that it is unlikely that you can consistently win enough to overcome the costs of trying.

DEGREES OF EFFICIENCY

Debate about the efficient market boils down into considering one of three models. At one end of the spectrum is the strong market theory: No one can ever get information that isn't known to the market. Even insiders cannot benefit from their position. Supporters point to studies of price movements before significant public announcements to prove that inside information leaks. The weak market theory acknowledges that insiders may occasionally profit from their information. The semi-strong theory cuts down the middle.

It would be hard for me to argue that markets are always perfect. Insiders do occasionally score big gains. Of course, they must be willing to risk jail. And quite often even insiders lose when their sure things don't pan out. Only the most naive among us would think that insider trading has been eliminated. However, as information spreads more quickly and further, it becomes more difficult to profit from insider trading and harder to conceal it from regulators. While occasional violations will continue to occur, the impact on the markets is probably minimal. Some economists today even argue that the prohibition of insider trading in unnecessary and counterproductive.

The more important issue is whether research and active management can add value to a portfolio. As we have noted, if markets are efficient, then all the research in the world will not improve an investor's results. If not, then research can be a valuable addition. If we can set up an appropriate benchmark for a market or a portion of it, then we can measure the impact of management. Fortunately, today we have hundreds of indexes that measure the performance of various markets and parts of them. If we don't like the available indexes, it's easy enough to generate others that capture a more specific portion of the target market. Indexes have no transaction, management, or other real-world costs. They are always fully invested. They offer the perfect investment style to use as a comparison.

Management offers not only style, but selection of individual securities and perhaps market timing. Management costs money, both in management fees and transaction costs. In addition, it is difficult for managers to stay fully invested even if that is their goal. Not counting taxes, management is generally assumed to cost at least 2 percent a year. If the investor pays taxes, the constant buying and selling will create substantial tax liability that becomes a heavy drag on performance.

Index funds are mutual funds that mimic an index. In the real world, they will have some transaction costs and other expenses. These expenses average between .2 percent and .5 percent, depending on the market and the sponsor of the fund. Index funds do not constantly buy and sell, so the tax drag will not be nearly so heavy. This can be a substantial benefit for taxpayers and occurs as a fortunate byproduct. If markets are efficient, index funds do not have to bother with all that pesky research. Is this a free lunch? No, not really. Other, less wise investors are paying for all the research that makes the market so efficient.

If markets are not efficient, in theory good managers will overcome all the direct and indirect costs that they generate and add value. A good manager exploits market inefficiencies to produce superior results and relies on research, experience, intuition, or superior skill and cunning to decide what and when to buy and sell.

TYPES OF RESEARCH

Market research divides itself into two types: technical analysis and fundamental analysis. Let's look at each of them.

TECHNICAL ANALYSIS

Technical analysis starts with the assumption that everything one needs to know about a stock or market can be learned from studying its price and past movements. By plotting or charting past movements, technicians believe that they can discover repetitive patterns that will suggest valid buy and sell signals. Discovery of the right signals will lead to effective market timing. Some of the "pure" technicians insist on studying charts without the name of the firm attached so that they will not be confused or distracted by their knowledge of the firm. Technicians use all sorts of data and combinations of data to generate their signals. They will study insider trading, consumer confidence, interest rates, yield curves, market volume, short sales, odd lot volume, ratios of new highs to new lows, and hundreds of other indicators to generate their signals. They tend to speak in terms of resistance levels, floors, breakouts, proprietary trading strategies, periods of increased market risk, and other mysterious terms. Often technicians attempt to add a layer of legitimacy to their work by having the data fed into computers for number crunching and analysis.

Technical analysis persists in spite of the total lack of any credible evidence that it is effective. One might as well examine the entrails of animals, chart the stars, or worship the tooth fairy. Looking back, one can always find patterns that led to market events. The only little problem is that when you want to look forward, those patterns are no help. Many technicians constantly revise their indicators as they fail in real life, then backcast using the new indicators, and publish the theoretical results. To give the backcast greater validity, it is common to have a CPA firm certify that, had you used these techniques, you would have had this result. The fact that real, live investors never obtained those results is seldom disclosed. Today there are several landmark cases winding their way through the courts concerning backcasting, and the Securities and Exchange Commission has taken a lively interest in the subject.

Wall Street loves technicians and continues to pay them lip service. Right or wrong, technicians generate huge trading volume. Whether the investor wins or loses, the house always gets their slice. The media gives the technicians undue attention in their unending quest for simple solutions to complex questions and pithy, quotable, seven-second sound bites. Investors often desperately want to believe that someone can protect them from market forces that they do not understand. Technicians prey on the risk aversion we all feel by seemingly offering protection against the market's downside. By offering an illusion of risk reduction, market timers and technicians appeal to conservative and fearful investors. They paint themselves as concerned and responsible, while giving the impression that a buy and hold strategy is somehow wild and crazy.

FUNDAMENTAL ANALYSIS

Fundamental analysis is far more rational. It concerns itself with examination of the firm and the economy. Fundamental research looks at financial data, sales forecasts, market share, quality of management, expansion plans, new products, competitive position, economic forecasts, and other data to search out the real value of companies and the prospects that they face. From the investor's point of view, there is so much fundamental research done and the results are so widely and quickly distributed that she must decide if available information will give her a unique edge. One must always assume that a million or more people already know what you have just discovered.

Fundamental research also has a fundamental problem: forecasting. The market and economic environment is far too complex to allow for accurate forecasting, even if we have perfect data and insight. At best we have a very poor understanding of how the economy and the world's markets work. Even worse, noneconomic events pop up randomly to confuse us even more. One well-placed bullet, typhoon, coup, drought, or earthquake can make shambles of the best forecast. As a result, earnings and interest rate forecasts are so laughably bad that anyone with a 40 percent success rate can qualify as an expert.

CONFLICTS OF INTEREST

There is a darker side to the research problem that investors must also consider. The motives of the research departments may not always be pure. Wall Street has its fingers in many pies. As a result, conflicts of interest creep in to the analysis. In one famous case, an analyst observed publicly that Donald Trump was in big trouble with his Atlantic City project. Covering the debt was likely to be a big problem. Trump complained. The analyst was fired. The analyst's employers had had visions of assisting Trump with yet another bond offering. So much for honest research. Trump's later problems in Atlantic City are well-documented. The story is only unusual in that it became public when the analyst sued over his wrongful termination.

Few things gladden the hearts of Wall Street's barons like a big, juicy underwriting or takeover. The fees a big takeover can generate are beyond the ability of most of us mortals to even imagine. Wall Street knows that sell recommendations hurt the feelings of the very managers who control underwriting and takeover business. Hurt feelings often translate into a diminished prospect for further business. So it shouldn't surprise us that the ratio of buy to sell recommendations is skewed and that a sell recommendation often comes far too late to be of any use.

Wall Street continues to hype its research, partly to generate trading volume, partly to justify the full-service fees, and for another, important, and self-serving reason. Brokers who rely on research for recommendations shed a good deal of their liability if the recommendation doesn't work out. Some brokerages have taken to publishing both technical and fundamental research, often with directly conflicting recommendations. Now, how much help is that?

AN ALTERNATIVE POINT OF VIEW

Detractors of the efficient market theory point to the often-strange behavior of markets. For instance, they argue that the market couldn't have been right both before and after the crash of 1987 when it lost 500 points in one day. They miss the point. Nobody is saying that the market is always right, or even rational. The real point is that if markets are efficient, it is very unlikely that you, or anybody else, will be able to consistently beat them.

Another problem with the efficient market theory is that clearly not all markets are operating at the same standards. Very small companies have fewer analysts; some issues are thinly traded. Foreign and emerging markets have different disclosure and financial reporting criteria, enforcement may be lax, or corruption endemic. Some markets do not even have insider trading restrictions. All these complaints are valid, and all give comfort to managers who argue that they can exploit the inefficiencies to obtain above benchmark returns. In fact, these arguments weaken each day as the inability of active managers to deliver becomes clearer and clearer.

The lines are clearly drawn. If markets are not efficient, then managers should have an easy time beating their benchmark. If markets are efficient, then we should consider firing the managers and hiring the index. The proof is in the pudding.

In Chapter 9 we will examine the real-world performance of managers. We will also want to consider if overperformance is the result of skill and cunning or just dumb luck. Finally, does performance matter, and can managers repeat it? Will last year's heroes be back? Or will they fall into well-deserved obscurity after their fifteen minutes of fame? I'll give you a hint: Don't bet against the efficient market!

NINE

CAN MANAGERS ADD VALUE?

n the context of the efficient market debate this statement is true: If markets are efficient, then management may not be able to add value. More to the point, all the evidence supports the argument that investors waste billions of dollars each year in management fees with only additional risk and reduced returns to show for it. The performance fairy strikes again!

Playing tennis, golf, or chess are all activities that require skill. We can quickly identify the skilled players. On the other hand, craps and roulette are pure games of chance. Skill plays no part in the outcome. What about managing a stock portfolio? Can managers beat the market? If so, can we tell if they are skillful or lucky? Can we use past performance to predict future performance? Do winners repeat?

Measuring performance for management results requires a benchmark. It's important to use the right benchmark or we will hopelessly confuse ourselves. It's not very useful to compare apples and oranges, or foreign to domestic stock performance. As academics and consultants have delved deeper into the performance issue, the benchmarks have, by necessity, become more elegantly defined.

It's vitally important to have clean data. No one wants to do a study only to find out that the data used was corrupt. The ultimate nightmare for the academic is to have someone else point out that the data is corrupt. Fortunately, we have a great deal of clean data available from reliable third-party sources that most of us can agree on. For example, the private consulting firm SEI maintains the largest database on investment performance of institutional managers. Morningstar supplies extensive data on the mutual fund industry, and the Center for Research in Securities Prices (CRSP) maintains a database on individual security pricing.

A QUICK TEST

Let's start with a very crude test of management performance. We will compare the domestic growth equity mutual fund performance supplied by Morningstar against the S&P 500 index for one-, three-, five-, and ten-year periods looking back from December 31, 2000. The S&P 500 index is a fair comparison for large domestic companies. Of the 2,150 domestic growth equity mutual funds that Morningstar covered for the one-year period, 1,284 beat the S&P 500 while 866 of the funds fell short. Results ranged from 84.67 percent to –75.96 percent, while the S&P 500 attained a –9.10 percent return.

During the three-year period, the S&P 500 returned 12.26 percent while results in the funds varied from 60.82 percent to –37.67 percent, compounded annually. Of the total 1,430 funds, 811 beat the S&P 500.

Shifting to the five-year period, of 799 funds, 298 beat the S&P 500. Results ranged from 37.45 percent to –23.46 percent while the index racked up 18.32 percent.

At ten years, only 110 of 267 funds managed to beat the index, and results varied from 26.14 percent to 3.82 percent compounded annually against 17.45 percent for the S&P 500.

If beating the S&P 500 is a valid test of management ability, then a lot of managers are clearly not worth their salt. Fewer of them appear to be winners than we might have expected.

THIS TEST MAY NOT BE ENTIRELY PRECISE, BUT...

Let me be the very first to say that while this little study makes the point, and it is valid, it isn't perfect. In all cases, the average fund result fell below the index. However, the average result doesn't take into account the size of the fund. A few small funds could throw off the average in either direction, so perhaps we shouldn't be too concerned about the average.

Another reason we might be concerned about our little exercise is the issue of survivor bias. Funds that fail during the measurement period are not measured in the results. Mutual fund companies often make poorly performing funds disappear by merging them into more successful funds. Fund performance is not merged, and the companies succeed in burying their mistakes. The survivors presumably have a better record than the total number that started the measurement period. Voilà! A little bit of marketing magic allows the fund companies to show performance better than their shareholders actually experienced. A better study would account for this distortion.

A problem that disturbs me in this type of analysis is that a single year may account for extraordinary results. If that one year occurred last year, then it will show up in all time periods. The results will appear far more consistent than they actually were. A fund that had nine very average years followed by a great last year will look good for the past one, three, five, and ten years. If the great year occurred during the first year, then the ten-year result would look good, but the one-, three-, and five-year periods would look only fair. It is a far different picture, even though the total results would be the same. We haven't adjusted for consistency of results. Finally, we haven't adjusted for risk. Both the big winners and losers may have taken large risks to get where they are.

WHAT ABOUT THE WINNERS?

Some managers did beat the averages, a few by a very wide margin. All of them may claim superior skill and cunning. What about them? Is it possible to conclude that they are wise and the other managers are fools? By extension, are the people who invested with the winners wiser than the rest of us? Could we have predicted the winners?

Probability theory accounts for a number of winners and losers in any random series of events. If a million people each attempted to toss heads with a coin for several rounds, we could reasonably predict the number of winners after the first round. For instance, after ten rounds we would expect 976.563 winners. Each person has come up with heads ten times in a row. Because this is a random event, we would not expect exactly 977 survivors. We could, however, consult with a statistician and predict a very tight range for the number of winners. In an event that requires no skill, we can predict with some confidence that there will be survivors after ten rounds. We would also have a fair idea about how many winners there should be. Should one of our survivors become convinced that his skill contributed to his success, we might have a difficult time convincing him that he is deluding himself.

One way to determine if skill contributed to the outcome would be to see if there were significantly more winners than probability would have predicted. Suppose instead of about 977 winners, we ended up with 5,000 or 10,000? Then we might have to concede that an element of skill was involved.

If markets are efficient, we should expect to see a random distribution of results. When we study mutual fund performance, we should expect to see some winners. Probability theory demands it. We would be very disappointed and concerned if an occasional Magellan Fund (the most famous and successful fund in the whole history of the universe) didn't turn up. What we find is much fewer than a random distribution would predict. However, if we adjust the fund results by about 2 percent to add back their average costs of management and trading, then we get just about the bell-shaped curve that we would expect for performance distribution.

Since we have fewer rather than more winners, it is very difficult to support the argument that the winners got there by superior skill and cunning instead of with pure, dumb luck. This is a powerful but not totally conclusive argument. Like our deluded coin tosser, Peter Lynch (former manager of the Fidelity Magellan Fund) will never agree with the premise.

IF IT WAS GOOD YESTERDAY, WILL IT BE GREAT TOMORROW?

What about track record? If management skill adds value, can past performance give us an indication of future performance? Do winners repeat? How successful will I be if I only buy the funds with the best (that is, past) five-year track record?

A recent study examined mutual fund performance by category over several five-year time periods. Funds were divided into quartiles by past-total performance, and then followed for an additional five years. The results were enough to blow your mind! A top-quartile fund had just less than a 50 percent chance of being in the top half during the following five years. A bottom-quartile fund had just slightly more than a 50 percent chance of being in the top half during the following five-year period. Similar studies with similar results were completed by a large pension fund on the performance of its managers and a large consulting company on the results of the managers whose performance they tracked. In other words, we can't count on either winners or losers to repeat.

WHERE ARE THEY NOW?

I often encounter investors who still believe that the most important criteria for selecting an investment manager is past performance. This can lead to some mighty strange encounters. When I tell them that past performance is useless information, they look at me as if I were just a few bricks short of a full load. "Performance is all there is," they say, with more than just a little irritation, impatience, and condescension.

I hear myself in those words. That was what I was saying just a few years ago. I assumed that investment management skill was like landing an airplane or hitting a tennis ball. Selecting individual stocks with greater than average potential. Avoiding market turndowns could be learned. Some folks could master these skills and the few masters at them would be evident to all. Of course, the primary indication of investment management genius should be past performance. Superior past performance should be a reliable predictor of above-average future performance. Any fool can see that, right?

Just in case there is some misguided soul somewhere on this planet who still thinks that managers add value consistently or that past performance is an indication of future performance, I performed the following test.

We pulled out our rusty old Morningstar Disk with results ending December 1997. We then asked the Morningstar software to rank returns of the Morningstar category "Large Growth" for the previous five-year period, screening out any funds that held more than 10 percent foreign equity. We found 226 funds. Of these 226, we nominated the top twenty funds as our active manager heroes.

Figure 9-1. Top 20 growth funds from January 1993 to December 1997.

Order	Fund Name	Tot Ret Annualized 5Yr	% Rank
1	Spectra	23.81%	1
2	Robertson Stephens Val+Gr A	22.64%	1
3	Enterprise Growth A	21.77%	1
4	White Oak Growth Stock	21.63%	2
5	Enterprise Growth and Inc Y	21.56%	2
6	Founders Growth	21.13%	3
7	Putnam Investors A	20.71%	3
8	Harbor Capital Appreciation	20.27%	4
9	Pioneer Growth A	20.16%	4
10	MFS Massachusetts Inv Grth A	20.08%	5
11	Papp America-Abroad	19.62%	5
12	Vanguard Index Growth	19.46%	6
13	Gabelli Growth	19.43%	6
14	State St Exchange	19.35%	6
15	Universal Capital Growth	19.28%	7
16	IDS Growth A	18.87%	7
17	Fidelity Adv Eqty Grth Instl	18.74%	8
18	AIM Blue Chip A	18.73%	9
19	Janus Growth & Income	18.62%	9
20	Diversification	18.40%	9
220	Fund Average	20.21%	
	Index : S & P 500	20.25%	

BIGGER WAS BETTER

Domestic large companies were the place to be during the covered period. In fact, in some circles the S&P 500 index was considered the complete balanced portfolio. Big was definitely better. Back then, tech stock/dot-com/new economy/new metrics mania hadn't arrived quite yet.

It was a tough environment for managers. The domestic markets were unbelievably generous, but the largest of the large dominated performance. Few active managers were able to beat the S&P 500. The best-performing managed fund came in with 23.81 percent annual return. The

Figure 9-2. Growth funds, January 1993—December 1997, performance of $10,000 compared to S&P 500.

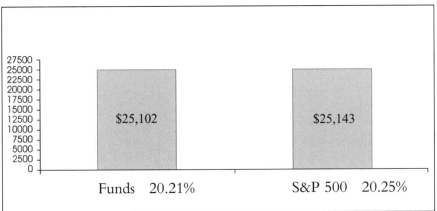

S&P 500 turned in a stunning 20.25 percent, while the average of the top twenty funds turned in 20.21 percent. While eight of the top twenty beat the benchmark, on average the top twenty funds fell short. If you are following the math here, in the total group, 218 of 226 fell short of the index!

Frankly, we normally find that more managers to beat the index. While hardly a ringing endorsement for active managers, it gets even worse.

If, however, you still believe that active managers can add value and that past performance is any indication of future performance, then you would assume that a subsequent time period would find these twenty funds rising to the top of the heap again, right?

Active managers are fond of saying that even if they have a tough time beating the market in good times, they can protect capital through skill and cunning during bad times. The following five years gave them the perfect opportunity to prove it. This was a time of great turmoil and transition. The dot-com bubble built and burst, taking a large part of the previous decade's gains with it. If ever there was time for active managers to shine, this should have been it.

This argument flunks convincingly when we examine the date. We fast forward five years to look at the five-year results as of December 2002. The group of funds passing our screen with a five-year track record has grown from 226 funds to 1172 funds. After a wild and hairy ride, the S&P 500 returns shrank to a very disappointing –0.58 percent.

Of our original twenty top funds, two funds have disappeared or been merged away. Another fund changed its investment objective, leaving just seventeen. We didn't /couldn't calculate their returns, probably distorting

Figure 9-3. Where are they now? Growth funds, Jan 1997–Dec 2002.

Order	Fund Name	Tot Ret Annualized 5Yr	% Rank
250	Spectra	-1.90%	43
#	Robertson Stephens Val+Gr A	#	#
153	Enterprise Growth A	-0.44%	26
412	White Oak Growth Stock	-4.52%	71
126	Enterprise Growth and Inc Y	-0.08%	27
518	Founders Growth	-7.57%	89
361	Putnam Investors A	-3.81%	82
204	Harbor Capital Appreciation	-1.16%	35
510	Pioneer Growth A	-7.37%	87
162	MFS Massachusetts Inv Grth A	-0.60%	28
376	Papp America-Abroad	-4.05%	65
191	Vanguard Index Growth	-1.09%	33
328	Gabelli Growth	-3.13%	57
62	State St Exchange	1.18%	16
*	Universal Capital Growth	*	*
483	IDS Growth A	-6.31%	83
157	Fidelity Adv Eqty Grth Instl	-0.48%	27
342	AIM Blue Chip A	-3.35%	59
43	Janus Growth & Income	3.96%	6
*	Diversification	*	*
	FUND AVERAGE	-2.40%	
	INDEX: S&P 500	-0.58%	

Disappeared. No data available.
*Merged with other funds.

the results (in favor of the active managers) due to the survivor bias. Of the remaining seventeen funds, two maintained top quartile performance against their peers, seven fell to second quartile, and eight fell to bottom half. Four funds found themselves in the bottom 20 percent of the pack, and the worst sank to the 89th percentile against its peers. The average of all seventeen funds fell to –2.40 percent, or not significantly different from the –2.68 percent that the entire 1172 funds experienced.

The worst fund from the original surviving seventeen (Founders Growth, which was number six during the first period) fell to a compound return of –7.57 percent, or about 5 percent compounded below the index, convincingly demonstrating that active management adds rather than reduces investment risk.

Figure 9-4. Growth funds, January 1997–December 2002, performance of $10,000 compared to S&P 500.

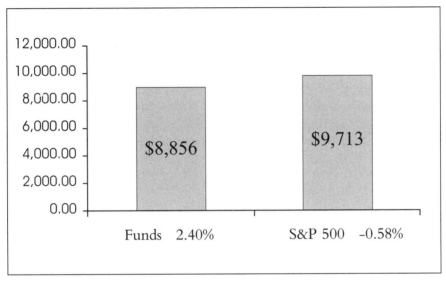

We would have predicted that all funds would have trailed the index by about 2 percent, an amount equal to their expenses and trading costs. That's almost exactly what happened.

We also would have predicted that the top performing funds during the first period would have random results in the trailing period that were not significantly different from the total group. That's almost exactly what happened.

If the first period results were any indication of skill and cunning, then we would expect them to be duplicated in the second period. But the seventeen surviving top-performing funds from the first period were able to collectively underperform the index by a about 2 percent.

It's worth mentioning that the above results are computed before we consider the impact of taxes. But active managers generate so much turnover while futilely pursue their holy grail of outperforming the relevant benchmark index that they systematically destroy capital for taxable investors.

Active management generates enormous fees when compared to passive or index investing, so we can't expect active managers to give up without a fight. They don't. Rather than admit it's all a hoax, they invest part of their fees in marketing to promote active management as a value-added service. This enormous marketing effort preconditions investors to do just the wrong thing. But rational investors looking at the facts should overwhelmingly choose passive, or indexing, as the lowest-cost, lowest-risk, lowest-tax-cost, most effective method to achieve their investment goals.

So after just a few moments of reflection, we should all absorb these four lessons:

1. Past performance is no indication of future performance.
2. Active management will produce an average return of about 2 percent below the appropriate index.
3. Choosing between active managers on the basis of past performance is a brain-dead, proven losing strategy.
4. Active management adds rather than reduces investment risk.

If past performance is not a reliable indicator of future performance, then the whole case for management skill collapses. Past performance may simply be a random result indicating luck, not skill and cunning. The implications for active managers' future employment are pretty grim. If investors ever catch on to the reality that management selection is an unpriced risk with high, negative expectations, lots of fund managers will have to obtain different employment.

Viewed from another perspective, the investor must consider the proposition that markets bring returns. It is not the skill and cunning of active managers. Market or index returns are very fine indeed. The dumbest investor alive will attain those returns by simply buying an index fund.

If investors can't be highly confident that the decision to hire a manager will result in better net performance than his benchmark (the appropriate index), then they should certainly choose the index approach. The index offers the lowest-cost and lowest-risk approach to obtaining market returns.

We started out asking the question, "Where are they now?" Yesterday's heroes are doing quite nicely, thank you. As a result of their past good fortune, investors threw money into their funds at record levels. With those giant cash inflows, fees for the lucky-few managers grew exponentially. While the skill of fund managers is questionable, a fund's reputation, suitably enhanced by deft marketing, has great measurable persistence and value. Past performance is a remarkably reliable predictor of future cash flow into a fund. While the new investors suffered below-average returns, the managers grew truly rich. It's almost enough to challenge your faith in the efficient-market theory.

Again, this isn't a conclusive argument. We can't say for certain that a top- or bottom-performing fund won't repeat, just that it doesn't appear to be more likely to continue its performance than random chance might dictate. These types of arguments take on near-religious intensity on Wall Street. I don't expect them to be solved in my lifetime. I do think that the overwhelming weight of the evidence suggests that markets are efficient and that management has a rather small chance of reliably exploiting inefficiencies. Given the egos and profits involved, you can expect further spirited debate.

In a nutshell, here is how I see the argument: You can accept the market rate of return. For instance, in the large companies that return is about 11 percent. You can try to beat the market. If you try to beat the market, you have only about a 20 percent chance of winning. Playing that game will cost you by lowering your average rate of return by about 2 percent. There is no reliable way to determine which manager might beat the market tomorrow. Somebody is always going to be on a roll. However, information on yesterday's winner is all but useless. Chasing yesterday's hot managers is clearly an uncompensated risk and a loser's game.

SOME RECENT DISSENTING VOICES

To further complicate the issue, two of the heavyweight thinkers who might be expected to support efficient markets have just published studies that show that in the very short term, less than two years, winners may tend to repeat. Both Roger Ibbotson and William F. Sharpe have international reputations in finance, and Sharpe has a Nobel Prize in economics, so they speak with some authority. Both of them recently made similar observations on short-term performance. Sharpe, in particular, goes out of his way to point out that the data may be ambiguous.

I personally believe that factors other than skill and cunning can extend a fund's winning or losing streak over a short multiyear period. For instance, during the early 1990s, a large overweighting in healthcare stocks resulted in significant over-benchmark performance for several years. Several mutual funds built reputations based on that one call alone. Since the decline of the healthcare sector stocks, most of those funds have descended into a disappointing level of mediocrity. I'm not sure that chasing last year's winner does anything other than position you as next year's loser.

During the last half of the 1990s managers that loaded up on S&P 500 and tech stocks had similar overperformance. Those funds that concentrated their bets looked brilliant for a while, then melted down before our eyes in 2000 and 2002. It's the same story with the same ending.

It's easy to pick last year's winner. It's difficult to pick next year's. A number of magazines routinely make mutual fund recommendations. Perhaps the most sophisticated of the popular business publications is *Forbes*. One would suspect that if recommendations can be done, *Forbes* has the resources to do it. For years the magazine has published an honor roll of mutual funds. If you had invested steadily in the *Forbes* funds, you would have had very disappointing results. This underperformance is so consistent and widely known in the industry that the award is considered the kiss of death.

TOWARD BETTER BENCHMARKS

We can build a benchmark for just about any market or portion of a market. For example, suppose we divided all the publicly listed stocks in the United States into ten different sizes by market capitalization on one axis and ten different segments based on book to market ratio on the other axis. We now have 100 different possible submarkets. We could call each submarket an investment style. Each style could have its own index or benchmark. If we studied the performance of each style, we would find that they were sharply different from each of the others. Each style would have distinct rates of return and exhibit different risk or standard deviation. Each would also have different correlations with the others. Each style could go through a market cycle with dramatically different results for each time period. In other words, there isn't just one domestic market, but many.

Most, but not all managers, confine themselves to a distinct style. Very few operate in all parts of the market or switch from one part to another. For instance, they may be large-cap value, mid-cap growth, or small-cap market. This is the area of the market they claim to know best, think has the greatest potential, or perhaps were hired to manage. In any event, over time most of the performance they obtain may simply be attributable to where they invest in the market. It wouldn't be fair to compare a small-cap value manager with the S&P 500, which is basically a very large-cap index. To test whether this is so, we can compare their results with the index that matches their area of investment. This type of benchmark is much more precise than just arbitrarily choosing an index like the S&P 500.

These benchmark designs can become very precise and elaborate. One large consulting firm examines the unique style of a manager within the market, builds an index of all the stocks in the style, and then has a computer construct 1,000 hypothetical portfolios from the index. They then average the results of the hypotheticals to create the benchmark to measure the manager. In the vast majority of cases, managers are unable to demonstrate that they add value against the benchmark.

The conclusion that investment style is much more important than management within the style become harder and harder to ignore. Even when a manager beats his benchmark, we are left with the problem of figuring out whether he was good or lucky. The revolving door and continuing management searches within large institutions for managers who add value lend credence to the idea that maybe it can't be done consistently. The migration from active management to indexing or passive management indicates that many large institutions have concluded that adding value either can't be done, or isn't worth trying to get.

TAKING BIG BETS AGAINST THE BENCHMARK

Even within a carefully defined style, investors are still faced with an alarming variation of results in both the short and long term. Looking again at the ten-year result for domestic equity funds, there is a surprisingly large variation in outcomes. Part of this is attributable to style differences within the markets. But a large amount of the variation can also be attributed to sector or timing bets by the managers. When a manager decides to overweight or underweight the firms or sectors in his style group, he expects to improve results. He might decide that General Motors will do better than Ford. Or he might decide that cars will do better than banks. Finally, he might decide cash will do better than stocks. From my perspective there is a chance that he will be wrong. If so, he will not make even the benchmark return.

Most of us are risk-averse. If at the beginning of the ten-year period we were given a choice of a sure return of 16.58 percent or one that might run from 33.37 percent to −12.79 percent, most investors would go for the sure return. Looking back, most individuals never came close to the benchmark and wish they had chosen it. The benchmark would have been better than all but 126 of the 294 funds. A totally passive approach to selection and a policy of no market timing would have delivered very satisfactory returns. The thing is, we don't have to be either skillful or lucky to get them.

CAN MANAGERS ADD VALUE? DON'T BET ON IT!

Based on the dismal record of managers to outperform benchmarks, we have to take the argument that markets are efficient very seriously. While we will never be able to prove our case to the satisfaction of everyone, the evidence is pretty strong. This evidence is supported by studies of markets all over the world. Even if some other markets around the world are not as efficient as ours, they are still fairly efficient. If all the information isn't as good as what we are used to here, at least all the players are being equally deceived.

When we go about building our investment strategy, benchmark, style, or passive investing may be a very viable approach. After all, what's wrong with top-quartile results?

In my own practice, I use only institutional-class index funds. Today it is possible to index almost the entire world. I think that approach gives us the highest probability of a successful outcome with the lowest risk. To the extent possible, I want to see predictable results. I hate underperforming the benchmark more than I would enjoy overperforming. That makes me pretty much like my clients: risk averse. My conclusion: Do the right thing—index.

MORE ON STYLE INVESTING

So we're back to the thesis that asset allocation is a much more important question than which stock to choose, when to choose it, or which manager should handle it. If it's more critical to be in the right market or style than any other question, how do we choose the markets? What do we know about style-investing results? How will they will help us construct our own portfolios? We will focus on how size of the firm affects returns and the debate on growth or value style in Chapter 10.

TEN

DOING IT WITH STYLE

ost investors want to know where to invest their money for the best return and the lowest risk. That sounds like a pretty reasonable request.

Until just a few years ago, the investment business resounded with genteel arguments between managers with different investment approaches. Each manager would give compelling reasons why his methods were the best. Growth managers assumed that rapidly increasing sales, profits, and/or market share would lead to a rapidly growing stock price. Meanwhile, value managers argued convincingly that overlooked, or out of favor, companies would provide steady growth while high dividends and a large asset base would ensure downside protection. Small company managers spoke fondly of discovering one or two of tomorrow's Microsofts. Large company managers favored liquidity and well-established companies. Midsize company investors argued that second-tier companies offered stability, growth potential, and the opportunity to exploit market inefficiencies. The few foreign stock managers were busy trying to convince Americans that international investing wasn't crazy. (Emerging market managers were still in diapers.)

These arguments were wonderful entertainment, but seemingly doomed never to be resolved. The debaters lacked even common definitions. The discussion was devoid of appropriate yardsticks, without the necessary tools to measure performance or risk. Each management approach yielded acceptable, positive results, but each result excelled at different times. Comparisons between markets were necessarily difficult. Each manager stressed the time frames where his approach excelled.

Investors could hardly be blamed if they didn't find solid guidance from Wall Street's competing gurus. The truth is that all the gurus were blowing smoke. Nobody knew what markets gave the best results at the lowest risk. (The idea that various types of investments might be complementary hadn't been considered.) Let's look at how all this "smoke" affected returns.

A MODEST PROPOSAL

In 1992 two University of Chicago professors, Eugene Fama and Kenneth French, found an elegant way to help resolve the problems of investing. In doing so they touched off one of the liveliest debates, and biggest dog-fights, finance has seen in years. Their results were surprising, and their arguments were compelling. Markets appear to have a sweet spot where higher returns can be expected without additional risk.

Under the capital asset pricing model (CAP-M), stock prices and expected future returns are related to both the market risk and a unique risk that each stock has that is called beta. Beta is a measure of the volatility of the individual stock in relation to the market as a whole. Everyone in finance loved CAP-M. It was elegant and relatively easy to understand and explain. There was just one little problem: Beta didn't do a very good job of explaining either price or returns. In particular, CAP-M and beta left large anomalies in two areas: Small companies and low-price companies had higher than expected returns.

In their article "The Cross-Section of Expected Stock Returns," published in the June 1992 issue of *Journal of Finance*, Fama and French set out to find a better way to explain prices and returns.

Beta is a single-factor variable. Fama and French tried a number of other factors in combination to see if they could provide a better fit. They found that, together, size and book-to-market (BTM) ratio did the best job of explaining stock performance. BTM is the ratio of the firm's book value per share to the stock price. If you are particularly observant, you may have noticed that BTM is the inverse of price-to-book ratio (P/B). This was necessary because book value may sometimes be zero, and a ratio with zero on the bottom is impossible to use in calculations.

A firm with a high BTM has lots of assets per share compared to a low BTM firm. As it happens, high BTM firms have characteristics associated with value and low BTM firms tend to be growth firms. Growth and value are somewhat fuzzy terms. Everyone seems to agree that Microsoft is a growth company, but value seems to be in the eyes of the beholder. BTM provides an objective measure.

"Value investing" may be one of the great public relations terms. Value firms are sick puppies. High BTM firms (low price-to-book ratio) tend to have low price-to-earnings ratios (P/E), low return on equity, low return on assets, slow or no growth of sales, disappointing profits, and other discouraging financial results. Even though they have large assets, the market has driven down the price of the stock. Because management often has no clear idea how to generate additional business growth, many high BTM firms pay large dividends. They are troubled firms. Often they have been troubled for some time and will continue to be troubled in the future. The risk of business failure is higher than healthy, growing firms. High BTM firms are companies under stress. At the very least, their prospects for rapid growth are considered dim. Examples of large company value stocks are General Motors, Sears, Archer Daniels Midland, Burlington Northern, Allstate, Loews, and Federated Department Stores.

Low BTM firms (high price-to-book) are just the opposite. They have high P/Es, return on equity, and assets. Usually they have histories of exponential growth of profits, sales, market share, and other healthy, desirable attributes. In general, they have so many internal investment opportunities that they do not pay high dividends. They are healthy companies. We all think of Microsoft and Intel as examples of glamorous growth companies.

DIVIDING THE MARKET BY SIZE AND BTM RATIO

Fama and French took all the stocks in the New York Stock Exchange and divided them into ten groups, or deciles, by market capitalization. Market capitalization is the total value of all the securities of a firm. It is found by multiplying the price of a share times the number of shares outstanding.

Having established arbitrarily sized groups, they took all the stocks traded on all the exchanges and distributed them into the appropriate size groups. Because of the smaller average size of the non-NYSE stocks, the groups now have many more stocks in the smaller deciles than the equal distribution of the original NYSE deciles.

Now, think of the size groups as being from top to bottom. Fama and French then horizontally sliced the result into deciles according to BTM. We now have a square grid, cut into ten by ten groups, or one hundred portfolios or styles. Each portfolio was followed for one year, after which the procedure was repeated. The performance of each of the one hundred portfolios as annually redefined was followed for an extended time— twenty-eight years, from 1964 to 1992.

The results were amazing. Small company stocks had higher rates of return than larger company stocks, but they had a much higher risk as measured by standard deviation of returns. However, high BTM stocks (value stocks) had higher rates of return than low BTM stocks (growth stocks) without any higher risk, as measured by standard deviation. This occurred at every size level. The value guys were right all along.

Investors in the bottom three deciles by size might expect a total return of about 5 percent higher average return than the top three deciles. However, these investors will experience greatly increased volatility. At every size level, investors in the highest three deciles by BTM will receive about 5 percent greater average return than the bottom three. Value investors will not experience any significant increase in risk, at least as measured by volatility.

EACH NEW STUDY CREATES NEW PROBLEMS

The implications of this study, if validated, are staggering both for economists and for investors. CAP-M and many of its implications are discredited. Investors can now construct portfolios with better performance than the market as a whole. Economists are stuck with the problem of explaining how value stocks can provide higher total returns without being subject to additional risk.

William F. Sharpe, the author of CAP-M, seems to be enjoying the debate. He has stated that he thinks Fama and French are on to something. He has also said that he thinks CAP-M, for which he won the Nobel prize in economics, was a pretty good first effort, and he's glad that the committee can't take back the prize. The rest of the academics appear to have worked themselves into a frenzy, either attacking or defending CAP-M. You can find plenty of papers posted on the Internet at various universities, if you care to follow the battle.

One of the implications of CAP-M was that the superefficient portfolio, the one that generated the most return per unit of risk, was the total world market basket. An investor who wanted more or less risk could take this global market index and either leverage it or water it down with a risk-free asset. This led to the spread of global indexing as an investment technique. Now it turns out that investors can do considerably better than the world market index by heavily weighting their portfolios with small company and value stocks.

ECONOMIC JUSTIFICATION FOR THE THREE-FACTOR MODEL

The idea that investors can expect additional returns without additional risk has even Fama and French struggling. It smacks too much of a free lunch. Since they are from the University of Chicago, we must expect them to cheerfully die before they admit to the existence of a free lunch. They are trying to identify other factors besides volatility that could explain the paradox.

Fama and French believe that their findings are consistent with an efficient market. They relate the differences in pricing and performance to cost of capital. If you run a large company and either borrow money from the bank or issue bonds, you will generally pay a lower interest rate than a small company because of the lower risk that you appear to offer. In the same manner, if you issue stock, you will generally command a higher price than a small company. As we might expect, large companies have a lower cost of capital.

In a like manner, well-run firms have a smaller cost of capital than poorly run or stressed firms do. High cost of capital means depressed stock prices and translates into higher expected returns.

A BAG FULL OF SICK PUPPIES

I have to admit it's difficult to get very excited about an investment philosophy that advocates buying sick firms. It goes counter to the grain, and the whole idea takes a little getting used to. It's hard to imagine generating much envy as you describe your portfolio of downtrodden losers. However, the returns generated by a diversified portfolio of distressed companies more than make up for the glamour of trying to uncover tomorrow's Microsoft. It appears that investors have been paying too much for growth firms and paying too little for value firms.

Of course, the Fama and French research was subjected to all the normal indignities of any revolutionary study. However, enough studies in other markets and other time frames have validated the original work. Value stocks appear to perform equally well in global markets.

The three-factor model goes a long way toward explaining the returns of many mutual funds and portfolio managers. By examining the manager's style as defined by size and BTM ratio of her portfolio, we have another powerful tool to evaluate management effectiveness. It's even possible to examine the pattern of a fund's past performance and make a very close guess as to the portfolio composition. In most cases, style accounts for far more of the performance than skill, cunning, or luck.

Investors receive another benefit from the Fama and French three-factor model. By incorporating explanations of stock returns based on size and BTM ratios, we are able to more confidently predict expected returns when modeling portfolios. This methodology represents a measurable improvement over using unadjusted raw data past returns as the expected future rates of returns. Historical raw data is subject to unusual nonrecurring, noneconomic events that can dramatically distort its usefulness as a forecasting tool. Improved rates of return forecasts will lead to much improved optimization models and better-performing, lower-risk portfolios.

While long-term data strongly suggests the superiority of small company and value investing to maximize returns, we must still be aware that growth and larger companies may experience extended periods of market favoritism. For instance, small companies did far below average in the decade of the 1980s. In the short run we can expect significant year-to-year variation. Accordingly, it appears wise to continue to hold some of both investments in a well-constructed plan to minimize risk at the portfolio level. However, the best-available data indicates that a strong tilt to value and a higher representation of small company stocks in equity portfolios will handsomely reward long-term investors.

Fortunately, there are a number of index funds that invest in both small companies and value. As we construct our portfolio, we will be incorporating them into the mix to accomplish the desired tilt.

FUN WITH NUMBERS

In Chapter 11 we will be shifting gears to examine some basic techniques that investors should utilize as they begin to build an investment strategy to carry them into the twenty-first century. These are what I call no-brainers. The magic of compounding, dollar cost averaging, the joys of tax deferral, and why the time to invest is the time when you have the money—all will be discussed.

ELEVEN

MORE FUN WITH NUMBERS

The U.S. Census Department estimates that more than 1 million baby boomers will live to more be than one hundred years old. Yet few of the boomers have begun to save for retirement or even know how much it will cost. Savings rates have fallen, and life expectancy is increasing. Like two trains hurtling down a track toward one another, there is bound to be a crash between the two factors. And, it will not be pretty!

Boomers who wish to avoid the financial disaster of outliving their money have two realistic chances: They can beat the odds and die early or begin saving in a serious manner now. As we shall see, delay in beginning to save is not a viable option. When they save and invest, they had better get close to a market rate of return. Otherwise, there are going to be a lot of very old, very broke people wandering around. Given the demographic trends, it's not likely the government is going to be in a position to bail the boomers out.

One of the most powerful concepts in finance to assist investors is the magic of compounding. Compounding investments looks like magic.

Rather than increasing in a straight line, compound investments increase geometrically. Not only does principal increase each year, but this year's earnings become next year's principal and accrue even more earnings. The process repeats as long as the money is left to grow. What seems like a small difference in input generates a giant difference in the final result. In other words, what appears to be a small change in rate of return, or slightly longer time period, will make the difference between poverty and comfort in your old age.

Let's have a little fun with numbers to see how compounding can work for us. Applying what we can learn about compounding will give us some guidance in our accumulation planning.

First Things First

I have to warn you to have your basic financial house in order before you start a long-term investment plan. No one should invest until they have a three- to six-month cash reserve for emergencies and the proper insurance protection. It won't do you or your family any good at all to get a 30 percent rate of return if you lose your job, wreck your car, die, or become disabled tomorrow. In a very real sense, life and disability insurance buy you time. It's also important to have your basic estate planning completed. At a minimum, make sure that your will, trusts, power of attorney, living will, and directions to healthcare providers are in place and up-to-date.

Credit card and other high-interest consumer debts are just plain ugly. It's not reasonable to expect a higher return on your investments than the cost of your credit card interest. Clean up high-interest consumer debt, the earlier the better!

Put Time on Your Side

Here's an example of how compounding can put time on your side: Suppose that on the day you were born your father decided he wanted you to have a nice retirement when you turned sixty-five. Each year for ten years he deposited $1,000 into an account for your retirement. Assuming that he earned a reasonable 10 percent net, your retirement plan grew to $15,937.42 by your tenth birthday. At this point your father stopped making contributions. The fund continues to earn 10 percent net and you are able to resist the overwhelming urge to cash it in for a new Corvette when you reach twenty-one. The fund grows to $3,013,115.83 over the next fifty-five years.

With adjustment for inflation, we assume that inflation ate away about 3.5 percent of the nominal yield and the real value of the accumulation in terms of dollars when you were born is $322,027.60. The real value of the inflation-adjusted income available to you is $20,931.79 for the rest of your life. (We are assuming that you withdrew 6.5 percent beginning at age sixty-five and left 3.5 percent to grow to hedge the inflation rate.) All this was accomplished with a total cost to your father of only $10,000. Compounding worked its magic.

Now let's assume that your father waited until your tenth birthday to begin a savings program for you. If he deposited $1,000 a year for the next fifty-five years, he would only accumulate $1,880,591.43 for your retirement. Waiting ten years cost the accumulation more than $1.2 million, even though he contributed $55,000 to the program.

If your father still wanted to accumulate the $322,027.60, he would have to contribute $1,602.22 per year for fifty-five years at 10 percent interest. As a result, the total cost of the program has grown to $88,121.94.

Let's change the example again. You are now twenty years old, just out of college, and want to save for your own retirement. How much must you save each year at 10 percent to accomplish the same goal at age sixty-five? A few seconds with a financial calculator will show you that it takes $4,191.26 per year. The price is going up, but it's not out of reach. However, you are entitled to a new car and you don't have a stereo yet, so you put saving off for a little while.

At age thirty you briefly toy with the idea of starting a retirement plan, but you now have two children, a wife, and a new condo. You are a little distressed to see that the annual cost of meeting your goal has grown to $11,117.51.

Age forty finds you with a new home in the suburbs. For your birthday you fulfill the right of every American to have a wide screen television to grace the family room. At half time during the Superbowl, you pull out the old financial calculator and find that with twenty-five years remaining to age sixty-five, your cost to fund your retirement supplement is now a serious $30,637.58 each year. The shock sends you to the refrigerator for another brew. Maybe next year, you think, as the halftime show winds down.

At age fifty the kids are away at college and there's a new Infiniti in the driveway. Your company may lose a big contract, and there is disconcerting talk about downsizing, so now doesn't look like a great time to start a serious savings plan. You are too stressed-out to check, but if you did you would be shocked to see that, with only fifteen years to go to your planned retirement, you will need to deposit $94,823.14 each year!

At age sixty you have the "children" living at home again. They don't seem to be in any big hurry to leave, although there has been a trial balloon floated to borrow the funds for a down payment for their own condo. The $189,059.14 required each year to fund your retirement plan is clearly out of the question, and you are wondering how it will feel to still be working at eighty. You catch yourself daydreaming about winning the lottery.

LESSON ONE: START EARLY

The first lesson we learn from our little exercise is to start to invest early. Put time on your side. The earlier you start saving, the easier the burden, and the more likely you are to have a successful outcome. It's never to early to invest for retirement. It can get too late. Of course, it's always easy to put it off. There is always a good excuse. Don't let it happen to you. The cost of reaching your goal goes up each day.

LESSON TWO: PLAN FOR A REASONABLE RATE OF RETURN

The next lesson we can learn from an exercise like this is the importance of getting a reasonable rate of return on our investments. While I used 10 percent as a fair rate, I don't think many Americans actually come close to this as a net rate of return over time. Far too much money is committed to safe, low rate of return asset classes and far too little to the higher-risk, higher-return classes.

Going back to our twenty-year-old, it took $4,191.26 each year for him to reach his goal at 10 percent, but if he expects to make only 9 percent he must save $5,729.90 per year. Of course, if he expects to earn 11 percent, he can reduce his funding cost to only $3,053.92. A one percent change in earnings has a huge impact on funding costs.

We know that risk in an equity portfolio falls as the time horizon increases. Certainly a retirement plan is a long-term horizon. Investors should consider shifting assets to where they will get higher rates of return. That means fewer bonds, CDs, and annuities, and more stocks. Within the stock classes, research would indicate that a tilt toward value, small cap stocks, international, and emerging markets increases rates of return. Properly mixed, these asset classes should generate handsome increases in return without undue risk. In later chapters we will construct a portfolio to demonstrate the possibilities to both increase rates of return and reduce risk.

LESSON THREE: CONTROL COSTS

Rate of return is not exclusively a function of risk. Cost can have a major impact on an investment program. Markets are reasonably efficient. It is not likely that you can beat them by much or even anything at all. Each market can only return so much. That return is reduced by cost. You must adopt an effective cost control program as part of your overall strategy. We will have much more to say about how Wall Street can get in your way later. For now, I will observe that the average client of a full service brokerage house can save an easy 3 percent per year by dispensing with the dubious advice of the Street.

LESSON FOUR: CONTROL TAXES

One of the least understood costs in an investment portfolio is tax. In the real world most of us have to pay tax. Many times our investment plans increase our tax burden. Each time we receive a dividend, interest payment, or capital gain, Uncle Sam has his hand in our pocket.

Tax can become a very serious drag, but it doesn't have to be. In many cases, taxes on investments are voluntary. Or perhaps we should say they are a tax on ignorance, because they can easily be avoided.

In real estate the prime considerations are location, location, and location. In tax strategy the prime considerations are defer, defer, and defer. The longer we can defer paying a tax, the longer we have investment dollars compounding for us rather than going to the government. If you buy a stock and never sell it, you will never have to pay a capital gains tax. When you die, your heirs will receive the stock with a new basis from your estate. (They may or may not have to pay an estate tax. That is a separate consideration.)

Mutual funds present a couple of interesting wrinkles. Many funds have huge portfolio turnovers. As you are probably aware, each time a fund manager sells a stock in his portfolio, you get a pro rata share of the gain or loss. All the transactions are totaled at the end of the year, and you get a 1099 tax form for your share. A copy goes to your favorite uncle, Sam. This can often result in a tax to you even in a year when you have losses in account value. The cumulative effect of taxes each year can seriously erode the returns that equity funds can generate. Some of the mutual funds rating services have included information on tax efficiency. This is a very rough estimate of the capital gains already built up by a fund. Few investors are aware that when they buy a fund that has a substantial, unrealized gain, they may soon get to pay taxes on the gain as if they had held the fund from the time it first bought the stocks. This is hardly what we would consider an optimum outcome. Help is at hand. By their very nature, index funds don't turn over their assets. Taxes will be minimal compared to an actively managed portfolio.

Some index funds have taken this a step further. They have a stated objective of never incurring a capital gain for the shareholder. The only time they expect to incur a capital gain for the account is when a company is acquired for cash. In that event, they expect to be able to sell sufficient stocks with a loss to prevent a net gain for the shareholder. So only dividend income and nominal interest income are subject to tax. In an equity portfolio, this should be a very small amount compared to the total appreciation over time.

Everybody knows that taxes are a drag on performance, but I am constantly surprised at the number of investors who blithely pay taxes each year on their investment earnings without considering the impact on accumulation or the alternative strategies that they could employ. It's never a good idea to let the tail wag the dog, and a rational investor shouldn't seek tax avoidance or tax minimization per se. Nevertheless it makes sense to pursue the highest after-tax return. Generally if we can defer taxation till a later date and convert a high tax rate to a lower one at the same time, we will have more after all the taxes are paid. Every dollar that leaves the field early to pay taxes is a dollar lost to future growth and enjoyment.

BUILDING A TAX MODEL

Let's build a simple model to examine the impact of taxation, which varies with tax rates and the length of deferral. Our investor has a lump sum of $100,000 to invest for thirty years, after which he either liquidates the accumulation to buy a yacht or keeps the capital intact and uses annual income or gains to finance his retirement. Assume his investments have a nominal (before tax) annual return of 10 percent.

We will deduct federal taxes from the account as income is distributed or gains are realized. We will also assume that the investor's marginal tax rate is the account's effective rate (which would not be true for an investor who had little or no other income). Income and short-term gains will be taxed at 39.6 percent and long-term capital gains at 20 percent.

CASE ONE: DEFERRED LONG-TERM GAINS

In this case, our investor could buy and hold shares of stock that do not pay dividends. The effective tax rate on unrealized gains would be zero. At the end of thirty years, his investment would have grown to $1,744,940, and he will not have paid a penny of tax. (If our investor dies now or anywhere along the way, income tax, though not estate tax, is forgiven, and he will never have paid any tax on the gains. A moral victory, at least.)

If our investor sells his entire account at this point to buy a boat, his gain of $1,644,940 is taxed at 20 percent so his net accumulation is $1,315,952. That money would purchase a luxurious, new 60-foot trawler with intercontinental range.

By instead selling appreciated shares equal to the annual return of 10 percent, our investor grosses $174,494 annually. Assuming his investment was for 10,000 shares at $10 per share, each share is now worth $174.49. He must sell 1,000 shares his first year. After adjusting for basis, his profit per share is $164.49. His net annual income (after the 20 percent long-term capital gains rate is applied) is $141,595. Darling, ask Jeeves to break out the Dom!

CASE TWO: DEFERRED ORDINARY INCOME

Here our investor finds an inspired manager who can overcome the enormous internal costs of a variable annuity (VA), so he earns returns at the same 10 percent rate before tax, as in the first case. There are no annual tax bills, so the gross accumulation is also $1,744,940.

If the account is liquidated as a lump sum, all but the original $100,000 is taxed as ordinary income at 39.6 percent, and the remaining after-tax accumulation has shrunk to $993,543. A well-maintained, ten-year-old cruiser in the fifty-five-foot class isn't out of the question.

Alternatively, our investor has a gross annual income of $174,494, which is reduced by the ordinary income tax rate of 39.6 percent. So, he will net $105,394. The higher tax rate on withdrawal bites into income, but there is plenty left thanks to the deferral. Darling, shall I get you some champagne?

CASE THREE: ANNUAL REALIZED LONG-TERM GAINS

In this case our investor purchases a mutual fund or managed account that has high annual turnover. Say the fund generates no interest, dividends, or short-term gains. The effective turnover is 100 percent, and all gains are realized and taxed each year. The investment account thus compounds at just 8 percent per year, and the accumulation is $1,006,266.

Because our investor paid taxes on gains all along, the net sum after liquidation is also $1,006,266. The boat budget is about the same as for case two. Otherwise, our investor's annual income on his remaining $1,006,266 would be $100,627, netting $80,502 after long-term gains taxes. The annual tax during the accumulation period reduced the pie available to convert to retirement income. Darling, where's that bottle of wine we've been saving?

CASE FOUR: ANNUAL ORDINARY INCOME

Finally, the investor might opt for a fully taxable investment that generates its entire return in taxable income or short-term realized gains (see Figure 11-1). (An extremely high turnover mutual fund might produce the latter scenario.) The effective compounding rate is only 6.04 percent, because 39.6 percent of each year's gain is taxed away. Over the years our investor has to cough up $315,283 for the government. Gross accumulation is $580,887.

Because he has paid taxes on all appreciation already, the net amount after liquidation is the same $580,887. A nice used boat is still a possibility, but a galley chef is out of the question.

The net annual yield from this investment will be $35,085 after income taxes are paid at the 39.6 percent rate. The smaller accumulation and the larger annual tax bite are devastating. Darling, pass me a beer.

Figure 11-1. Sizing up tax strategies.

STRATEGIES	Pre-Tax Accumulation	Post-Tax Accumulation	Annual Post-Tax Income
Deferred long-term gains	$1,744,940	$1,315,952	$141,595
Deferred ordinary income	$1,744,940	$993,543	$105,394
Annual realized long-term gains	—	$1,006,266	$80,502
Annual ordinary income	—	$580,887	$35,085

Investors should favor long-term deferrals and capital gains treatment, as in the first case.

CONCLUSION

Our model isn't real-world perfect, but it shows that taxes matter—a lot. Investors should favor long-term deferrals and capital gains treatment. The closer your portfolio can get to case one, the more money you will accumulate.

Even if you don't buy into the efficient market hypothesis, you may want to consider index funds for your taxable equity investments. Actively managed funds generate higher turnover than index funds, which can lead to bigger tax bills. New tax-managed index funds (including several from Vanguard) are somewhat actively managed in order to control taxes. Hold periods are increased so that most gains are long-term. Highest-cost lots are always sold first, and losses are harvested occasionally to offset realized gains.

Death and taxes may be inevitable, but taxes are manageable. To maximize your own benefit from this strategy, keep records of each purchase so that you can identify the shares you sell as the highest-cost ones in your portfolio. That will minimize the gain and the taxes.

BEATING THE TAX MAN

The government offers us one great way to beat the tax man for long-term investors. Pension plans, 401(k) plans, IRAs or SEP-IRAs, and self-employed pension plans (HR-10) all offer total tax deferral. There are no taxes on interest, dividends, or capital gains as long as the funds remain in the retirement plan.

You should take advantage of any tax-favored retirement plans available to you. The combination of current tax deduction and tax deferral is the best thing since sliced bread. Hopefully you will pick up some matching contributions from your employer, which will really sweeten the deal.

Stuff every penny you can afford into your retirement plans as early as you can afford it. As the Nike ads used to say: "Just to do it!" Invest in equities for the long haul. Don't get hung up on trying to time the market or be too concerned about the normal market variations. They work in your favor.

DOLLAR COST AVERAGING

Dollar cost averaging has been described as one of the oldest, least exciting ways of investing. Yet almost everyone agrees on its validity. Actually it is a simple discipline. It requires investing a set amount of money at regular intervals in a particular investment over a period of time. (Dollars invested at regular intervals x time = dollar cost averaging.)

Studies show that investors who use this strategy average a lower cost per share on their purchases than if they try to time their purchases to buy at the lowest prices. Most experts agree that it takes a minimum of eighteen months for dollar cost averaging to be effective.

The advantage of dollar cost averaging is apparent when you sell a larger number of shares at a higher price. Remember, you accrued more shares because your investment bought them over time at a lower price.

AN EXAMPLE OF DOLLAR COST AVERAGING

A simple example of dollar cost averaging developed in the May 1993 issue of *Worth* magazine illustrates the concept: You decide to invest $1,000 on the first of each month for three months in your favorite stock. The first month, the stock sells at $100 a share. You buy 10 shares. The second month, the stock falls to $50 a share, and you buy 20 shares. The third month, the stock recovers to $75. Your $1,000 investment buys you 13.3 shares.

You now have 43.3 shares that you bought at three different prices for a total outlay of $3,000. The stock is currently selling at $75 a share, so your 43.3 shares are worth $3,247.50. That's an 8.25 percent profit. Also, your average cost per share is less. If you divide the average price per share by your total investment of $3,000, your average cost per share is $69.23.

Figure 11-2. A dollar cost averaging sample.

Amount Invested	Price Per Share	# Shares
$1,000	$100	10.0000
$1,000	$50	20.0000
$1,000	$75	13.3333
Total: $3,000	$75 (Average)	43.3333
Amount Invested:	$3,000 ($1,000 x 3 months)	
Current Value:	$3,250 ($75 x 43.3333)	
Average cost per share:	$69.2308 ($3,000 / 43.3333)	

Of course, this is a hypothetical illustration. It does not imply a guarantee of a specific return on any particular security. It does not take into consideration taxes, inflation, or costs in purchasing stocks that should also be factored in when you figure your return on investment.

A 401(k) plan is an excellent way in which to implement dollar cost averaging. Since each pay period money is deducted from your earnings for that period and placed into the 401(k) plan, you will find that you have paid less per share over time if your choice of investments remains constant for a substantial length of time.

Reinvestment of dividends and capital gains is a form of dollar cost averaging and one of the smartest things investors can do. Also, with few exceptions, reinvesting costs you nothing as far as loads or fees.

Finally, if you do decide to dollar cost average, you need to bear in mind that, although it has been a highly successful investment technique in most instances, it neither assures a profit not protects against losses in a down market. Dollar cost averaging works only if you continue to systematically purchase, whether the market fluctuates down or up. As such, you have to stick with the program to get the best benefits.

FORCING YOURSELF TO SAVE

Nobody enjoys toys more than I do. I just know I am entitled to each and every one of them, so I have had to trick myself into saving. I am constantly searching for ways to keep my grubby little hands off the money. The best way for me is to set up ways that I won't see it, and I use a maximum pension contribution to make sure I don't convert all my earnings into boats.

The best way to make sure you have the funds when you need them is to set up a payroll deduction every month. This will put the tremendous power of dollar cost averaging to work for you and painlessly reinforce your wise decision to start saving now. One of my friends wants a bill each month from his financial advisor for his savings goal. Another gives the funds to his wife to invest. Just find a method that works for you. If you need further discipline, just remember that the only thing worse than being dead may be to have outlived your money!

So there it is: Put time on your side, start saving early, invest for high rates of returns, control costs, control taxes, use dollar cost averaging, and use a forcing system if you need to. Designing an investment strategy is one thing, implementing it is another. In Chapter 12 we will begin to implement our strategy. We will start by examining the profound changes in the financial services industry over the last generation. These changes allow knowledgeable investors to execute sophisticated strategies in a very economical manner. You don't have to be a multibillionaire, but you do have to know what is available. Wall Street isn't going out of its way to show you how to economize. Business as usual is just too profitable for them. Until you demand better, Wall Street is only too happy to sell you the same old stuff.

TWELVE

MAY DAY AND BETTER MOUSETRAPS

Congratulations! You now have the broad general outlines of your investment strategy. However, there's still a long way to go before you achieve financial success. Implementing your strategy is just as critical as design. There are lots of ways we can still screw up. The devil is in the details, and the news is almost all good. If you know where to look, you will find that there are resources available to you that our fathers couldn't have imagined. Obstacles may be placed in your way, but if you know what to expect they are easy to avoid.

How Deregulation Opened Up Wall Street

Before we turn to the nuts and bolts of implementation, it's time to shift gears for a little while. We need to examine the landscape of the financial services industry. It's an industry undergoing radical change. We have talked about some of the advances in financial economics over the last forty years, but there is another driving force to the sweeping transformation taking place.

Deregulation opened up financial markets, drove down the cost of transactions, and brought in new suppliers of financial services and products. The end result is that now you can execute your strategy much more efficiently and economically than ever before. If you are a do-it-yourselfer, you can bypass much of the old Wall Street structure. If you want advice and service, your choices are far better today. Either way, under deregulation, you win big.

VIVA LA REVOLUTÍON!

You may be forgiven if you happened to miss the revolution that began on May Day. No, this revolution isn't celebrated each year with a giant march through Red Square. Nor is it marked by shots of tequila with our southern neighbors on Cinco de Mayo. I am unaware of any epic poems that chronicle the events of this glorious revolution, or any anthems or ballads that we might sing. The heroes never received a parade, and the whole thing passed almost unnoticed by an indifferent public. There is no holiday, no statues, and no fireworks to mark it, but May Day was an important revolution, and you should celebrate it. As an investor, this revolution set you free, and today you have options you couldn't have dreamed of previously. Let's see how this revolution happened by taking a short history lesson.

THE DUTCH MAKE A PURCHASE

A few hundred years ago, the Dutch made a small real estate deal to acquire a little island of the coast of North America. The price was certainly reasonable. The island was nicely located at the mouth of a great navigable river, sheltered by a fine harbor, and opened to a fine sound that was sheltered by another long island.

Given the great location, it wasn't long before the Dutch began to trade with their new neighbors on the southern tip of the island. At first, trading was primarily confined to commodities that the surrounding area had in abundance. These commodities were then shipped home through the harbor facilities. Soon trading expanded to finance a lively commerce.

New companies were formed, and investors were invited to purchase speculations in the fledgling ventures. These speculations were certificates of ownership or debt and would much later be called stocks and bonds. The certificates were placed on open-air tables. Investors wandered the area, examining the certificates, gossiping, bargaining, and eventually buying or selling.

ENTER THE PIGS

A problem developed. Pigs from an adjacent common area ran through the trading area, splattered the traders, knocked over the tables, and trampled the speculations. After some short consultations, a wall was built to keep the pigs out. Later the street where the trading took place was named after the wall. Later still, the area grew to become the financial capital of the world.

Early on, the securities traders formed an association to govern their business transactions. It was decided that the association should have a monopoly on trading and that no traders should undercut the prices of their competitors. Traders who violated the agreement were banished from the association, an action that effectively ended their careers. This arrangement greatly enriched the traders, but certainly couldn't have been considered unusual given the business climate at the time. At the least, there was very little recorded dissent or comment from economists on the negative implications for market efficiency. Later the trade association was given government sanction, and commission price-fixing became the law of the land.

MAY DAY

In any event, that's how business continued until May 1, 1975. "May Day," as it is called in the industry, changed all that when the Securities and Exchange Commission allowed negotiated commissions.

May Day was greeted with howls, gnashing of teeth, and predictions of doom by the brokerage houses. These institutions of capitalism couldn't imagine that they could survive competition. May Day was the beginning of the end of Wall Street's guaranteed good deal. As you can guess, Wall Street brokerages didn't exactly fall over themselves to advertise discounts to investors. Nevertheless, the genie was out of the bottle, and you couldn't get him back in. Little by little, Wall Street was being dragged into the real world of competition.

Initially benefits were unevenly distributed. Large institutions could immediately trade blocks of stock for a tiny percentage of the previous costs. Since May Day, small investors' trading costs actually increased at the full-service houses. Soon discount brokers appeared, offering sharply lower trading costs to retail investors. At first, discount brokerages provided few services. But both the quality and quantity of the discount brokerage's services increased little by little. The success of early entrants such as Charles Schwab attracted additional players. Competition did what it usually does: further reduced prices, increased quality of service, and multiplied consumer choices. Keep tuned. The story is far from over, and things keep getting better and better.

Meanwhile, other institutions are also keeping the heat on. Banks, insurance companies, and mutual funds are cutting into Wall Street's traditional turf. In particular, no-load mutual funds have provided attractive alternatives to traditional brokerage houses and broker-dealer operations. Independent investors have embraced them in amounts that are hard to imagine. However, no-load means no help, and many investors lack time, inclination, or confidence to chose from the many offerings. Today we have over 11,000 non-money market funds in the United States alone. As a result, the selection process can appear rather daunting.

Change wasn't just confined to the brokerage industry. Insurers and bankers have undergone a parallel experience. In the good old days, long before voice mail, and before the break up of the phone companies, stockbrokers sold stock, insurance agents sold insurance, and bankers took deposits and made loans. Today everybody does everything, and it is difficult to distinguish who the players are, even with a program.

Until just a few years ago, bank, savings, and loan interest rates on deposits were capped by federal law. Yet bankers were free to charge whatever they could get away with for loans. Individuals had few alternatives for savings. Most could not afford to purchase individual T-bills. Savings bonds required long-term commitments. The advent of money market funds changed all that. When interest rates began to rise during the 1970s and 1980s, banks found themselves hemorrhaging deposits. "Disintermediation" became the buzzword of the day. A succession of extraordinary policy blunders followed. To compete against the money funds, deposit interest rates were unfrozen. The banks then found themselves in the unfortunate position of paying high rates to depositors while many of their older loans were fixed at very low rates. Banks were encouraged to make high-risk loans and enter other lines of business to increase their earnings. Federal deposit insurance protected savers. The resulting frenzy of foolishness, greed, corruption, and the inevitable near collapse of the banking system has been well documented. (To be fair, the banks didn't make the inflation that drove up interest rates. Lyndon Johnson's Great Society, the Vietnam War, and the oil embargo did that.) Today, after a zillion-dollar bailout program provided by the taxpayers, banks have adjusted to a system where they pay reasonable rates to depositors. While banks have not exactly rushed to increase deposit rates, the availability of money market funds enforces a market discipline that keeps rates in the ballpark.

Insurance companies lived for a long time in a world protected from price competition. While no federal regulations governed their rate-making, each state reviewed rates with an eye to protecting the solvency of the insurance industry. In practice, the State of New York was able to set rates for most insurance companies nationwide. As a condition for doing business in New York, insurance companies had to charge uniform rates and pay uniform commissions in every state in which they did business. Few companies wished to be locked out of New York, so they happily went along. Like the securities business, an industry ethic developed that considered price competition dirty. It simply didn't exist. Policies were carefully designed to provide comparable but not superior value to the insured. Insurance departments rewarded any attempt by companies to lower rates, provide discounts, or offer rebates with license suspensions. Fair policy comparisons were just about impossible, and the widespread use of dividend projections rendered the entire exercise meaningless in any event. Agents were carefully trained to sell high-cost, high-commission products, and avoid the use of term at all costs. Loyalty to the company was considered superior to loyalty to the client.

Eventually the insurance companies succumbed to the same market forces that affected banks. Rising interest rates in the 1970s and 1980s coupled with the widespread acceptance of money market funds provided savers with far more attractive alternatives to insurance policies. "Buy term and invest the difference" became a popular philosophy for savers. Little by little, the insurance industry was forced to increase policy values. New types of policies like universal life, variable life, and lower-cost term were introduced to recapture the market. Internal expenses were cut and mortality charges adjusted to reflect longer life expectancy. Today, a dollar of life insurance costs about one third of what it did twenty-five years ago, and cash values are greatly enhanced.

THE PRICE OF CHANGE

All this change comes at a price. Change brings noise and confusion. It takes us awhile to sort out the new benefits. Nevertheless, the trade-offs are overwhelmingly favorable. Investors astute enough to look beyond the traditional sources found themselves richly rewarded with lower costs, increased options, and fewer conflicts of interest.

MONOPOLY AND REGULATED INDUSTRIES

Many regulated industries share common characteristics. A great many people get paid far too much to do far too little. Innovation is stifled, and the consumer pays far more than is fair. Wall Street was no exception. Prior to May 1, 1975, price competition in the securities industry was illegal. Wall Street was one big gentleman's club raking in inflated monopoly prices while worshipping the status quo. Commissions were fixed. Competition, such as it was, revolved around peripheral services such as research or other advice. Prices for services were bundled together. You paid for the research and other services whether you wanted them or not. Even if you considered Wall Street's advice worth far less than zero, you paid.

The discount brokerages unbundled the services and slashed the pricing. Investors who had the time and inclination to go it alone reaped enormous benefits. For instance, several years ago brokerage houses offered to trade and hold no-load mutual funds in their accounts. Initially they charged a small transaction fee to cover the cost of the service. More recently, they have introduced a no-transaction fee service for selected mutual funds. (As you will recall, there ain't no such thing as a free lunch. The brokerage houses receive direct compensation from the mutual fund company for acting as a distribution channel and providing certain shareholder and administrative services. These payments average about .25 percent to .35 percent per year. However, no additional cost is incurred by the investor who utilizes a brokerage account over what a direct purchaser would pay. As long as a fund has a 12(b)-1 fee of .25 percent or less, they are allowed to call themselves a no-load fund.)

Even if the investor pays a transaction fee to the brokerage house, it is a small portion of the cost of purchasing a typical load fund. For example, at $100,000 a typical front-end load commission would be $3,500, while a transaction fee at a discount brokerage would be below $30.

This seemingly simple service is a giant advance for investors. Prior to this, investors had to identify a fund, open an account with the fund through the mail, and transfer funds to purchase shares. The entire process could take weeks. Redeeming shares involved much the same process and time. Funds could be out of the investor's control for extended periods while in the mail, waiting for redemption, or waiting for the checks to clear. Transferring from one fund family to another was a nightmare of paperwork and delay. Tax accounting was too dreadful to contemplate. Each fund family provided their own reports. Managing a diversified portfolio was a complex task indeed. Now, a single account can hold many funds or families of funds. Funds clear overnight, and transferring requires a single telephone call. The brokerage provides a monthly consolidated report, and managing the funds becomes a reasonable task. A consolidated tax statement comes once a year. More recently, the discount brokerage houses have introduced software for twenty-four-hour trading and account monitoring from the comfort and convenience of your home or office computer.

When discount brokerages began to offer their back-office facilities to independent, fee-only investment advisors, retail investors could obtain professional unbiased advice and efficient execution at a total cost far below what was previously offered. By providing a clear separation of the brokerage functions from the advice function, investors who sought advice avoided the conflicts of interest that poisons the commission-based brokerage business. This arrangement offers such enormous, readily apparent advantages that it threatens the way Wall Street has done business for generations.

The person who said, "Build a better mousetrap, and the world will beat a path to your door," didn't understand much about business. The inventor of the new, improved mousetrap must contend with the manufacturer of the old mousetrap. Even if his product is demonstrably better, he will face inertia and indifference by the buying public and a well-orchestrated public relations campaign by the established company. After all, they are raking in a fortune selling the old mousetraps. Often, the established company is well capitalized and has a strong brand name. They are not likely to just roll over and give up their market share. They will fight like crazy to keep going on with business as usual.

Even if the new mousetrap must eventually and totally replace the old, the established company still has many options. Often the best option is to harvest the business. The old company can continue to profitably sell the old mousetraps for years to anyone who is foolish enough to buy them.

Another option is to introduce their own new mousetrap with some of the features of the competition. However, in the process they risk cannibalizing their older product sales. If the older product is more profitable, they will attempt to maximize sales of the older line as long as possible. This course maximizes profits and buys time to adjust to the new environment.

Wall Street's traditional brokerage houses and broker-dealers are both harvesting their business and attempting to improve their offerings. However, they are clearly being dragged kicking and screaming to the party. Even if they wanted to join the new world, Wall Street faces some formidable problems. Their overhead in terms of real estate, systems, and people is enormous. They will never be able to compete on a cost basis with discount brokers and independent advisors. Their used stock sales force is poorly trained in basic economics and finance and determined to preserve their antiquated commission structure. In addition, they suffer from a well-deserved image problem.

Meanwhile, the public is becoming increasingly disenchanted. Better mousetraps are available, and market share is flowing at an ever-increasing rate in that direction.

The revolution in the financial services industry began with a deregulation of the brokerage, banking, and insurance industries. Because the May Day Revolution was so poorly understood, not all investors are fully aware of the many benefits that have resulted. Retail investors were slow to grasp that the game changed. Unaware of the new rules, they initially failed to press their new advantages. As investors learned of the advantages that additional choices brought, the revolution picked up steam.

In many ways, a quarter century after May Day, the process is still just beginning. As one by one investors vote with their feet, they transform the industry in their favor. The one and only thing that Wall Street really understands is loss of market share. Demand better, and you will get it. The choices are already available. All the tools necessary to implement a superior investment strategy are there for the choosing. Your father never had it so good.

THIRTEEN

IT'S A JUNGLE OUT THERE!

In the world of finance there are traps, pitfalls, and perils that could ensnare an unsuspecting investor. A general awareness of them, plus a healthy dose of skepticism, will stand you in good stead. I will be your guide for this little tour through the pitfalls of Wall Street. I've survived in this swamp for twenty-five years, so I can point out a few things that might help ward off disaster.

Before we start, I want to say that things are good and getting better. The capitalist system and Wall Street's markets that make up an integral part of the system are the economic miracles of the world. However, even miracles aren't perfect. One thing about this miracle is that it doesn't rely on saints or even particularly good guys to make it work. In a very real sense, the markets are always under construction, and self-improvement. As we saw in Chapter 12, improvement has been gradual but relentless. Consumers always want more and better deals. By demanding better, they force change. Just by voting with their feet, or dollars, they make the whole system better. Neat system, isn't it?

Make no mistake about it, I'm proud to be a capitalist tool. However, there are a few flaws left in the paradise, and we might as well admit it. What we need to do is to discover how to either work around them, or turn them to our advantage.

This chapter is devoted to showing you how to avoid totally unnecessary disasters as you execute your investment strategy. In particular we will discuss nonmarket risks that could separate you from your hard-earned money. To be more precise, we will examine scams, rip-offs, conflicts of interest, and other dastardly deeds.

HORROR STORIES

We have all heard familiar horror stories about investments gone bad. These stories may include the following ones:

- A Miami "investment advisor" leaves his family, cleans out a large number of client accounts, and disappears. He is found months later living in a house of ill-repute in Taiwan. Returned home for trial, he is promptly convicted and sentenced. The money is not recovered. Some of Florida's top physicians are wiped out.

- Three airline pilots in Atlanta lose their entire retirement accounts after their airline folds. A total of $1.3 million disappears from accounts controlled by a "financial planner."

- In Texas, a small state-chartered trust company with strong ties to a major air carrier fails. Accounts are frozen for over a year while the state literally digs through shoeboxes to construct records that are several years in arrears. It is discovered that the trust company carries only $1 million total insurance to cover more than $100 million of deposits. After the failure, the insurance carrier cancels coverage, claiming fraud. There is no state fund to cover deposits. Fortunately, most of the deposits are recovered.

- Some of America's largest brokerage houses have settled multi-million-dollar claims for fraudulent sales practices, inappropriate investment recommendations, failure to supervise account executives, and churning of accounts.

- Boiler-room operations swindle thousands of unsuspecting investors out of millions of dollars each year in total scams.

■ Thousands of investors have complained that banks have misrepresented mutual funds as government-guaranteed investments.

■ One of the nation's largest insurance companies is accused of selling high-cost insurance policies as retirement accounts.

The list is almost endless, but you get the idea. Those kinds of catastrophes don't have to happen. If you think about it, a few basic precautions would have prevented each of the tragedies. Here are a few of Frank's rules of survival:

■ *Never give any investment advisor a general power of attorney over your account.* Use a limited power of attorney to authorize your advisor to make trades within your account for your benefit. There is never a reason to name an investment advisor as owner, contingent owner, or joint owner of your account. It shouldn't be possible for any other person to ever receive a disbursement from your account. Your brokerage or trust company should only disburse to you at your home address or to your bank account. Insist on confirmation of all account activity and statements directly from your custodian. Check your statements for unusual or unauthorized activity. Never use your investment advisor's address as your address to receive statements. As President Reagan used to say: "Trust but verify."

■ *Select strong custodians for safekeeping of your assets.* Use major brokerage houses or trust companies that are properly insured, audited, and regulated. Don't let some Mickey Mouse, little financial institution act as custodian of your assets.

■ *Remember that if it sounds too good to be true, it probably is.* The markets are far too efficient to allow for excess profits in excess of the risks taken. Con artists almost universally appeal to investors' greed and unrealistic expectations. They can't exist without rubes willing to believe the unbelievable. By now you should have a good feel for the range of reasonableness in various investment markets.

■ *Consider carefully whether you need a guide.* Many investors shouldn't try to go it alone. Investing funds professionally is a full-time job. It takes specialized knowledge and significant resources. The field is rapidly evolving. It takes a great deal of time just to keep up with the research. Evaluate whether you have the skill, judgment, discipline, and experience to do a proper job. Your investment plan is your future. It's too important to leave to amateurs. I once read a Robin Cook novel, but I don't think I'm ready to do brain surgery.

■ *Avoid commission sales.* All financial professionals get paid. And, of course, all of them have an interest in attracting your business. You can't expect any of them to send you to the competition. How they get paid, however, can have a very significant effect on the nature of their recommendations. In fact, how you pay for advice may be much more important than how much you pay.

THE ROLE OF COMMISSIONS

The commission sales process opens the door to a host of potential consumer abuses, including serious conflicts of interests, inappropriate investment recommendations, very high costs, and excessive portfolio turnover or churning. With all the hidden agendas possible in the sales environment, it would be extraordinarily naive to expect objective advice.

Business Week's February 20, 1995 cover story "Can You Trust Your Broker?" lists an entire catalog of investor abuses. Here's how the magazine summed up the story in a sidebar called "The Case Against the Brokerage Industry":

■ *Pressure.* The compensation system at brokerage firms creates intense pressure on brokers to generate a high volume of commissions.

■ *Incentives.* Brokers are given extra incentives to sell special, high-profit-margin products with little regard to their suitability for customers.

■ *Bad advice.* Firms push brokers to recommend in-house mutual funds (where the firm earns management fees) instead of funds run by outside managers. Most in-house funds have mediocre performance records.

■ *Bonuses.* Many firms recruit top "producers" from other firms with huge upfront bonuses and extra-high commissions. That gives the producers an added incentive to promote excess trading.

■ *Poor information.* Firms don't provide customers with information on the overall return on their investments and aggregate commissions they've been charged.

Commissioned sales have been good to Wall Street. It's a great way to distribute products. Investors, on the other hand, are often poorly served. The brokerage system is inadequately policed and rife with built-in and undisclosed conflicts of interest between broker and customer. Hardly a day goes by without disclosure of another violation of trust. Unable and unwilling to repair an extremely profitable system, Wall Street responds with slick public relations and advertising.

Wall Street's large brokerage houses are very complex businesses. What you see at your local office is just the tip of the iceberg. The retail operation is essential to support many of the more profitable lines of business. Commissions are the mechanism that allow the house to manipulate the broker. With the right commissions, incentives, and bonuses, Wall Street can get their brokers to sell anything.

CONFLICTS OF INTEREST

The common thread that runs through many of the worst abuses is the commission-based system of compensation. Commissions create the conflicts of interests between the broker and client. For instance, many brokerage houses also act as market makers for NASDAQ stocks and bonds. In this capacity they buy and sell for their own accounts. It's a neat little business where, like Las Vegas, the house almost always wins. The brokerage houses buy at one price from the public and sell to them at another. The difference is called the spread—the profit the house makes for bearing the risk of holding an inventory of stocks.

It turns out that making a market is generally very profitable. It also doesn't have very much risk. It turns out to be a lot more profitable than some brokerages on the New York Stock Exchange. If the house has a lot of transactions where they act as market maker, they can make big profits. That's why many brokerage houses pay higher commissions to brokers for selling stocks where the house makes a market than stocks where they don't make a market. A little disclosure on the bottom of your confirmation that the brokerage may make a market in the stock is supposed to alert you to this little conflict of interest. Most investors never consider why they get so many buy and sell recommendations where the house just happens to make a market in the stock.

BONDS AND THE COMMISSION SYSTEM

Another interesting peculiarity of the commission system is the way bonds are treated. While commissions on NYSE stocks are tightly controlled and disclosed on the confirmations, bond salespeople are allowed to tack on just about anything they think the market will bear. Bond commissions are never disclosed on confirmations. The buyer just gets a statement that he purchased a bond at a particular price. Of course, most brokerage houses make a market in bonds. More obscure and thinly traded bonds have higher spreads. In general, very liquid bonds have about a one- to two-point spread, but it can go much higher. Occasionally a bond sales representative can sell a bond with a 6 percent spread. These six-point bonds are often referred to as touchdown bonds. In some offices whenever a touchdown bond is sold, they ring a bell. If there aren't any customers about, everybody cheers. Perhaps this explains why brokerages seem so partial to bonds.

MUTUAL FUNDS

Any brokerage house or broker-dealer worthy of the name has a family of mutual funds. They all love this business because it becomes an annuity for them, paying them fees forever almost without regard to performance. As a class, brokerage funds have some of the highest expenses and worst performance being offered. For instance, the aforementioned *Business Week* story showed a table with the largest brokerage house funds compared to the largest independent families of load funds. The worst-performing family of the independent funds had better performance than the best-performing brokerage house funds. Most large brokerage houses pay higher commissions for sale of their funds than outside funds. (A few have recently and very publicly abandoned the practice.) Nevertheless, you shouldn't be too surprised to learn that most brokerage accounts have a high percentage of house-brand funds in them.

Not content to receive the sales allowance alone from outside mutual funds, many brokerage houses have begun to demand and receive a portion of the fund's ongoing management fee and other allowances from outside mutual funds. Some mutual funds have refused to pay, or have internal expense charges too small to allow a continuing fee to the brokerage house. So some brokerages have established dual lists of outside fund families. Those who pay get preferred treatment, whereas those who don't have the commissions paid to the salespeople get cut.

INITIAL PUBLIC OFFERINGS

Initial public offerings (IPOs) generate lots of fees for brokerage houses. Strangely enough, the offering allowance to the brokerage house and the salesman is never called a commission. This offering allowance is a multiple of the commission that a salesman could earn on a NYSE trade. Notwithstanding the tremendous frenzy that Internet IPOs once generated, most investors in IPOs have very poor results over the subsequent few years. Perhaps driven by the high offering allowance, Wall Street's brokers rarely fail to generate tremendous enthusiasm for IPOs.

NEW UNIT INVESTMENT TRUSTS

New unit investment trusts (UITs) and new closed-end funds are similar to IPOs in that brokers earn a multiple of what they could earn from the sale of an existing UIT or closed-end fund. In addition, the offering allowance doesn't have to be called a commission. Because of the high offering expenses built into UITs and closed-end funds, the overwhelming majority of the time a new offering begins to trade, the price falls to net asset value or below. Most investors would be far better served to wait a few days or weeks after the offering trades and then buy at the far better prices. Almost everybody on Wall Street knows this. Unfortunately, the commission is very small compared to the initial offering. So new UITs and closed-end funds continue to be manufactured and sold as if they were some kind of great, neat deal.

OTHER CARROTS HELD OUT TO STOCKBROKERS

So far we have just described cash payments to stockbrokers and registered representatives. But there are other neat ways to lead them around by the pocket. Many firms offer deferred compensation in addition to direct commissions. Invariably, these plans are tied to proprietary products and other high-profit offerings. Private offices, secretaries, titles, and other perks depend on selling enough of the right stuff.

Firms have a whole hierarchy of offerings depending on profitability to the house. Highest on the totem pole are proprietary products. The firms not only garner sales commissions, but lock up management fees forever.

Other products, while not proprietary, offer the house an enhanced interest. These enhanced interests include increased dealer reallowance, sharing of management fees, generous support for conventions and meetings, and directing trades to the house.

Next there are funds that do not support the profit objectives of the firm but must be available for competitive reasons. Sales of these products are tolerated, but certainly not encouraged.

Finally, if an adequate profit isn't available from a product, the firm doesn't enter into a sales agreement with it. Because law only allows salespersons to sell products that are licensed by the house, that excludes the product from consideration.

As a general rule, commissions follow the profit potential for the house and are inversely related to the expected return for the customer. High commissions cannot coexist with low profit margins.

If the carrot doesn't work, there is always the stick. Brokers who fail to meet quotas, including minimum production of proprietary product, just don't seem to last long. Managers whose offices don't produce don't last much longer, and so on up the food chain.

The single ethic and obsession in the brokerage industry is: Sell more! Success or failure is measured by commission dollars, not client returns or satisfaction. Most stockbrokers can tell you to the penny what they earned in commissions last year. Few stockbrokers have the foggiest notion what their clients made as a result of their advice.

These conflicts of interest are not just incidental to the business. Rather they are a fundamental part of traditional commission-based, transaction-oriented brokerage. Conflicts of interest and failure to disclose define the process.

THE FLAWED SYSTEM OF LARGE BROKERAGES

There are a great many talented and ethical people in the business, but the system is fundamentally flawed. The system makes it very difficult for brokers to do the right thing by clients. A broker who practices long-term buy and hold strategy is not liable to endure for long. She can never get paid for recommending that a client do nothing at all, but we all know that often that's the best course of action. Finally, a broker who institutes a rigorous cost-containment and control program for his clients has just signed his own retirement papers.

You may say that the value of this professional advice makes up for any flaw in the system. These aren't just used-stock salespeople; they are highly trained financial consultants, right? Well, not quite. We have examined the quality and integrity of Wall Street's research efforts. In my opinion, that advice is worth far less than zero. Wall Street's research efforts are both a fine justification for excessive trading and a defense against litigation for the house. And for this they expect the investor to pay!

However, what does the stockbroker or registered representative bring to the table? It's a mixed bag, but it would be a mistake to assume that they are all highly competent. The best of them got that way through their own efforts in a system that demands very little. You wouldn't be far off if you considered entry requirements to be a total sham.

It turns out that almost anyone without several felonies can qualify. There are a couple of short exams administered by the feds. But plenty of schools offer three-day cram courses that carefully cover only the basic questions and answers. Anyone with a few hundred bucks is guaranteed to pass the test or repeat the course as many times as necessary. Fortunately, the cram courses have the questions wired, so few suffer that indignity.

While many brokers are very bright, it's not a requirement for the job. Neither is advanced or related education. Several successful brokers I know have never seen the inside of a college or taken a finance course.

Once the aggravating formality of the exam is out of the way, the real training begins. Most brokerage in-house training courses could fairly be described as 10 percent product knowledge and 90 percent sales training. It's then on to getting on the phone to sell. The technique, described as either "smiling and dialing" or "dialing for dollars," is the fundamental education for new-hire stockbrokers at most houses. It's strictly sink or swim. Attrition is high. You shouldn't be surprised to learn that once the entrance exams are passed, there is only a token requirement for continuing education. Most of the continuing education provided generally comes from the house and consists of about the same proportions of product knowledge and sales training. Controlling the education process rather effectively limits the options to the house preferences. As a result, many brokerage houses actively discourage their salespeople from pursuing independent professional training. For instance, one very large brokerage prohibits its salespeople from displaying the Certified Financial Planner (CFP) certification on their cards, letterheads, or any other client contacts. Whatever their reasons, the brokerage houses certainly aren't bullish on education.

So what are the qualifications? The single biggest attribute the brokerage houses or broker-dealers are looking for is sales experience. It doesn't matter what you sold, if you can sell, the brokerages want you. At a Florida brokerage one of the top producers' only other experience and qualification was selling swimming pools.

In the real world, financial advisors must get paid. Otherwise they will all close shop and go sailing or play golf. How that compensation is structured can play a large role in determining the quality and integrity of the advice received. Wall Street's failure to resolve the commission compensation issue in a manner favorable to investors has led to the rapid erosion of their market share to independent, fee-only investment advisors. Let's face it, nobody really likes the big brokerage houses. Investors just didn't know they had alternatives. But they are beginning to learn.

ALTERNATIVES

Not all investors need or want investment advice. For those, books like this one will help to define strategy. Discount brokerages and no-load mutual funds provide eminently satisfactory solutions to the custody and execution problems that weren't available just a few years ago. Web-based trading drives down transaction costs and bypasses salespeople entirely.

Other investors who need and want professional advice but are not satisfied with the traditional "churn and burn" brokerage tactics also have better solutions. (Later in this book we will discuss some criteria for selecting and working effectively with financial advisors.) Voilà! All that is necessary to keep the improvements rolling is to keep demanding better. Pretty neat!

In Chapter 14 we will start to develop an investment policy by defining our objectives, time horizon, and risk tolerance.

FOURTEEN

SETTING YOUR GOALS

A clear definition of objectives, time horizon, and risk tolerance goes a long way toward suggesting the appropriate investment strategy. The better we can define our objectives, the better plan we can craft to meet them. The more precisely you can define your goals, the better plan we can design to meet them. It's not enough to say "I want to make a lot of money" or "I don't want to take a lot of risk."

Of course, in real life you might be expected to have several, distinct financial goals, each with different parameters. A young family may be saving for a down payment for a home, retirement, and their children's college education all at once. An older couple may be focused on retirement and estate conservation. Each objective may have different time horizons and risk parameters. Let's look at several decisions that investors should make at the outset.

SETTING MONETARY GOALS

Setting monetary requirements for each goal is a pretty straightforward process:

- ■ *Inventory your resources.* Be certain to include pension plans, Social Security, other existing investments, and real estate. Add in any other planned investments.
- ■ *Project your income needs and capital needs in today's dollars.*
- ■ *Add an appropriate inflation adjustment.* This will give you a target in inflated dollars.

From this process you can determine your minimum required rate of return on your current assets and planned investments. That required rate of return must be feasible, attainable, and within your risk tolerance. If that rate of return isn't feasible, you better go back to make adjustments in your lifestyle or increase your planned investments. Based on what we know about long-term returns, I wouldn't be very comfortable if your retirement strategy required an 18 percent return on your portfolio. It's just not likely that you will be able to find a combination of assets that will reliably deliver that rate of return. Often investors feel driven to take excessive risk when they are unable or unwilling to invest enough to meet their goals. They become prime targets for scam artists with inflated promises. The elderly often become victims of fraud when they see that their existing assets will not be enough to support their lifestyle.

Finally, we can design a portfolio with an expected rate of return adequate for your needs. Most of you will find that you must develop a required rate of return higher than bonds and savings can generate. The next question is, can you live with the risk required to meet your goals? If you can't live with the risk, we have to go back and adjust your lifestyle or increase planned investments.

HOW SOFTWARE CAN AID THE PLANNING PROCESS

If all this sounds like a very complicated exercise, relax. We have the software to do these calculations. It's very powerful and allows for instant comparisons of alternative scenarios. You will be able to see instantly if your assets will support your desired lifestyle, what rate of return is necessary to keep you from running out of funds, and how much risk you will have to assume to get the desired rate of return.

Widely available programs can guide you through many of the items you must begin to consider as you build your plan. They make quick work of budgeting, Social Security forecasts, inflation adjustments, assets available, time to go to objective, rates of return required to meet objectives, and risk required to meet rate of return requirements. You can build in known expenses like college, or a new boat, and expected future receipts like the sale of a home or inheritance. You can see the effects of tax rate changes and play "what if" with investment returns or risk levels.

Your age and financial situation will impact how you set your goals. It's silly for a twenty-five-year-old to try to forecast his retirement budget exactly. At that age, few of us know how our lives and careers will develop. In addition, the very long time frames mean that if our estimates of rate of return, inflation, or expenses are off just a little, the resulting error will be enormous. But while our future may be a blank sheet, the need to provide for it is not.

As we saw in "More Fun with Numbers" (Chapter 11), it is vital to begin to invest as early as possible. Small periodic savings early in our career will grow to really meaningful balances given the magic of compounding. So a twenty-five-year-old might content herself with a goal of saving 20 percent of her gross income, obtaining a rate of return of at least 6 percent over inflation, and avoiding tax on her investments. If she continues this discipline throughout her career, she may reasonably expect to attain financial independence and security.

The concept of saving 20 percent of gross pay may seem a little revolutionary to many American consumers. With credit cards showered on us, it is difficult to resist the temptation to spend, spend, spend. Keep in mind that no matter how little you think you earn, many others would be happy to have 80 percent of it. If we don't establish the discipline to live on less than we make, no one else can do it for us, and no amount of investment advice will help.

All investors with access to a tax-favored retirement plan for a current tax deduction, as well as tax-deferred accumulation for the life of the plan, should take maximum advantage of it. It will reduce the real cost and increase the benefits of your hard-earned investments. By providing both a carrot (in the form of tax deductions) and a stick (in the form of tax penalties for early withdrawals), retirement plans increase the chance that money will be saved and used for the intended purpose.

Many people find it helpful to commit their goals to paper, then signing the document as a contract with themselves. This gives them an extra sense of purpose. As I have said before, if you are anything like me, any extra discipline helps when I crave another toy.

As we grow older, we should be better able to get a handle on our career progression and lifestyle. By age fifty, it's possible to forecast retirement requirements. Most of us have some fuzzy idea about where we would like to live, in what style, what size boat we want, how many children are left to put through college, and other needs. By now we also have some assets in inventory. We can begin to put numbers on our requirements. The assets available, the extent of the need, our past investment success, time remaining to retirement, future investment levels, and required rates of return can begin to be estimated. Hopefully we have accumulated a good-size nest egg. This nest egg will continue to grow and, along with planned additions, provide for our future security. If we have no nest egg, it's not too late to begin a serious investment program.

As we approach retirement, our planning can become more refined and precise. Along the way we will need to adjust constantly. We may develop new requirements or need to incorporate new research into our plans. A good plan is flexible, but focused and disciplined at the same time.

Just because they are retired, investors must not assume that their need for income will automatically decrease. Many young retirees (under seventy-five) often find that they need more income than they did before retirement because they travel and pursue other interests that were put on hold during their working and child-rearing periods. In any case, it's probably not realistic to plan for less than 75 percent of your preretirement income in real or inflation-adjusted dollars.

Somewhere between the ages of seventy and eighty-five, retirees may begin to slow down their travels and reduce their income needs. However, around seventy many retirees find that their income needs increase again as their health care and long-term care expenses accelerate.

My own experience with retirees bears this out. Few choose to sit on the rocking chair on the porch and drink iced tea all day. A friend of mine recently invited me to jog with him one morning at a fishing camp. I run several miles three to four times a week, but after a few miles I had to quit while he continued on for another three miles. After breakfast we went fishing all day. Then he led an evening hike after dinner, followed by a card game that went on well into the night. He was up early the next morning to go fishing. His age? A mere seventy-five!

So don't assume that your income needs stop when you retire. If your retirement is going to be "golden," you will need money. If you set your sights too low, you can absolutely guarantee yourself poverty in your old age.

TIME HORIZON

Time horizon is a critical factor in investment planning, but often not properly understood. Time horizon ends when you plan to liquidate an entire portfolio to meet a goal. For instance, if you are saving for a down payment on a house in two years, the time horizon left is two years. However, if you are investing for retirement, the time horizon is the rest of your life. Let me say that again. The time horizon for a retirement plan does not end the day you retire. The average married couple at age sixty will have at least one survivor reach the age of ninety-three. That means that half of them will have a survivor older than ninety-three. By definition, that's a very long-term time horizon.

One of the most inane ideas regularly foisted upon the American public is the idea that retirees should invest only for income and that, as investors grow older, they must become more conservative. Even *The Wall Street Journal* occasionally quotes some brain-dead financial planner reciting the formula that the percentage of bonds in a portfolio should equal the age of the investor. Hogwash!

Many financial planners specializing in investing for retirees insist that their clients invest for both growth and income until their late nineties. Given the very long lifespan of retirees, a planner who recommends a heavy percentage in safe, fixed assets (such as bonds, annuities, or CDs) might later expect to be sued for malpractice as the investments and income fail to keep place with inflation.

As we have previously observed, if you have a short time horizon (anything less than five years), you have no business in the market. In the short term, risk to your nest egg is too high. So if you are two years away from building a new house, or your daughter is about to enter Harvard, your funds for those goals probably ought to be in CDs.

Market risk falls as the time horizon increases. It actually falls as the square root of the time horizon. That means that the difference between the best-case/worst-case expectations for a one-year time horizon is only one-third as large after nine years, or one-fourth as large after sixteen years. We have also seen that with very long time horizons, the worst-case expectation in the stock market may be better than the best-case with safe assets.

Retirees who anticipate living off their capital, and those close to it, should consider that they have two time horizons. In the short run they will need income, and in the long run they will need a growth of capital and income. They should arrange their asset allocation accordingly.

Nothing is any worse than having to sell assets at depressed prices to meet a need that we should have forecast and provided for. For retirees who need a steady income, this could result in the portfolio self-liquidating during a very bad period. Accordingly, I recommend that my retired clients set aside at least five years of income needs in very short-term bonds and money market funds to meet their known income needs. (Seven years is better.) The balance can be set aside to grow. For instance, if we are withdrawing 6 percent a year for our income needs, then we would have about 30 percent to 42 percent set aside for five to seven years, needs. In a bad year, we can liquidate the short-term bonds to provide our income needs. In a good year the stock market funds can be reallocated back to bonds. The resulting mix will suffer a small total return penalty, but because of the short-term bonds the portfolio picks up a large increment of safety. In a bad market, the bonds allow us to "live off the fat of the land" while the stock market recovers.

Some fortunate retirees do not anticipate having to draw against their capital for extended periods of time. Perhaps they have a large, fixed pension or other guaranteed income. In that case there is no particular reason for them to invest more conservatively than they did before retirement and no particular reason to load up on bonds. The market will neither know nor care what their age is, and the asset allocation decision can be determined solely by their risk tolerance.

DEALING WITH RISK, THE FOUR-LETTER WORD

Risk tolerance is the final dimension of the goal-setting process. We have discussed the unfortunate effects of excessive risk aversion. Retirees face a far greater risk of outliving their capital than losing it in a properly designed, equity-based, global, asset allocation plan. On the other hand, excessive risk at the portfolio level can lead to real and permanent losses. Where we take risk, we want to achieve the highest rate of return per unit of risk. So even if we have a high tolerance for risk, we shouldn't just throw stuff against the wall to see if it sticks. The idea is to get rich or at least achieve financial independence, not generate cheap thrills.

From my perspective one of the biggest problems of risk is that when the market goes down, as it surely must do occasionally, clients will lose faith and bail out in a panic. Sometimes I suspect that when we speak of risk to the investing public, they filter out some of what we say. They may think that risk doesn't apply to them, or that the professional's role is to eliminate it in their portfolio, or that they will otherwise be immune. So when the inevitable market decline comes, the investor feels betrayed, shocked, confused, and frightened. It shouldn't happen. In this frame of mind, the investor is primed to do the very worst possible thing: sell and retreat to the "safety" of cash. All thoughts of long-term objectives vanish. The investor locks in his loss and guarantees that he won't be on board for the inevitable recovery.

Market risk means that sometimes your equities will go down. It is only a function of when, and we can't know that. The market, doesn't care whether you just invested, or if you are above your starting capital, or how close you are to your goal. Thus, if you are in the market, get used to the idea. If you can't get used to the idea, don't go into the market. Better to have not been in the market at all than to panic and sell when the market dumps.

Decide in advance how much risk you are willing to tolerate. You may define it in many different terms. You could say to yourself that you want to be 95 percent certain (that's two standard deviations) that you will never have a loss exceeding a given amount. Or, you could say that you can accept a risk level about halfway between the S&P 500 and short-term bonds. Or you could even say to yourself that you are willing to tolerate whatever risk is required to achieve a long-term result that's 3 percent better than the large company stocks.

However you define risk, remember that savers sleep well while investors eat well. The relationship between risk and reward is almost a physical law. If the worst result you are willing to accept is a CD result, then that is also going to be your best possible result.

Now that we have decided where we want to go, we can begin to examine roads that will get us there. A clear statement of objectives, risk tolerance, and time horizon should be reduced to writing to form the first portion of a policy statement for your investment strategy. The law requires that fiduciaries have and adhere to a written policy statement. However, every plan should have a policy statement, and I strongly recommend that you put yours in writing so that you can refer to it later. (A sample investment policy statement that I use with my clients is included as Appendix 4.) It will help keep us focused on achieving our goals that will in turn help us to keep a clear head in times of stress. If you think that you can administer a long-term investment plan without occasional days of stress, either you are very laid-back indeed or you haven't been paying attention. The next step in developing your strategy is to begin to formulate an asset allocation plan that will satisfy the requirements we have just laid down.

FIFTEEN

BUILDING YOUR PORTFOLIO

ow it's time to put it all together. Let's see how what financial economists have learned over the last twenty years can help us to build a portfolio.

IN THE REAL WORLD

When we are building an investment strategy, we must acknowledge that we operate in an uncertain world. Few variables are under our control. Because we cannot foretell the future, any strategy we are able to devise is unlikely to turn out to be the "best" strategy in retrospect.

However, we can build a very good strategy with what we do know. Rather than trying to beat some yardstick or every other investor around, a superior strategy has the highest probability of meeting our long-term goals. It also will subject us to the least risk along the way, attempt to maximize our returns for the risks we are willing to take, and systematically whittle down the risks and costs of being wrong.

In the short term every portfolio will be "wrong" a great deal of the time. With the benefit of hindsight, at the end of each period we will wish that we had been more (or less) committed to each asset class. For instance, we might have wished for more stocks in a year when the markets do well and more cash in a year when they do poorly. We will just have to accept this in order to be "right" for the long term.

A QUICK REVIEW OF SOME BASIC PRINCIPLES

Capitalism is the greatest wealth-creating mechanism ever devised. As we serve our own interests, the value of the world's economy increases. The markets that are an integral part of capitalism rise to reflect the increase in the world's economy. We expect this trend to continue. Markets offer each of us the surest opportunity to participate in the growth of the global economy.

Risk cannot be avoided, but it offers an investor the opportunity for higher returns. In particular, equities offer investors the highest real returns over time. Most investors cannot expect to meet their reasonable goals without accepting some level of market risk.

Asset allocation decisions explain the vast majority of investor returns and offer the investor the biggest chance to control his investment results. The impact of market timing and individual security selection pale by comparison to asset allocation. It follows that the greatest share of the investment process and attention should be devoted to the asset allocation problem.

Risk can be actively managed. Diversification is the primary investor protection. Asset allocation between stocks, bonds, and cash allows an investor to tailor a portfolio to meet his risk tolerance. Modern portfolio theory offers an investor the chance to obtain an efficient portfolio that maximizes the return for each level of risk he might be able to bear. New research by financial economists (Fama-French) examines the expected cross-section of returns and gives us an opportunity to predict expected returns by categorizing stocks by their size and book-to-market ratio. The practical implication of the Fama-French research enables investors to construct portfolios with higher expected returns than the market as a whole by tilting their holdings to smaller companies and value stocks.

Risk happens. Investors must accept and expect reasonably regular market declines. These events should be viewed as perfectly natural. At worst they are a nonevent to long-term investors. At best they may represent buying opportunities. It is vital that investors maintain a long-term perspective and exercise discipline if they are to avoid the dreaded "buy high, sell low" behavior.

Markets are efficient. Attempts to either time the market or select individual securities have not been effective or reliable methods of enhancing returns or reducing risk. Active management cannot demonstrate sufficient value added to offset their increased costs. Deviations from benchmark portfolios can explain the variability of mutual fund and institutional performance.

Market and economic forecasts are notoriously unreliable. Accordingly, strategies based on forecasting have not been successful when compared to a long-term buy and hold strategy. The only forecasts we make are that the world is not likely to end, the world economy is going to continue to expand, and the world's stock markets will continue to be an efficient mechanism to capture this growth in value.

Past performance of investment managers is not a reliable indicator of expected future performance. Neither this season's big winner nor loser is any more likely to repeat than pure chance might predict.

Cost is a major and controllable variable in investment management. Low cost is strongly correlated to higher investment returns. Management fees, transaction costs, and taxes all serve to reduce investor return. Cost must be rigidly controlled.

METHODOLOGY

Our discipline to attack the investment problem is called strategic global asset allocation, a long-term strategy that will divide the investor's available wealth among the world's desirable asset classes. Naturally enough, our first task is to decide which assets to include and which to exclude.

We will confine ourselves to liquid, marketable securities. This policy represents a major constraint, but not a particularly burdensome one. It allows us to price each asset in our portfolio on a daily basis. Should we wish to liquidate any or the entire portfolio, we can cash out for full value within one week. Right off the bat we have excluded many asset classes, some of which might be frivolous, some desirable. Baseball trading cards, diamonds, postage stamps, rare coins, antique automobiles, and commemorative plates are all out.

Other asset classes are excluded for different reasons. Most individuals will not be comfortable with options, commodities, futures, and the more exotic derivatives. Few "professionals" understand the complicated trading strategies, as is evident by the occasional multibillion-dollar losses endured by major institutions. If Barings bank can't monitor their trading strategy, how can you and I hope to? Managed commodities pools are sometimes touted as prudent diversifiers for balanced portfolios, but results have been distinctly underwhelming. Generally all investors, no matter how sophisticated they judge themselves, should restrain the occasional overwhelming urge to invest in things they don't fully understand. Looking back on my own career, I've found that the more I adhere to this general guideline, the better job I have done.

To me gold is just another commodity, an asset with a limited expected rate of return, and a very high risk level. Many managers include gold as an asset class in their portfolios. They are attracted by its very low correlation to other asset classes. While I understand this point of view, I cannot make myself tie up any percentage of my clients' wealth in an asset with such a dismal return history. Lots of gold bugs are still holding on to "treasure" purchased at prices of almost $800 an ounce twenty years ago.

By now, you are probably beginning to suspect that asset class selection may be rather arbitrary. If so, go to the head of the class. Mine is a very stick-to-basics approach and subject to my own value judgments. As a manager of other people's money, I must respect their constraints. For instance, some clients may dictate that their portfolios contain no emerging markets.

◆❖❖❖❖❖◆

CASE STUDY

THE JONESES: A CASE STUDY

Mr. and Mrs. Jones are age sixty and fifty-five, respectively. Mr. Jones is about to retire with a fixed pension of $50,000 a year from a major corporation. Recently Mr. Jones received a substantial inheritance resulting in total accumulated liquid assets of $1 million. The Joneses lead an active lifestyle and will need an income from their liquid assets of approximately $60,000, fully adjusted for inflation. The Joneses expect that inflation will run at least 3.5 percent on average over the rest of their lives. They are very reluctant to consider invading principal to fund their income needs and feel an obligation to pass on their wealth to their children, if possible. Above all, they do not wish to outlive their income and would like to remain financially independent. They would describe themselves as conservative investors and their financial goal to be focused on inflation-adjusted income and conservation of wealth. They are sophisticated enough to realize that they cannot accomplish their objectives using guaranteed investments, but do not wish to assume excessive risk.

My first observation is that the Joneses have a very long time horizon. As we have observed, the average life expectancy for the survivor of this couple (from a government table used widely for tax calculations) exceeds thirty-four years. Because this is an average life expectancy, about half of such couples will have a survivor longer than this. In addition, the Joneses do not want to invade principal, so amortizing the funds over their projected lives is not an option. Furthermore, the Joneses will need a fair withdrawal (starting at 6 percent of initial capital) each year in order to sustain their projected lifestyle. Because they expect inflation to run an average of 3.5 percent, their minimum acceptable return must be at least 9.5 percent.

A look at the long-term data on bond and CD returns confirms that the Joneses are not going to be able to come close to meeting their objectives without accepting some equity risk. On the other hand, their known withdrawals for the next several years are high. They cannot accept the risk of a 100 percent equity portfolio. In a bad market they might run the risk of depleting their capital to finance withdrawals.

As a first cut, we could examine a traditional institutional asset mix of 60 percent equities and 40 percent bonds (see Figure 15-1). A very naive or simple strategy would be to buy the large company index for 60 percent and the long-term treasury bond for 40 percent. Once a year we could rebalance the funds to account for withdrawals and the natural market value fluctuations.

This strategy is certainly simple enough to execute. It doesn't require expensive consultants or a giant staff. It has low cost, meets our minimum required rate of return, sets aside enough in bonds to meet our known income requirements for almost seven years, and has a tolerable risk level.

Wait a second. This is for the dumb guys, right? Large institutions must do better! How can we brag at cocktail parties? We want a sophisticated power strategy with lots of consultants to impress our friends and get those big returns we always read about in *Money* magazine.

As it turns out, this would be a very good strategy indeed. During the five-year period ending December 2003, this strategy would have outperformed twenty-seven of the largest thirty pensions in the United States. While the media is full of stories touting enormous returns and legendary managers, perhaps only one percent or 2 percent of individual American investors actually obtained investment results this good.

Figure 15-1. Typical retirement plan, portfolio 1.

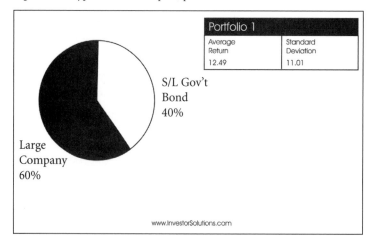

If the Joneses adopt this simple strategy, they will meet their objectives, outperform most large institutions, and be way ahead of their fellow investors.

Using this little portfolio as a benchmark, let's see if we can use what we have learned to form an even better portfolio. We will hold the original asset allocation of 60/40 stocks to bonds constant, but expand our asset class choices to see if we can lower risk or improve return (see Figure 15-2).

First let's look at the bonds. The primary reason to hold bonds in a portfolio is to reduce equity risk. As you will recall, long-term bonds have a reasonably high risk and offer a very limited return. Bondholders generally demand increased interest rates for longer maturities to compensate them for the increased risk. An in-depth examination of bond returns would indicate that there is very little extra return associated with increasing maturities. What would happen if we dumped the long-term treasury bond portfolio and substituted it with a much shorter maturity? Let's substitute a high-quality bond portfolio with a maximum average maturity of two years. In this case, we'll use one-year T-bills.

Figure 15-2. Shorten duration of bonds, portfolio 2.

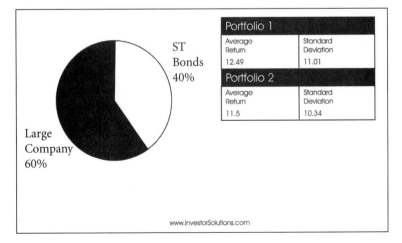

Portfolio 1	
Average Return	Standard Deviation
12.49	11.01

Portfolio 2	
Average Return	Standard Deviation
11.5	10.34

ST Bonds 40%

Large Company 60%

www.InvestorSolutions.com

The new portfolio exhibits a very satisfactory decrease in risk without suffering much decrease in expected return.

Next, let's look at the equities. It has long been established that international diversification will decrease risk in a domestic-only portfolio. So, we test the effect of splitting half the equity portfolio into the EAFE (Europe, Australia, and Far East) index and the large companies. True to our expectations, we note a gratifying decrease in risk (see Figure 15-3).

Figure 15-3. Diversify internationally, portfolio 3.

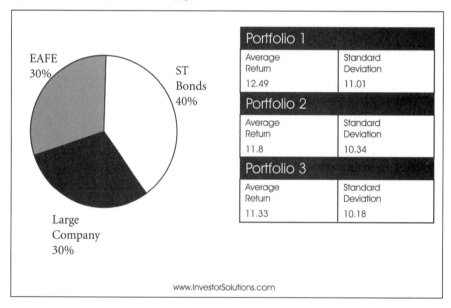

| Portfolio 1 | |
Average Return	Standard Deviation
12.49	11.01

| Portfolio 2 | |
Average Return	Standard Deviation
11.8	10.34

| Portfolio 3 | |
Average Return	Standard Deviation
11.33	10.18

EAFE 30%

ST Bonds 40%

Large Company 30%

www.InvestorSolutions.com

The EAFE and the large company index are comprised of large companies in developed countries. Small companies offer much higher returns than large companies, so let's divide both our domestic and foreign portfolios to capture some of this extra return (see Figure 15-4).

Most of the index is comprised of growth stocks (stocks with low book-to-market ratios). The Fama-French research points out that value stocks (stocks with high book-to-market ratios) have a much higher rate of return without additional risk. So let's split the equities again to add a strong value tilt (see Figure 15-5).

Figure 15-4. Think small, portfolio 4.

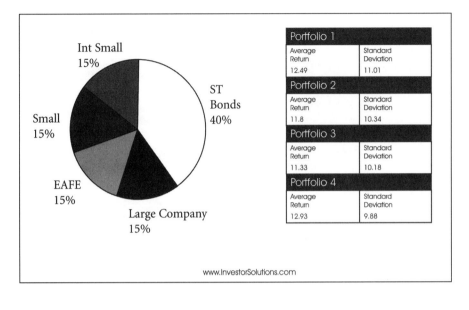

The process could continue to test the effects of including such asset classes as emerging markets or real estate (in the form of equity REITs). However, this example does not include them because I lack reliable twenty-year data. As new asset classes are defined, their usefulness will be determined by whether they increase return or reduce risk at the portfolio level. If they can increase return or reduce risk, they add a valuable diversification effect. An appropriate data series, a little trial and error, and a little judgment will identify which of them add enough value to justify inclusion. I use a healthy dose of emerging markets in my portfolios but no real estate.

We know that expected returns in the emerging markets are very high. Risk level is also high on an individual market basis. But emerging markets have very low correlation with each other and with other developed markets. Including emerging markets as part of our foreign allocation further increases rate of return without adding additional risk to our portfolios.

On the other hand, real estate investment trusts (REITs) seem to behave somewhat like interest-sensitive stocks

Figure 15-5. Think value, portfolio 5.

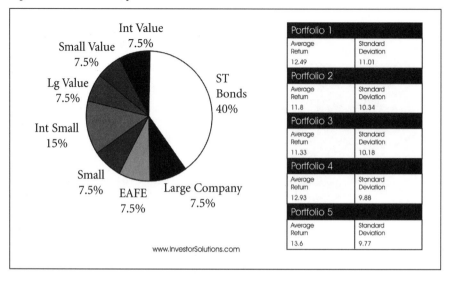

www.InvestorSolutions.com

and utilities and somewhat like small cap stocks. Inclusion in the portfolio doesn't add much in the way of diversification benefit.

CONCLUSIONS

While our initial 60/40 mix of large company stocks and the long-term treasury bond was a pretty good portfolio, we have been able to substantially improve it. We have met the clients' minimum required rate of return, stayed well within their risk tolerance, and improved both risk and return over the initial portfolio.

Our improved, balanced account has maintained and enhanced performance while slashing risk. We accomplished this by making no forecasts and selecting no individual stocks, and without attempting to time the markets. We didn't try to pick the best asset class, and we didn't trade frantically. We just put a number of attractive asset classes together in a way that made sense. You don't need to watch the market twenty-four hours a day, and you don't need to be wired to your PDA while you play golf.

The last twenty-eight years have been good to equities, though our time period (1975 to 2003) included a few anxious moments. We witnessed the final fall of Saigon; three minor police actions in Panama, Haiti, and Grenada; and an all-out war with Desert Storm. We had nuclear confrontation and the fall of the Berlin Wall. We had low inflation, high inflation, booms, and recessions. We had high interest rates and low interest rates. We had a strong dollar and we had a weak dollar. We had Democrats and Republicans in both Congress and the White House. We had good markets and a couple of spectacular "crashes." We had a president impeached but not convicted, who survived to watch his chief tormentor retire in disgrace. In short, it was a little-better-than-average time for investors. Depending on your particular personality, it will take courage, faith, or a very laid-back attitude to stay fully invested every day. Whatever it takes, remain fully invested in a diversified portfolio. It's a key element in success.

The portfolio we designed is on the leading edge of financial research. But research continues, and the story is far from over. As new, state-of-the-art research tools are developed, they will first be available to the large institutions and investment advisors. How fast they filter down to the retail level is purely a function of demand. Until enough investors demand them, only professionals will have the best tools.

Demand is a result of education. Wall Street has little interest in educating investors to prefer low-cost, low-profit-margin investment strategies. The old ways are so much more profitable—for them. To the extent that Wall Street has enormous advertising and public relations budgets, they shape the debate and discussion in the popular media. Independent investment advisors advocating low-cost, low-profit-margin investment strategies tend to have rather smaller budgets for advertising and PR. It's rare to see an intelligent discussion of value versus growth investment style. Or, to see anyone advocating index fund investing either on television or what passes for sophisticated financial press. But it's not unusual at all to see yesterday's hero sharing tidbits, gossip, and speculation. This type of activity may have great entertainment and amusement value, but it is of little help in assisting investors to formulate their plans. Some of the more popular Wall Street television programs have little trouble giving a half-dozen conflicting strategies in a single half hour.

Investors have to get used to the idea that they must educate themselves and go beyond the traditional Wall Street sources of investment advice, if they want to utilize the most effective investment strategies. Many of you will decide to work with a professional. However, you still must know enough to choose between the scam artists and the true professionals.

As you educate yourself, demand better strategies, lower costs, and better research. Don't settle for what Wall Street wants you to know. Don't settle for what Wall Street wants you to have. That's the financial equivalent of letting the foxes guard the hen house.

The portfolio designed in this chapter won't meet the needs of every investor; however, it can easily be tailored for many other investor needs. Chapter 16 will illustrate how to adjust the relative proportion of bonds in the portfolio to increase rate of return or decrease risk. We will also take an in-depth look at how our portfolio performed and the implications of the strategy we designed.

SIXTEEN

❖❖❖❖❖❖❖

PORTFOLIO TACTICS

Chapter 15 introduced the story of investors Mr. and Mrs. Jones. Let's see how our portfolio would have performed for the Joneses during retirement and how that portfolio would have compared to either a CD or full equity account. Then we will look at how other investors may modify the portfolio to meet their individual needs for liquidity and risk tolerance preferences.

OLD-SCHOOL INVESTING

We have been conditioned to think of market timing, stock selection, and manager performance as the keys to success. Because these beliefs are deeply ingrained, even superior investment strategies like strategic global asset allocation take a little getting used to.

Building a successful investment plan for the twenty-first century requires a fundamental change in the way we think about investing. New advances in investment and finance offer us solutions both simpler and more elegant (and very, very different) than what we grew up with.

What I'm advocating is so different from public expectations that sometimes people look at me as if I'm not quite right. As an investment advisor, I'm expected to have an opinion on where the market is going. Well, I have an opinion, but it's no more likely to come true than yours or your dog's. Some people are offended and disappointed when I tell them that.

We are exposed daily to countless experts who are worried about the market. Their indicators and forecasts point to a possible correction. They are prepared to retreat to the safety of cash. This allows them to look responsible, conservative, and caring. By pandering to the public's fear, they hope thousands of anguished investors will decide to trust them with their money. On the other hand, advisors who insist on remaining fully invested at all times are perceived as reckless.

Advisors are supposed to beat somebody or something. Often the first question people ask is: "What kind of numbers have you achieved this year?" Those numbers become the chief yardstick to determine if the advisor is good or bad. I'm still waiting for the first investor to ask: "What's the best long-term allocation?" or "How much risk do I need to take to meet my goals?"

Without tools to evaluate risk or choose between alternative strategies, investors are left with just one number to compare performance. By default, year-to-date or last year's performance figures are the only criteria for measurement. If those figures alone determined a successful investment plan, we could all buy one copy of *Money* magazine each year, pick the single, top-performing mutual fund, and go sailing. Unfortunately, the *Money* magazine approach is often the worst way to form a strategy.

TURNING YOUR GOALS INTO A STRATEGY

Every strategy has certain performance implications. The word strategy implies a conscious effort to achieve stated goals. As we saw in Chapter 15, the goal for the Joneses was not to beat the large company, any other index, or person. They were not interested in maximum performance. Their concern was to at least meet their minimum acceptable return levels without taking excessive risk. They wanted a comfortable and stress-free retirement.

The asset allocation design will determine results in both short- and long-term periods. What's more, both risk and returns will be driven far more by asset allocation than stock selection or market timing.

We could have looked at the twenty-year, asset class returns and seen that foreign, small company stocks produced the highest return. But putting all the Joneses' money in foreign, small company stocks will not produce a comfortable and stress-free retirement. Any asset class can and will have extended periods of serious underperformance from its long-term trend. And, foreign, small company stocks can and do have wild swings in short-term performance.

LET'S GET RISKY

So why put any of that risky stuff in the Jones plan? Why not just buy them a few utility stocks and forget it? The reason is this: When we measure risk at the portfolio level, we can see that the best way to construct a conservative portfolio is not to have all safe assets, but to have a conservative mix of attractive assets. A risky asset with a low correlation to other assets in the portfolio can actually reduce risk in the portfolio. It's a question of trying to get as much bang (return) for the buck (risk) as possible. A diversified portfolio offers much higher returns per unit of risk than does a utility or blue-chip portfolio.

If we individually examine each asset class, we will see that some have considerable risk (see Figure 16-1). I have used the traditional definition of the risk-reward line as falling along the points between the risk-free T-bill rate and the large company stocks. Any point falling above or to the left of the line is good, while below or to the right of the line is not. Investment managers all strive to have their performance fall somewhere in the northwest quadrant.

Figure 16-1. Portfolio building blocks, 1975-2002.

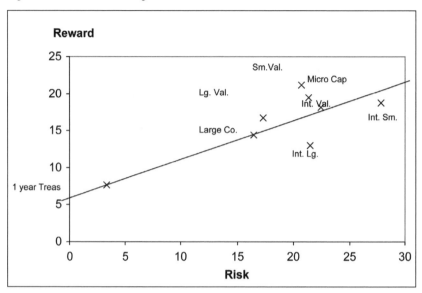

Over the long term, investment markets and portions of markets generally sort themselves out just about as they are here. In the short run, we might expect just about anything. It's not terribly unusual to see a negative-sloping, risk-reward line for short time periods. That just means the market went down and that stocks performed worse than T-bills. In the business we tend not to put many of those charts on the wall, but you should know that they exist. You must think of these temporary reverses as just another nonevent on the way to meeting your goals.

BALANCING RISK WITH RETURN

While looking at the chart, you might notice that the statistics generally confirm that small stocks have a higher return and risk than large ones, and that value has a higher return without any more risk than growth. During this particular time period, value stocks had higher risk than the S&P 500, but turned in higher returns. Foreign stocks, adjusted for currency back to U.S. dollars, have had lower returns than domestic stocks.

EAFE (Europe, Australia, and Far East) had somewhat lower returns than we might have expected, but this occurred while the S&P 500 was on a once-in-a-lifetime tear. Because it is primarily a large-growth portfolio, it falls considerably below the large foreign value stocks. Foreign small company and value stocks are particularly attractive in terms of return, generating much higher rewards than EAFE. Fortunately, they also have low correlation to our domestic stock markets. Notice how far below the line the long-term bond portfolio falls. Long-term bonds show much higher risk for no more reward than a short-term portfolio.

What is important is how much risk the portfolio has and that the risk is reasonably conservative. From another perspective, few portfolios with this level of risk will offer better total return. While the efficient frontier is a constantly changing target, we must conclude that our superior portfolio is reasonably efficient. Here's another view of our efforts to improve the starting portfolio in Figure 16-2.

Figure 16-2. Portfolio construction, cumulative results 1975-2002.

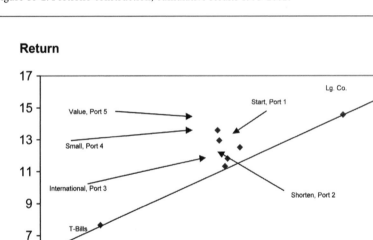

How did each of our improved portfolios perform over the twenty-six-year period? Check out the year-by-year performance of each of the portfolios along with the T-bill and S&P 500 returns. (See Appendix 1.)

The word strategy also implies a long-term approach. Even the best long-term strategy will not be the best each year, or even each five years. And, since we are dealing with equities, and equities have risk, it's important to understand that even the best strategy isn't a guarantee against occasional bad (negative) periods. Remember, risk happens.

EXPECTING PERIODIC DECLINES

One measure of risk that investors use is chance of loss. Let's face it, none of us like even temporary declines. In a twenty-six-year period, our portfolio had only two losses. The large company index had four losses and portfolio 1 in Chapter 15 had three losses. However, that doesn't mean that worse performance wasn't possible.

For instance, had the data been available to build our model, we would have seen larger losses in the dismal 1973 to 1974 period. The possibility for larger losses is incorporated in the model. We have enough data points to build a reliable model and have faith in our standard deviation measurement. Just keep in mind that performance can and will exceed one standard deviation about three years in ten. Of course, few complain if the performance exceeds a standard deviation on the upside.

Investors also seem to have any number of mental yardsticks that they employ relentlessly either against themselves or their financial advisors during periods of underperformance. Investors want to do better than CD rates, and they want to do that every day. Of course, even a superior portfolio will not outperform CD rates every day or every year. In fact, this portfolio fell short of that yardstick a total of five times.

NO MORE SECOND-GUESSING

Investors often have one more mental yardstick for comparison. The temptation to second-guess yourself or your strategy is enormous. After all, investors are human, and they believe, quite reasonably, that they should have it all. For instance, often they want to beat the S&P 500. We have gone to a great deal of trouble to build a portfolio that doesn't look anything like the S&P 500. The S&P 500 is made up of large domestic growth stocks. These tend to have a relatively low return per unit of risk that they endure. (The performance from 1995 to 2000 was an aberration and not likely to be sustainable during the long run.)

Our strategy has been to seek out asset classes that have a higher rate of return and very low correlation with domestic, large company, growth stocks. It stands to reason that our portfolio will not track with the S&P

500. This means that sometimes the S&P 500 will outperform our superior portfolio. When foreign, small company, or value stocks are having bad years, it is not likely that we will outperform an exclusively domestic, large company, growth portfolio. In fact, the S&P 500 outperformed our portfolio fifteen out of twenty-five years! In summary, our superior portfolio had two losses, failed to beat CDs five times, and failed to beat the S&P 500 fifteen times. (See Appendix 1.)

Investors often tend to narrowly focus on any yardstick that exceeds their portfolio performance for the moment. This practice can lead to some interesting conversations between investors and their advisors. Unless investors focus on their own goals, risk tolerance, and strategy, performance becomes an impossible moving target. Investors must understand that a superior portfolio will underperform from time to time, no matter what mental yardstick they use. If they are prepared for this disconcerting reality, they are less likely to find themselves abandoning their superior portfolio in favor of Wall Street's deal of the day.

ADJUSTING THE PORTFOLIO FOR INDIVIDUAL PREFERENCES

As good as this portfolio is, it won't be right for every investor. Some will want more return, some will want less risk. It's pretty easy to modify the portfolio to meet most objectives. For investors seeking lower risk, we can just shift the proportion of assets from equities (stock) to short-term bonds. We started with a 60/40 mix of stocks to bonds. More conservative investors might opt for a 40/60 or even 20/80 mix of stocks to bonds. However, they ought to hold each of the asset classes, even the riskiest in their portfolios. They will just hold a smaller percentage of each class.

Investors wanting higher risk and reward can just reduce the proportion of bonds. Once they get to zero bonds, they have two potential courses to follow if they want still higher returns. First, they could shift the asset allocation to more value and small company stocks. While our example didn't include emerging markets, we can assume that they might opt for a healthy portion of them in their portfolio as well. As an alternative, these investors might consider purchasing the portfolio on margin.

As a practical matter, most investors would not be comfortable with these higher levels of risk. (Very few of my clients have complained that we aren't taking enough risk.) My view is that, properly practiced, investing should be reasonably boring. Perhaps there are some intrepid souls out there craving excitement, but they don't find their way to my door in large numbers. While I have a number of investors fully invested in equities, I have exactly zero investors on margin.

THE PROOF IS IN THE PERFORMANCE

Here is how the portfolios would have performed (see Figure 16-3). Each portfolio containing equities is comfortably above the old risk-reward line. You should also notice that the most conservative, balanced portfolio with 20 percent equities has both lower risk and higher performance than a pure, short-term, bond portfolio. (Each of our adjusted portfolios is a very good strategy at a particular level of risk.) (See Appendix 3).

Figure 16-3. Customizing portfolio results, 1975-2002.

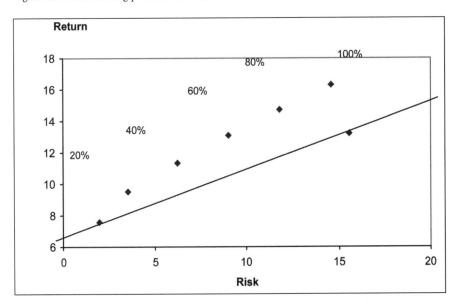

HAPPINESS THROUGH ASSET
ALLOCATION

Back to the Joneses. How would the portfolio have performed for them? Would it have met their need for income, an inflation hedge, and an increase in real value? And, how should they turn this portfolio into an income-generating machine?

If the Joneses had looked at their total capital each December 31 and withdrawn 6 percent for the following year's income needs, the income stream would have been very favorable. (See Appendix 2.)

Growth above the 6 percent income withdrawal is reinvested to provide an inflation hedge and long-term growth of capital. The healthy level of short-term bonds keeps us from having to consume stocks during market declines. The process of reallocation each year back to the original proportions will result in selling bonds following bad years and stock following good years. Reallocation actually contributes to total return, while holding the risk level constant.

Income under the plan began at $80,052 and grew to $362,529 last year. Income from CDs started at $66,300 and trended up until 1981, when it reached $172,700, then tapered off to $17,800. Total income under the plan of $7,736,599 compares favorably to income of $2,014,900 with the CDs.

The Joneses had a clear choice, and they could have gone the safe route. The CDs are still only worth $1 million, and the example portfolio has grown to $5,679,626 by the end of 2002. Rather than nibbling caviar and toasting champagne, the Joneses would be out cashing in McDonald's discount coupons. While they are there, they can check out employment opportunities behind the counter. Not all those smiling older faces are there just because they're bored with retirement. That million dollars didn't go as far as you might have thought if you simply put it in the bank twenty-five years ago.

REALITY REARS ITS NASTY HEAD

Please don't read too much into this model. The time period we were forced to use was considerably better than normal. (Data is not available in all the markets we wanted to demonstrate for longer than twenty-five years.) Falling interest rates, falling inflation, and superior stock markets characterized the time period. Both nominal and real rates of return were significantly higher than long-term trends. For instance, if we had included the dismal 1973 to 1974 years, our rates of return would be lower.

No one should base their planning on attaining anything like the rates of return here. As a rule of thumb, don't expect long-term results higher than 8 percent above the inflation rate. (Many economists believe that even 8 percent is far too high.) If you do better, celebrate. Just don't base your whole strategy on attaining returns that are so much higher than normal.

A STRATEGY FOR EVERYONE

We have demonstrated a superior investment strategy. Looking forward, our strategy should yield superior results while limiting risk for long-term investors in almost any economic environment short of unlimited nuclear war or total global economic collapse. Appendix 3 gives year-by-year and summary performances for each of the six portfolios.

Whether you are playing tennis, flying fighters, or practicing medicine, you should be constantly looking for the highest probability shot. The combination of strategic global asset allocation and modern portfolio theory (with an appreciation of the cross-section of expected returns in various parts of the world's markets) offers investors the highest probability shot of making their objectives a reality.

Chapter 17 will expand on specific tactics to meet the needs of funding education.

SEVENTEEN

EDUCATION

The vast majority of investors I work with have two primary concerns: Retirement or college education for their children. They have every right to be concerned. Both concerns will require startling amounts of resources. Neither is likely to receive increased government assistance in the foreseeable future. Individuals are on notice that they are going to be on their own to provide for both.

EDUCATION IN THE GOOD OLD DAYS

As an in-state student, in 1962 my first semester's tuition at the University of Virginia was $214. Out-of-state students paid about twice that amount. I was never able to conspire to spend more than $2,200 for an entire year's expenses including books, car, insurance, gas, rent, food, clothes, and pocket money. Most of that could be earned at a good summer job.

Those days are gone forever. For more than a generation, education expenses have inflated at more than twice the rate of the economy as a whole. Working your way through college isn't possible for most kids. The available jobs just don't pay anything close to what is needed. Only a few fortunate families can afford to fund college expenses from their current income. Many boomers and yuppies failed to provide an education fund for their children. So today many graduates start life with debts in the $60,000 to $100,000 range.

While education may be expensive, ignorance is unthinkable. Education isn't optional. In the twenty-first century the fault line between rich and poor will be determined by schooling. And all degrees are not created equal. Anyone who thinks a local community college degree is worth the same as Harvard's is deluding himself.

Software is available from many mutual fund companies to assist parents in estimating the future cost of college. The packages I have seen have a database of current college costs by type of institution and information on past inflation factors. Plugging in the child's current age will generate a total estimated future expense. Once we know that figure and current investments allocated to meet the college expense, it's a small step to back off and determine the amount that must be invested each year to meet the education goal.

These packages are great tools. However, they are all very sensitive to assumptions about future inflation and investment rates of return. So use a little discretion when plugging in those factors. Otherwise the numbers can get a little strange.

The college-funding problem is compounded by two factors: time horizon and taxes. Time horizon may be a very important factor in setting our investment policy for education. Assuming we begin to fund the day of birth, we only have seventeen or eighteen years until we need our first big checks. Then we need big checks on a regular basis for an additional four years (at least). That's the best-case scenario. In Chapter 11, we have already discussed the overwhelming advantage that an early start has when investing for any financial goal. Education is no exception.

Often young families feel they cannot afford to begin funding college from birth. Delay, of course, compounds the problem. Given what we know about variability of market returns, it's not comfortable to maintain a fully invested equity portfolio as the time horizon shortens. We are going to have to come up with a lot of money on a very tight schedule. Sometime (about five years out from our goal) we will need to look hard at reducing the risk in the portfolio. After all, we don't want little Suzy to miss Harvard because the market went into a funk when she was sixteen. So any family with limited resources may wish to begin moving assets from equity to short-term bonds or CDs. (Of course, if you are really well-off, you may not be so concerned with short-term market conditions. Wealthy people always have more options.) For most parents (even those that are very comfortable with market risk) at best there may be only a thirteen-year window to invest in an all-equity portfolio.

Taxes add another wrinkle to the investment policy decision. Many parents' careers are just hitting their stride as the college years approach, so they often find themselves in a high-tax bracket. It's annoying to have to pay taxes on the investment earnings of your child's college fund. This sets up a situation where many bright financial planners propose cures worse than the disease.

ANNUITIES FOR COLLEGE FUNDING? NOT!

Another inappropriate solution to the tax problem is the use of an annuity. Under today's law, withdrawals suffer ordinary income tax and a 10 percent penalty if the owner is under age fifty-nine and a half. Most parents will be younger than this during their child's college years. I find it hard to imagine that the tax-deferral value of an annuity could overcome the additional cost of the annuity shell, ordinary income tax treatment, and a 10 percent penalty in any reasonable time frame associated with college funding. In my humble opinion, only ignorance or greed could account for the prevalence of annuity recommendations as a college-funding vehicle.

HELP FROM THE GOVERNMENT?

Under Section 529 of the tax code, state college plans now enjoy tax-free growth and estate tax advantages. As a result, more states are starting to offer college savings plans. This new breed of college plan is a major improvement over both the Uniform Gifts to Minors Act and the prepaid tuition plans that have been established by a number of states. (Though Section 529 also grants estate and tax benefits to prepaid plans, they are unlikely to cover the complete cost of tuition.) These state savings plans are a great way for grandparents to help their children and grandchildren and lower estate taxes at the same time.

Almost all states have already set up college savings plans. (You can check the College Savings Plan Network for details.) Eligibility, schools that are covered, exemption from state income tax, investment policies, costs, and other important provisions will vary widely, so read the fine print.

State-by-state comparisons aren't only of academic interest. One of the advantages of these wonderfully flexible plans is that you can choose one regardless of where you live and where the recipient of your gift plans to attend school. Furthermore, under federal legislation, there are no pesky income restrictions and no age limits. You don't even have to be related to the beneficiary. Remarkably, although a gift invested in one of these plans is treated as a completed gift under estate and gifting tax law (so donors can deduct their gifts from their taxable estates), the grantor still retains control of the funds. No need to worry about the grandchildren blowing the funds all on an around-the-world motorcycle trip.

There is an advantage to making large gifts early, if you can afford to do so. In line with the annual gift tax restrictions, you can donate up to $10,000 a year, and your spouse can donate another $10,000. But you may gift five years' worth at once, up to $50,000 plus another $50,000 from your spouse. (In that case, you'd need to survive for five years for the entire gift to be removed from your estate.) Once an account reaches the maximum $100,505 (a limit that will be adjusted for inflation), no more gifts may be made, but there is no upper limit to the size that the account can grow to. If you gifted $50,000 to an infant, the account might grow enough to provide for undergraduate, graduate, law, and medical school.

Suppose I live in Florida and my granddaughter lives in Philadelphia. She has it in her mind to go to school in Nebraska, and I want to help her. I can give up to $50,000 to the New Hampshire Fund this year ($100,000 if my wife joins me in the gift). The funds will appreciate tax-deferred and, when used by the child for post–secondary education expenses including room, board, fees, tuition, and supplies, the money will be tax-free. If she later decides to go to school in Alaska or Hawaii, that's all right, too. Eligible institutions include almost any qualified higher education program including undergraduate, graduate, and accredited trade schools, not only state public schools.

What if she doesn't go to school at all? I still retain control of the funds, and I can decide to use them to send one of her other relatives to school. The approved list of who counts as a relative is very liberal, including parents, children, and in-laws. If none of her relatives want to attend school, I can take the money back and pay income tax on the appreciation and a 10 percent penalty tax. (The 10 percent penalty is waived for death or disability of the beneficiary. If the beneficiary wins a scholarship, then an equal amount can be withdrawn without penalty.)

Plan assets must be invested by the states. (This may explain why these plans have been kept such a secret. Stockbrokers, registered representatives, and financial advisors can't figure out a way to get paid and so have had little incentive to push them.) Once you pick the plan, you have no investment control. However, you can split your accounts among multiple states to diversify. For instance, you can pair New York's plan, managed by TIAA-CREF, with New Hampshire's Fidelity-run plan.

A child who is the beneficiary of such a plan may be less eligible for financial aid. But high-income, high-net-worth families don't have the same chance for financial aid. In fact, restrictions are so tight that many middle-class families are deluding themselves if they expect their child to get aid. You also may not contribute to an education IRA in the same year that you contribute to an approved state college funding plan. In most situations, however, that's hardly a sacrifice. All in all, college savings plans offer a unique combination of tax-favored college funding with estate and gift tax advantages that are hard to beat.

OTHER OPTIONS FOR EDUCATION

There are a number of viable alternatives to the education IRAs and Section 529 education funding plans that a family should consider as they plan their college-funding strategy. All trade tax advantages for varying degrees of control over the account, but most should be helpful to almost any family.

Good planning will help lighten the funding load. Still, there are no magic bullets. Families must budget and save to make it happen, and, as always, the earlier they start, the easier the task.

THE UNIFORM GIFT TO MINORS (UGMA) AND UNIFORM TRANSFER TO MINORS (UTMA) ACTS

There is little good to say about this option. Because minors can't own property, states have allowed parents (and others) to set up accounts for them. On the one hand, the gift is considered irrevocable and subject to the normal $10,000 or $20,000 limitations for gifting. The donor may not take it back, and the account may only be used to benefit the child. The child can even sue if the proceeds are used for any other purpose. When the child reaches the age of majority in the state of residence, he or she is free to use the funds for *any* purpose, whether or not it has to do with education. This potential diversion of the hard-earned funds from their intended purpose happens just enough that almost every financial advisor knows of at least one such horror show among their clients.

There are some tax advantages, of course. The first $700 of unearned income (gains, interest, and dividends) escapes taxation. The next $700 is taxed at 15 percent, but amounts over $1,400 in the account all accrue at the parents' highest tax rate until the child turns fourteen. After age fourteen, the tax rate is the child's. Even though the gift is considered final, if the custodian dies the proceeds are included in his or her estate.

OTHER IRAS

Contributions to a Roth IRA can be withdrawn free of penalty and taxes for education expenses. In eighteen years, a married couple, each making maximum Roth contributions at $2,000 each per year, would have deposited $72,000. If they had been successful in earning 10 percent during that time, the total value would have grown to $182,396.69. After withdrawing the basis for a qualifying education expense, $110,396.69 remains to grow for retirement.

The Roth IRA can be a handy source of education funds and allows the contributor to maintain total control of the funds, ensuring that they are spent as desired.

Don't forget that children can also contribute up to $2,000 a year to a Roth if they have earned income and can take advantage of the same tax-free withdrawals. (Those of you who have businesses may be able to find employment for a deserving family member while doing a little creative income shifting.)

Withdrawals from a regular IRA would not be subject to penalty if used for education expenses, but would be subject to regular income tax. This makes regular IRAs somewhat undesirable for college funding.

AN ACCOUNT IN A PARENT'S NAME

Holding an account in a parent's name ensures total control of the funds and, if properly designed, may still provide tax-favored accumulation. Of course, the parent would be taxed on any dividends, interest, or gains in the account, so individual stocks or mutual funds chosen for low turnover and dividends make a lot of sense. The S&P 500 index, a total market index, or a foreign index fund would be likely candidates. When the child is ready for school, shares can be gifted to the child. When the child sells the appreciated shares, they will be taxed at the child's lower capital gains rate, which could be as low as 10 percent.

STATE PREPAID COLLEGE TUITION PLAN

Under previous legislation, states established prepaid college tuition plans to cover tuition and perhaps room and board. Under a typical plan, a deposit equal in amount to current tuition is guaranteed to cover the cost of tuition when the child enrolls. If the child does not attend a qualifying school, a refund is available. However, gains and interest are forfeited. Many expenses are not covered by the plan, so that only about 30 percent of the total cost of college may be provided for. Not all schools participate in the plans.

Given the restrictions on the use of funds, limited coverage of expenses, and the forfeiture of profits if not used at a qualifying state school, these older state plans have been eclipsed by newer, more favorable funding methods.

HOPE AND LIFETIME CREDITS

As part of the 1997 Taxpayer Relief Act, Congress included the Hope Scholarship Credit and the Lifetime Learning Credit. These programs provide for limited tax credits for qualifying educational expenses.

The Hope Scholarship Credit is limited to $1,500 against tuition and fees during the first two years of college. Lifetime Credits are limited to 20 percent of the first $5,000 ($1,000) but may be used at any time. Only one family member can qualify for a lifetime credit no matter how many members are in college. Both credits are subject to income limitations ($100,000 joint/$50,000 single with the standard phase-ins beginning at $80,000/$40,000).

THE RIGHT PLAN

Any of the above alternatives will work. It may come down to personal choice. But here are a few considerations you may want to keep in mind:

> If estate and gifting tax considerations are important, the Section 529 plan is hard to beat. It's also a great way for grandparents and other family members to reduce their estate tax burden and still maintain control of how the money gets spent. All the other options (with the exception of UGMA accounts) offer attractive combinations of income tax advantages and control.
>
> Most families find college expense to be a high and moving target. In the final analysis, the decision of what plan to use may be far less important than the decision to start investing early and the discipline to actually get it done.

The best you may be able to do is start early and invest for high rates of return, especially during the early years. As college approaches, you may wish to consider reducing the risk in the portfolio.

EIGHTEEN

A COMPREHENSIVE APPROACH TO INVESTING DURING RETIREMENT

Few subjects provoke as much emotional stress as the later stages of retirement planning. Our jobs and money both become part of our self-image. Suddenly both seem at risk.

Until retirement, new checks usually arrive with great regularity. Most of them will be consumed. A small part of them will be saved for that far-off day. It seems that there is plenty of time to make up for an occasional bad investment decision.

One day the nature of the game changes irrevocably. Retirees realize that they won't have any chance to make up for poor investment decisions. Whatever assets they have accumulated have to last forever. In one sense, time has run out. In another sense, time appears to stretch out without limit. The natural inclination is to stop taking any risk at all.

There is a strange paradox at work here. The avenue that offers the highest probability of achieving long-term financial goals is not the one with the lowest risk. Of course cavalier self-confidence can quickly deteriorate into morbid concern as potential retirees ponder the questions,

"When can I retire, how much is enough, and how do I make it last?" Let's put what we have learned to work on the retiree's problem of making the nest egg last forever.

A DIFFERENT GAME PLAN

Investing during retirement is completely different than investing for retirement. The requirement to generate liberal, consistent, and reliable income over a long-term, indefinite time horizon changes the problem in a fundamental way. During the accumulation phase it is completely rational and consistent to take a full measure of global equity risk in return for the probable higher returns. The emphasis is correctly placed on attaining the highest possible accumulation. At retirement the objectives change: Generate income, and don't run out of money. An entirely different strategy is called for.

Retirees have several key concerns:

- How much can I safely withdraw?
- How can I make my nest egg last forever?
- Can I hedge the portfolio for inflation?
- If anything is left over, how can I get the most to the next generation?

In addition, several factors complicate these key concerns:

- Fixed-dollar withdrawal programs increase investment risk and introduce the possibility of self-liquidating the portfolio during extended market declines.
- Time horizons are extended, but cannot be predicted exactly in advance. The average life expectancy for a couple aged fifty-five to sixty is about thirty-two years.
- Inflation is embedded within government policy. We cannot count on it going away.
- Taxes are a dead drag on performance and the largest expense investors face.
- Because investment returns are finite, expenses must be rigorously controlled.

- IRA and pension-forced withdrawals at age seventy and a half may accelerate receipt of principal and its taxation far in excess of needs.
- Beneficiary selection and estate planning is complex due to the intersection of IRA withdrawal rules, income, and estate tax considerations.

Decision making is complicated by uncertainty. Most of the factors that determine success or failure are beyond our direct control. Retirees cannot control or predict market returns, interest rates, or even their own mortality. Consequently, we must focus on the things that we can control and devise a conservative investment strategy that will yield the highest probability of success.

SUSTAINABLE WITHDRAWAL RATES

No two retirees have identical situations or objectives. Each case must be individually considered. A comprehensive approach considers all the complicating factors before reaching a solution. No single facet can be considered in a vacuum. The process is a little like putting together a puzzle with many parts. Some compromise may be necessary, and retirees must face up to the possibility of midcourse corrections.

So, the first piece of the puzzle is how much can we safely withdraw each year for our expenses?

OLD ASSUMPTIONS ARE HAZARDOUS TO YOUR WEALTH

The traditional financial planning assumption about retirement income generation goes something like this: You will make 10 percent on average and withdraw 6 percent per year. Each year your account balance and income will grow by an average of 4 percent. You will die rich, and your children will receive a windfall. This sounds wonderful in theory, but it's a bust in the real world.

The fatal problem with the traditional assumption is that it does not account for the variability of returns the retiree faces in the real world. We know from past experience that projecting average returns forward in a straight line is totally inappropriate. Average returns count for nothing if your retirement precedes a period like the Depression or 1973 to 1974. Your nest egg stood a high chance of self-liquidating during those periods. The real world that you face is much more complicated and risky than an average return might indicate.

A PIONEERING STUDY

Three business professors from Trinity University of Texas, Philip L. Cooley, Carl M. Hubbard, and Daniel T. Walz, broke new ground with their paper "Retirement Savings: Choosing a Withdrawal Rate That Is Sustainable."[1] They employed historical back testing to demonstrate the relationship between withdrawal rates, time horizon, and asset allocation. Their results reveal that portfolio failure rates are directly related to time horizon and withdrawal rates and are influenced by asset allocation.

Using the S&P 500 and bonds in various combinations over varying time periods commencing in 1926, the study tracked failure rates against withdrawal amounts (see Figure 18-1). *Even in the best possible case where there were no taxes, no expenses or transaction fees, and the optimum portfolio was known in advance, significant failure rates occurred above 6 percent.*

Figure 18-1. The Cooley, Hubbard, and Walz study: failure rate with optimum portfolios (thirty-year periods).

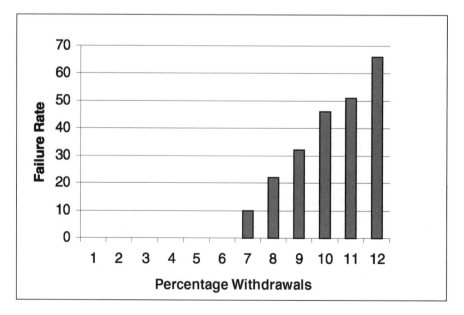

The Cooley, Hubbard, and Walz study highlights the need for conservative withdrawal rates and, by implication, the need to accumulate liberal amounts of capital to fund a comfortable retirement. Historical back testing is a useful tool and provides a powerful sanity check. Yet, like any modeling tool, it has its limitations. In this case, we are stuck with only one series of data. Unless we believe that the past results will reoccur in exactly the same sequence, our findings will not be as robust as we might hope. For instance, running the sequence backwards or any other reshuffling will result in entirely different results. Furthermore, historical back testing leaves us with no simple method to vary either rates of return or volatility in the sample set.

New and more powerful modeling tools confirm these principles and add additional insight, but do not replace the need for very conservative assumptions if the retiree wishes to have a high probability of success. The fact remains that the highest risk factor a retiree faces, and the only decision directly under control, is the withdrawal rate.

RECOGNIZING THE EFFECT OF VOLATILITY

Monte Carlo simulation and today's powerful spreadsheet applications give us far more insight into the problem and point out some additional solutions that would not have been possible with historical back testing.

Simply put, Monte Carlo simulation utilizes random draws of numbers from pools constructed with specified rates of return and volatility (risk). Much like a lottery, we build a pool of numbers and pull them out at random to construct a single test. We then repeat the process 1,000 or 10,000 times and summarize the results. The summary provides a quantitative estimate of the range and distribution of the possible returns. Varying the construction of the pools of numbers allows us to examine different strategies to see which ones give a higher probability of success.

For instance, we could construct pools of numbers that have an average return of 10 percent and a standard deviation of 10 percent. Then, starting with a $1 million dollar portfolio, we can test the survival rates of 4 percent, 5 percent, 6 percent, and 7 percent withdrawal amounts 1,000 times each. Our findings will generally confirm the Cooley, Hubbard, and Walz study.

What happens if we run the tests again using a pool of numbers with a 10 percent rate of return but a standard deviation of 10 percent, 15 percent, and 20 percent? The withdrawal rate is 6 percent per year. At thirty years only one percent of trials fail at 10 percent, but 22 percent fail at a standard deviation of 20 percent. Failure rates soar with the higher volatility. All 10 percent returns are not equal. (See Figure 18-2.)

Figure 18-2. Portfolio failures increase with risk, 30-year periods, assumed return 10 percent.

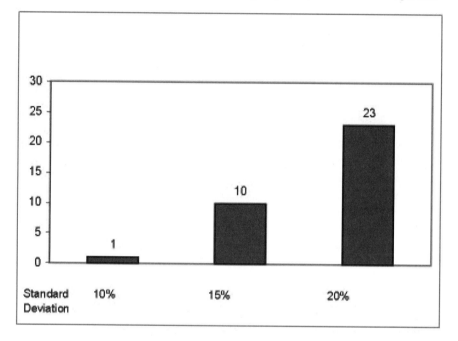

The simulation reveals a clear link between volatility and survival of the portfolio at any given time horizon. Anything we can do to reduce portfolio volatility (given the same rate of return and withdrawal rates) will significantly enhance the chance that a retiree's nest egg will survive.

TOTALLY SKEWED

In the traditional analysis you might think that half of all trials would result in greater than expected returns and half less. However, it's worse than that. The only case where each trial yields the average result occurs where there is no portfolio volatility. In that special case, every trial survives and gets the identical result.

With volatility, outcomes become skewed. Even though we obtain the expected rate of return across the sample, the median return is less than the average. The higher the volatility, the greater the sample becomes skewed at any time horizon. So while we get the average return we expect, the average result is less than what we expect. As the number of failures goes up, the number of extraordinary results also goes up. A small number of players obtain much higher-than-expected results, while a large number of players' portfolios either fail or obtain lower-than-expected results.

For example, suppose we expect a terminal value of $100,000 for a particular withdrawal rate, rate of return, and time horizon. If one result yields $1 million and nine results yield zero dollars at some particular risk level, we have achieved our average return. However, nine of ten retirees are broke!

SUMMARY

It's hard to overestimate the importance of selecting a realistic withdrawal rate for the following reasons:

- If capital is insufficient, the retiree may be tempted to increase the withdrawal rate.
- A high withdrawal rate increases the chance of going broke.
- Reaching for higher investment returns increases volatility that in turn increases the chance of going broke.

Constructing the Investment Policy

Every step of the investment policy must support the retiree's objectives. The ideal policy will support the required withdrawal rate while maximizing the probability of success.

The first problem that faces the retiree is that guaranteed investment products are unlikely to provide sufficient total return to meet the retiree's reasonable needs. Meanwhile, equities are far too volatile to provide a reliable income stream. A compromise must be reached. A combination of stocks and bonds will probably best meet the needs.

Because at least part of the portfolio will be volatile, the question of risk management moves to the forefront. Our first step is to construct a "two bucket" portfolio.

BUCKET ONE—ADEQUATE LIQUID RESERVES

Recognizing that equity investments are too volatile to support even moderate withdrawal rates safely, investors must temper their portfolios with a near riskless asset that will lower the volatility at the portfolio level and be available to fund withdrawals during down-market conditions. As a minimum liquidity requirement, I suggest high-quality, short-term bonds sufficient to cover five to seven years of income needs at the beginning of retirement (see Figure 18-3). While it is tempting to chase higher yields with longer duration or lower-quality issues, past experience indicates that the enormous increase in risk swamps the small, additional yield benefit.

So if you expected to draw down 6 percent of your capital each year for income needs, you might want to have 30 percent to 42 percent in fixed investments. That way, if the market takes a dive, as it probably will sometime during your retirement, you will have plenty of time for it to recover. Meanwhile you can draw down the bonds. This protects your growth assets during market declines.

Figure 18-3. The "two bucket" portfolio: adequate liquid reserves in bucket one.

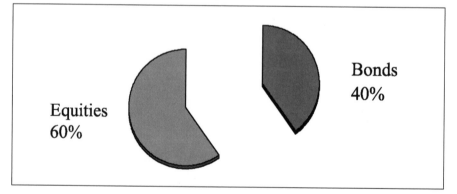

BUCKET TWO—A WORLD EQUITY MARKET BASKET

Our second bucket will contain an approximate, weighted, world equity market basket (see Figure 18-4). The design philosophy is to construct the equity portfolio with the highest possible return per unit of risk.

This investment policy recognizes the impact of volatility and employs standard portfolio construction concepts to reduce it. These well-known modern portfolio theory techniques include utilization of multiple asset classes with low correlations to one another. For example, I utilize nine distinct, global equity asset classes. These classes each have high expected returns at tolerable risk levels and relatively low correlation to each other. We overweight the United States for our domestic clients' currency preferences and overweight small and value stocks to increase expected returns while diversifying into dissimilar asset classes.

Figure 18-4. The "two bucket" portfolio: a world equity market basket in bucket two.

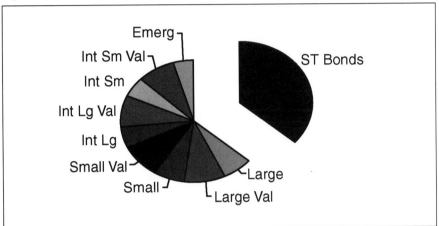

WITHDRAWAL STRATEGY—PRESERVING VOLATILE ASSETS IN DOWN MARKETS

A rational withdrawal strategy will recognize that equities are volatile and short-term bonds are not. So we employ a specific strategy designed to protect volatile assets during down-market conditions. Otherwise, excessive equity capital will be consumed during market downturns.

Most advisors have been content to treat retirement assets as a single portfolio. For instance, many would advocate a lifestyle portfolio comprised of 60 percent stocks and 40 percent bonds. However, this leads to withdrawals on a pro rata basis from both equity and fixed assets regardless of market experience. It does nothing to protect volatile assets during down markets.

A far superior, alternative strategy would treat the equity and bond portfolios separately, then impose a rule for withdrawals that protects equity capital during down markets by liquidating only bonds during bad years. During good years withdrawals are funded by sales of equity shares, and any excess accumulation is used to rebalance the portfolio back to the desired asset allocation. Again, using spreadsheet models with Monte Carlo simulation, we find substantial incremental improvement by imposing this simple rule.

IMPLEMENTATION

In all cases, implementation is via no-load, institutional-class index funds. This policy spreads risk as widely as possible in some of the world's most attractive markets while controlling costs, preventing style drift, minimizing taxes, and eliminating management risk.

EVALUATION OF ALTERNATIVE STRATEGIES

Finance has been silent on the question of where to invest on the efficient frontier. Monte Carlo simulation gives us a powerful tool to evaluate alternative strategies. For example, should an investor needing a 6 percent withdrawal rate invest in a portfolio with a 10 percent return and a 12 percent standard deviation, or one with an 11 percent return with a 15 percent standard deviation? Does this answer depend on the time horizon? Does the answer change if the withdrawal rate changes? Monte Carlo simulation can guide us to the best choice depending on the investor's unique requirements and goals. The correct choice is the one with the highest probability of success.

We can also conduct a stress test on our assumptions. For instance, what happens if we have volatility right but rate of return falls 2 percent short of our estimate?

TRANSITION PLANNING

The investor will want to transition from the full accumulation mode to the retirement asset allocation plan sometime in advance of the retirement date in order to assure that sufficient liquidity is available when needed.

For instance, with ten years before you retire, you still have a fairly long time horizon. While there is never a guarantee, the odds are greatly in your favor that a heavy exposure to equities will pay off handsomely. Think how you would feel if you had missed out on the market in the 1990s.

However, as you approach retirement, you probably will want to scale back to your preferred retirement asset allocation. Exactly how you manage the transition from stocks to a balanced portfolio is up to you. Too early and you are likely to miss out on a lot of growth, too late and you may be exposed to a market downturn at or near your retirement. Let me offer two suggestions that you can modify to meet your needs:

1. Determine your optimum asset allocation at retirement.

2. About five to seven years before you expect to retire, begin shifting equal amounts once a year into short-term bonds so that the year you retire you are at your preferred asset allocation.

MIDCOURSE CORRECTIONS AND INFLATION ADJUSTMENTS

The discussion's assumption that a retiree will continue a fixed dollar withdrawal program regardless of investment results is simplistic. (However, without that assumption, no guidelines can be derived.) In fact, a retiree may be in a position to temporarily decrease withdrawals during down markets until his capital recovers. Or, assuming early results in excess of expectations, the retiree may elect to increase her withdrawals as capital increases. In many cases, terminal values are a gratifying multiple of starting capital. Consequently, midcourse adjustments to withdrawal rates are possible and may very well be positive.

A built-in inflation adjustment increases risk in the same manner as a higher initial withdrawal rate. The lower the initial rate, the more likely that positive adjustments can be made to hedge inflation.

ALTERNATIVE WITHDRAWAL PLANS

If income requirements are variable or capital permits, an alternative policy of making fixed percentage withdrawals against the annual principal values may be an acceptable solution for many retirees. This policy will provide a variable income stream that is automatically adjusted for investment results.

Retirees who can accept a variable income and withdraw a constant percent of remaining capital (rather than make fixed dollar withdrawals) never face the prospect of zeroing out their accounts, no matter how bad their investment results are in the short term. Generally, this option is only acceptable to retirees with modest income needs relative to their available capital.

ADDITIONAL CONSIDERATIONS

Retirement planning cannot proceed in a vacuum. All aspects of the family situation and objectives must be considered.

TAX CONSIDERATIONS

Taxes are a dead drag on performance and the highest cost individual investors face. Every dollar that marches off the field to the IRS is no longer available to grow for your future. Two portfolios with identical pre-tax returns may have widely differing after-tax returns. The rational retiree will adopt an investment policy designed to maximize after-tax returns. There are a variety of useful techniques that can be employed to minimize the tax bite:

- Evaluate the use of tax-free bonds for income and safety requirements in nonqualified accounts.
- Generate income from sale of appreciated shares qualifying for capital gains treatment.
- Distribute high turnover funds like value and small company funds to qualified portfolios where possible.
- Minimize turnover in nonqualified funds.
- Utilize tax-efficient index funds.
- Benefit from Roth conversion opportunities.

LIFETIME DISTRIBUTION PLANNING

Required distributions at age seventy and a half may cause inconvenient or awkward income streams. Proper selection of distribution elections prior to the required beginning date (RBD) can ensure that funds are delivered in the quantity desired and at the times desired. Full or partial conversion to Roth may help alleviate the problem.

ESTATE PLANNING

Many retirees will want to ensure that their assets, including retirement plans, will not be consumed by unnecessary costs and transfer taxes. With proper planning a beneficiary may be able to defer income tax for many more years on the vast majority of an inherited IRA. Appropriate attention must be paid to beneficiary selection of qualified plans and coordination with a comprehensive estate plan. Roth IRA conversion may be the most powerful, overlooked, and underused estate-planning opportunity available for many retirees.

Use of properly designed intervivos trusts and/or a durable power of attorney for nonqualified assets will minimize potential estate tax and probate fees and provide a management vehicle in the event of incapacity.

COST CONTAINMENT

Market returns are finite, and costs reduce them. Professional advice, transaction costs, and other expenses are not free. But the market is competitive, and total costs can and should be closely controlled.

BE PREPARED FOR MIDCOURSE CORRECTIONS

In lieu of a crystal ball, the best mathematical models cannot anticipate all eventualities. By making conservative initial assumptions, we increase the probability that midcourse corrections will be positive.

NOTE

1. Philip L. Cooley, Carl M. Hubbard, and Daniel T. Walz, "Retirement Savings: Choosing a Withdrawal Rate That Is Sustainable," in *AAII Journal* Vol. XX, No. 2 (February 1998). Available at http://www.aaii.com/promo/mstar/feature.shtml.

NINETEEN

THE JOYS OF FUND SELECTION

The asset allocation decision is the heavy lifting in the investment process. Having decided on an appropriate asset allocation plan, our quest now turns to finding the appropriate funding vehicles to best represent each asset class. As it turns out, mutual funds are almost the ideal building blocks to construct your globally diversified investment strategy.

As designers of a superior investment strategy based on strategic, global asset allocation, we will select mutual funds that allow us to very tightly control our portfolio. We will be seeking very precisely targeted funds in diverse markets and investment styles. This will require us to leave behind any notion that there is a single best fund that might meet our needs, abandon the ever-popular but childishly simplistic and ineffective magazine ratings, and redefine our performance benchmarks.

THE MUTUAL FUND INDUSTRY

Mutual funds have become popular because they offer huge advantages to small and large investors. (Small investors are loosely defined as those with less than $50 million or so to invest.) The advantages of mutual funds are overwhelming. Today there are more than 13,000 nonmoney market funds. Rather than having too few choices, we are buried in them in most asset classes. With more than three new funds coming on stream each business day, just reading the new offering prospectuses becomes a full-time job.

Traditionally, we have thought of diversification, low cost, and access to superb managers as the chief advantages of mutual funds. The first two are certainly true. Where else can an investor purchase a portfolio containing hundreds or even thousands of individual issues across a market with as little as $500 or less? How can she do it without being destroyed by transaction fees? Now, of course, we have to wonder if management can add value. If the investor is convinced it can, then she can attract the attention of the best talent available by pooling her funds with thousands of others. If the investor doesn't believe management adds value, then she has the alternative of investing in index or passively managed funds.

FUND BASICS

Let's see if we can cut through all the noise and clutter to see how the fund industry works. Then we can develop a few simple criteria to drive your selection decisions. This procedure is fairly straightforward, and it allows you to get in control of the total investment process.

COST: THE NATURAL ENEMY OF THE INVESTOR

Cost is an important consideration for investors. Cost is also one of the few areas where investors can exercise a great deal of control. There seems to be a concerted effort by the fund industry to absolutely prevent investors from figuring out what their costs really are and what the implications of the various pricing strategies mean. Don't despair. It can be explained very simply.

MANAGEMENT FEE

Every mutual fund has a management fee. It is fully disclosed in the prospectus. This fee goes to pay the normal expenses of running the management team and the business. It includes postage, printing, rent, salaries, accounting, lights, telephones, equipment, and the like.

THE DREADED AND MUCH MALIGNED 12(B)-1 FEE

Some funds charge a second fee called a 12(b)-1 fee. The purpose of this fee is to promote the sale of more shares of funds to the public. The fund might use this fee for advertising or commissions to salespeople, or to pay custodian and service fees to a discount brokerage house.

It's not important whether the fund breaks out the 12(b)-1 fee in the prospectus. All funds have some type of promotion expenses. Some just choose to show them as a separate cost.

EXPENSE RATIOS

Both management fees and 12(b)-1 fees, if any, are included in the fund's expense ratio. Expense ratios are always fully disclosed in the prospectus. This is the number the investor should zero in on. There is a very strong inverse relationship between total cost and investor return. While purveyors of high-price goods invariably love to imply that you get what you pay for, on Wall Street it's often easy to get far less. As you might expect, low expense ratios are very, very good. Expense ratios can vary from under 0.25 percent to over 3 percent.

TRADING COSTS

Trading costs are not included in the expense ratio and are not disclosed. (More about the second point later.) We may impute some information about trading costs from the portfolio turnover. Some funds never trade, and some may turn the entire portfolio over several times a year. We know that lots of buying and selling is expensive. Just how expensive trading can be varies from market to market. Trading costs are generally very small for NYSE stocks. But when we get into small company, foreign, or emerging market stocks or bonds, prices can get very high. For instance, a "round trip" on a small company stock may exceed 7 percent. Consequently, an average of two trades a year on a small company portfolio can go a long way toward eating up the average profits.

Trading costs fall directly on the fund. When a fund buys a stock it carries the stock on the books at cost, including commissions. When it sells, it shows the net receipts after commissions. Neither commissions nor the spread are ever accounted for. Unless one can demonstrate a very positive benefit from trading (most managers can't), then small turnover is good.

THE BOTTOM LINE (WELL, PART OF IT ANYWAY!)

Simply put, the ongoing cost of running any mutual fund is the expense ratio plus the trading costs. Unfortunately, this definition doesn't include the impact of commissions.

COMMISSIONS AND THEIR IMPACT

Some funds are sold directly to the public. Others are sold by salespeople. The second type of fund has to figure out how to pay the salesperson. A number of interesting arrangements have developed to solve that problem.

In the bad, old days, many mutual funds were sold by contract. The investor paid a set amount every month for a number of years to satisfy her contract. During the first year, the salesperson got half of the investment. After that, the salesperson usually got about 4 percent of the continuing contributions. Perhaps that explains the slow acceptance of mutual funds by our parents.

Later, so-called front-end load products emerged with a top sales charge of about 8.5 percent. This sales charge was deducted from the total investment, and the balance ended up in the fund. So out of a $10,000 investment, $9,150 went into the fund and the balance ended up in the sales organization's pockets. Larger investments might qualify for a discount. For instance, at $100,000 the typical sales charge would be 3.5 percent. Front-end load products are often called "A shares" within the industry.

Over time, resistance to the high sales cost drove many companies to cut their maximum sales charge to around 5 percent. But as true no-load mutual funds cut into the market, funds began to look for ways to hide the sales charge. This effort reached its brilliant conclusion with the invention of the brokerage houses' no-load or "back-end surrender charge" funds (commonly called "B shares").

Until the investing public began to figure it out, the brokerage houses and broker-dealers had the best of all possible worlds. They were able to increase the average commission paid to the salesperson, and at the same time claim that the product was no-load. The broker got a 5 percent or 6 percent commission the first day, and the client saw all his money go to work in the fund at the same time. This little piece of Wall Street magic was possible because the sponsoring company fronted the commission to the broker. The company recovered their payment to the salesperson by increasing the charges to the fund about 1.5 percent per year. (This charge was the so called 12(b)-1 fee, named after the NASD's enabling regulation.) In the event the investor liquidated his fund prior to the company recovering the commission, interest, and a profit, the investor was charged a back-end surrender fee before his proceeds were paid out. This last part of the transaction was not often emphasized during the sales process, so many investors were in for a rude shock if they bailed out for any reason.

If investors took the time to do the math, they discovered that the back-end surrender funds could be a very expensive way to invest. For one thing, large investments got no discount. An investor placing $250,000 in a front-end load fund could expect a one time 3 percent charge. But if she held the same size investment in a back-end surrender charge fund until the end of the typical surrender period of six years, she would end up paying 9 percent in hidden fees. Assuming growth of the investment, the fees got larger! Finally, the hidden charges continued forever so the total cost could be huge. Of course in our example, the salesperson got twice the commission he would have earned in the more straightforward front-end transaction. It's not too hard to see why brokers loved the back-end surrender products.

If the evolution of the load fund industry had stopped there, our task would be somewhat simpler. But as investors began to wise up, fund families tried to stay one step ahead by introducing new types of shares with new pricing. The names they gave the pricing schemes aren't always consistent from one company to another. "C shares" look rather like "B" shares, but the internal charges fall after the surrender period. "D shares" have a level one percent charge paid to the salesperson each year, but have no surrender period or charge. Many "A" share funds have introduced a 12(b)-1 charge to finance a trail commission to the salesperson on top of the original sales commission. Still other companies are experimenting with reduced front-end charges but larger ongoing fees to finance increased trail commissions.

A few years ago, the NASD issued regulations that prohibit any fund charging a 12(b)-1 fee in excess of 0.25 percent from calling themselves no-load. The same regulations have allowed fund families to actually increase trail commissions to salespeople, who now presumably refer to their products as no front-end load—all in the name of consumer protection. At the same time, some true no-load funds have expense ratios high enough to choke a horse. Be certain to look beyond the labels.

If all this is beginning to make your head spin, there is a simple solution. Just buy no-load funds. Then all you need to be concerned about from a cost perspective is expense ratio and trading costs. Your broker may not care for that solution. However, it's not your job to keep her happy. Even if we ignore the effects of embedded conflicts of interest in the commission sales process, commissions have a direct economic impact on the investor. You may think of front-end load funds as being the equivalent of running a 100-yard dash from three to eight yards behind the start line. Back-end funds might be thought of as running the same race while carrying a 150-pound load.

Another problem with the traditional load products is the psychological feeling of being trapped in an investment by the large cost of moving. Investors will often stay in an inappropriate investment rather than endure a second set of fees required to bail out of the first poor choice. Families of funds mitigate this problem. They allow an investor to switch without penalty within a single family of funds. This still requires the investor to severely limit his choices. With true no-load funds, especially if held as custodian by one of the large discount brokerage firms, the investor may have more than 1,000 choices in over 200 fund families, and she can execute them with just a phone call. (Some transaction charges may be tacked on by the brokerage firm, but these are a very tiny portion of the commission charges on load funds.)

One great working solution to define a no-load fund is to inquire about the cost of a round trip. If you can buy a fund today for a dollar and sell it tomorrow for a dollar (assuming the market hasn't moved), you have something that looks, smells, and feels like a no-load fund. While this definition may not be technically accurate, it will uncover lots of deceptive sales tactics. You will quickly be able to quantify the costs of brokerage and trading costs.

TARGETING YOUR MARKET SEGMENT

The next big issue we face in building our investment plan is to select funds that reliably capture the performance of the market or segment of the market we have specified in our model. We know a great deal—but never enough—about the risk, return, and correlation of stocks based on the size of the firm and the stock's book-to-market ratio. This information is crucial in designing the asset allocation plan.

If we are going to have control of our asset allocation plan, we must seek out funds that will confine themselves to a definable style. For instance, we know that across most of the world's economies, the smallest 20 percent of the companies have about a 5 percent higher expected rate of return than the largest companies over long periods. Of course, this return comes with a higher risk and a correlation with other asset classes. If our asset allocation plan calls for a 15 percent weight in small companies, that is what we want to have. One person's definition of small may vary considerably from the next person's. So our terms must be objectively defined. For example, we might define a fund with a maximum size company of $500 million as small. Other observers might call these type of companies micro caps. However, if we want the performance that comes with small companies, we are just kidding ourselves if we buy the smallest firms in the S&P 500.

The same goes for value. Value is a harder term to pin down than size. Lots of managers call themselves value managers but own portfolios of stock with very low book-to-market ratios. If we want a strong, value representation, we must seek out funds with stocks in the highest third when ranking book-to-market scale for each size company.

STYLE DRIFT: THE NATURAL ENEMY OF ASSET ALLOCATION

It would be disconcerting to find that a fund we have selected to represent small companies is suddenly investing in General Motors, IBM, and AT&T. Many growth funds have now decided to add foreign stocks to boost their performance. That might or might not work out well for their particular fund, but it skews the model badly.

The tendency of managers to wake up one day and decide that an entirely different market segment looks more attractive than where they are is called style drift. Style drift is the natural enemy of the asset allocation plan. It goes without saying that we have no way to control risk if we don't know what is in the portfolio, or if the portfolio can change radically without any advance notice.

TRADITIONAL LABELS AND FUND OBJECTIVES THAT OBSCURE RATHER THAN ENLIGHTEN

Traditional labels and prospectus categories are not much help here. In fact, it's best to forget them. The categories are arbitrary and ambiguous. Just where is the boundary between a growth and income, a growth, or an equity income fund? These nuances have always escaped me. Many fund-rating services attempt to use these categories to compare fund performance. The funds often respond by redefining their objectives to fit a category where their relative performance is better.

Defining the investment manager's style provides us with a great deal more useful insight. Morningstar's style boxes allow the potential investor to determine at a glance the average size and growth/value characteristics of the portfolio. While far from perfect, this system is a big improvement. The style boxes are limited in that they describe only the average holdings in the portfolio. Some portfolios are hard to properly categorize, and the boxes are no assurance against style drift.

Many mutual funds have wide latitude to invest wherever they wish. Some have demonstrated either superior skill or cunning, or tremendous luck as their portfolio zigzagged. Magellan and 20th Century Ultra are famous for refusing to stay put. Their management will, of course, claim skill. Putting aside the question of skill versus luck, for each happy example, the landscape is littered with failed attempts.

Once we have made our asset allocation decision, we have absolutely no interest in the fund manager's market forecast. We want him to stay fully invested in the market we expect at all times. We have made the decision as to the exposure level we wish to have, and attempts by the manager to time her little part of the market are unacceptable to us. The mutual fund is simply a building block for our investment strategy, and the more predictable the building block, the better the finished structure. The days when we would turn over our money to a manager who could do whatever she wanted should be long behind us.

The asset allocation approach is a far cry from the traditional view of the role of the fund manager. Her role is reduced from exalted guru to subordinate technician. Her mission is to stay fully invested and widely diversified, keep her costs down, and reliably capture the performance of her assigned market segment. Should she stray from her assigned turf or attempt to market-time, she will be replaced. Should she fail to match her assigned market's performance, she can also be replaced by an index fund that will. On the other hand, it's not appropriate to blame the manager if her asset class shows poor performance. For example, Japanese small company fund managers are not to blame for an asset class that has shown a decade of dreary returns.

When it comes to picking funds, very little of what you hear in the popular financial media is useful, unless you just want to collect a few tidbits to exchange at cocktail parties. Lionizing last year's lucky manager is fun and probably harmless, but it tells us little about next year's performance.

Rating services such as Morningstar's star awards or the *Forbes* honor roll attest to the futility of applying past performance to tomorrow. Investments in either set of recommendations would have produced substandard results. If those two organizations can't make useful predictions with all their resources, how can the rest of us hope to? Why do people keep listening? When *Wall Street Week* starts interviewing next year's winners, I'll tune in. If successful investment management simply required counting stars or buying the *Forbes* list, we would all be rich and carefree.

On the other hand, there are some great resources that are widely available. For example, Morningstar's database on disk provides a treasure trove of information. It allows us to screen well over one hundred criteria including P/E ratio, P/B ratio (the reciprocal of book-to-market ratio), turnover, medium market capitalization, expense ratios, earnings growth, sector weightings, standard deviation ratings, estimated potential capital gains exposure, minimum purchase amounts, and even more data we can use in choosing our portfolio components. With just a few clicks of the mouse you can screen for no-load, foreign, equity funds (with an average firm capitalization not to exceed $500 million) that accept initial account sizes below $2,000. You can further define your search by checking for funds with expense ratios below 1.25 percent that are available through the Fidelity or Schwab brokerage systems. Then you can sort the funds in descending order of P/E ratios. Another click of the mouse allows you to compare your candidate funds with an appropriate index, check industry weightings in the portfolio holdings, and ensure that the funds hold enough issues for proper diversification. Morningstar even gives you the 800 numbers for most funds so that you can order prospectuses once you have identified a few likely suspects. Many city libraries have access to this or similar services. This caliber of information is much more useful than the type of article that touts "eight great funds" in *Money* magazine. With data like this, you can select and monitor your asset allocation plan segments.

ACTIVE VS. PASSIVE

The only reason to hire an active manager is if you are convinced that the manager can reliably improve over a passive benchmark. However, the only reliable thing about active managers is the consistency with which they fail to match the appropriate benchmark.

Unless you still believe in the tooth fairy, you will want to select an index fund for every asset category. The advantages are compelling. (These advantages include low expenses, low trading activity and cost, reduced tax exposure, and the assurance that we can reliably track our desired market segment.) And, you will never have to be concerned about style drift. Do the right thing: In every asset class where they are available, index!

AN ACTION CHECKLIST

Here is a checklist you may use to develop your fund selection process for individual asset classes. If you won't or can't use an index fund, my suggestions are:

- Define the market as tightly as you can—large, small, foreign, emerging market, Asia, Japan, Europe, etc. Make sure the manager stays fully invested and within the assigned market.
- Define style—growth versus value. (A strong value tilt should enhance performance and reduce risk.)
- Eliminate all load funds. (Never pay a load!)
- Check expense ratio. (The lower, the better—remember, some markets cost more than others.)
- Check portfolio turnover. (The lower, the better is the rule again.)
- Check the number of holdings. Funds with few holdings are taking concentrated bets against the market, increasing risk without increasing expected returns. The more diversification within the asset class, the better.

■ Compare performance to appropriate benchmark and competitive funds. Try to understand any variation from benchmark. (There is always a reason. Higher returns mean higher risk. For instance, 1999's big heroes were strongly concentrated in technology stocks. By year's end 2000, they looked like the worst dogs.)

LIMITED BUDGET

What do you do if you are just starting out? What if your budget is very limited? You can still build a champagne, globally diversified portfolio on a beer budget. While a $1 million portfolio might have twenty or more funds, you can do a reasonable job with just three or four index funds. For example, index funds such as the Vanguard S&P 500, Small Cap, and Total International would be a good start. As your portfolio grows, you can tilt toward smaller firms and value. Later you can add emerging markets. These are just examples. There are lots of great no-load families that accept very small initial purchases. Many will take on contributions as low as $50. The TIAA-CREF funds will accept as little as $25.

If you are making ongoing contributions to your investment plan, consider tilting your purchases to the most thoroughly beaten-up markets as you go along (after you have built up a good core).

JUST DO IT!

Remember that your investment plan doesn't have to be, perfect to be great. Don't wait for it to be perfect. It never will be, and you will still be waiting when you are old and broke. Get started now. If you need a little push to get going, use an automatic check withdrawal to your investment account. The important thing is to get started on a sensible plan and exercise the discipline to carry it out. Start small and build in pieces. Use your company savings and pension plans. If the choices aren't perfect, do the best you can. For instance, almost any growth fund in your company plan is going to pay off better in the long haul than any bond or guaranteed account. If the company plan offers foreign, value, small company, or emerging markets, use them. If not, balance your company plan with your own investment plan so that the whole thing looks like your ideal asset allocation.

Warts and all, no-load funds are still the best deal around. While I am one of the great mutual fund boosters, there are a few problems in the industry that you should be aware of. It's always a mistake to think that everybody on Wall Street is a member of the choir, even in the no-load mutual fund business. In addition, there are lots of alternatives to no-load funds, and a few of them even make pretty good sense as part of a balanced portfolio. We'll be taking a look at them, too. Remember, if we all demand better, we will get it. It's the one way to really get Wall Street's attention.

TWENTY

THE GOOD,
THE BAD,
AND THE UGLY

Somewhere over the jungles of Southeast Asia, I developed doubts about the perfectibility of man. Idealism was quickly replaced by pragmatism. Watching Wall Street at work for over twenty-five years has not restored my faith in man's perfectibility. Fortunately, as realistic and pragmatic investors, we can thrive and prosper in a jungle where not everybody wears white hats. Our job as good capitalists is to utilize the very best parts of a wonderful system and continue to press for improvements where necessary.

Forcing improvements is remarkably simple. We don't have to go on a mission or lead a charge. We can just refuse to patronize firms that abuse investors. A loss of market share will do more to help Wall Street's denizens develop ethical business practices than a million new regulators.

While our focus is on mutual funds, the problems we will discuss in this chapter are found in any form of managed account on Wall Street. Angels may not fear to tread on Wall Street, but they don't exactly flock there either. I don't want to imply that only devils reside there. There are plenty of honest and competent professionals who labor on Wall Street.

However, we must suspect that both devils and angels are as randomly distributed there as they are anywhere.

Mutual funds have been remarkably free from major scandal since Robert Vesco plundered IOS over thirty years ago. They are perhaps the best-regulated, audited, and straightforward investment mechanism available to us. As a result, fund managers have fewer chances to play around with your money than many other Wall Street enterprises.

Our mission is to explore the issues surrounding managed accounts and learn the right questions to ask about them. We have an absolute right to the answers. Then we can avoid those who either refuse to answer or give the wrong answers.

ADVICE FROM MOM

My mother once concluded a discussion about right and wrong with the observation that if I never did anything I wouldn't care to explain in church or see printed on the front page of the local newspaper, I would be all right. While philosophy isn't exactly my favorite subject, this still seems a remarkably good way to judge ethical behavior. It sets a much higher standard than simply complying with the law or following regulations.

The gulf between compliance and ethical behavior can be enormous. Richard Breeden, a former chief of the SEC, once remarked to an assembled group of investment advisors that before his term ended, he wanted "to convince Wall Street that there is more to ethics than getting through the day without being indicted." I hope he won't be offended if we observe that perhaps he finished his term before accomplishing his objective.

Most of the time Wall Street complies with the law, but there is plenty of activity that probably wouldn't stand well at the local church. And a discussion of many of these business practices in the local papers always makes someone squirm on the Street.

A SHORT HISTORY LESSON

As part of his campaign to restore faith in the markets, President Franklin Delano Roosevelt's administration had a series of laws enacted during 1940 and 1941 that regulated the securities markets. The Securities and Exchange Commission (SEC) was created and given broad powers.

However, the SEC was encouraged to delegate many of its powers to industry self-regulating organizations (SROs). And, as regulators, SROs fall far short of perfection.

NASD: THE NAME SAYS IT ALL

The National Association of Securities Dealers (NASD) is the SRO entrusted to regulate broker-dealers and dealers in the over-the-counter market (NASDAQ). As the name implies, the NASD is an association of securities dealers. The majority of the members hail from the securities industry. Protecting the interest of securities dealers is their primary concern. While token representation is required for investors, in practice these minority members are remarkably tame lap dogs.

There is a constant pressure from above as the SEC must approve regulations enacted by the NASD. Reform continues with each year a little better than the last. However, as with any good industry or trade association, true reform is resisted with great enthusiasm. So, what's good for business is not necessarily always what is best for the investor.

The appearance of high integrity is of the utmost importance. Confidence in the markets must be maintained, or investors will refuse to play. So an enforcement mechanism exists that occasionally doles out harsh punishment to the worst offenders. Some activities are clearly beyond the pale. A member who steals from clients or embezzles from his firm can expect to be banished with great dispatch. However, in gray areas we have come to expect very little moral sensitivity from the NASD. Unfortunately, there are lots of gray areas in the securities business. We can boil down the important issues to three areas with some overlap: cost, conflicts of interest, and disclosure.

COST CREEP

Given the enormous increase in assets under management in the mutual fund industry, we should expect to see a sharp reduction in expenses as a percentage of assets under management. Yet expense ratios have steadily increased. Consider the following: Assets under management by fund companies now exceed $2.7 trillion, an increase of 3,260 percent in fifteen years. Stock and bond mutual fund fees exceeded $19.4 billion in 1995. Yet during the same time frame, average expense ratios have increased from 0.71 percent to 0.99 percent (according to the November 28, 1995 editions of *The Wall Street Journal* and *Morningstar*).

There are some justifiable reasons for increases in expenses. New asset classes such as foreign, emerging market, and micro cap are more expensive and difficult to trade. Consumers are demanding more and more services from fund companies. And, funds that cater to smaller investors have higher expenses than funds with higher minimum investments. Each investor, no matter how large or small, represents a fixed expense for mailings, prospectuses, and so on. Yet, even given the economies of scale and the efficiencies introduced by technology, there just is no excuse for increases in expense ratios of that magnitude.

Late night talk show host David Letterman once joked, "Why does a dog lick himself?" The answer: "Because he can!" In a sense, it's the same with cost creep. Like the dog, mutual funds have found that they can. Investors have been remarkably docile when it comes to accepting these cost increases. As long as they will roll over for it, investors can expect more of the same. They have no one to blame but themselves. The cure is to focus on the expense ratios of mutual funds and reward funds and families that reduce costs.

THE MUTUAL FUNDS MARKETPLACES

When Charles Schwab created the mutual fund marketplace, investors and advisors flocked to embrace the concept. The convenience of being able to buy hundreds of funds with a single phone call, receive a single consolidated statement, and have next day settlement and the safety of an exceptionally strong custodian justified the nominal transaction fees for many investors. The service was a runaway sensation. The participating fund families received a marketing windfall. Schwab became an unbeatable distribution network at no cost to the funds.

As custodian of the funds, Schwab was required to assume many of the administrative chores that the funds normally supported. It became Schwab's responsibility to mail out prospectuses, semiannual and annual reports, proxy requests, and tax information. Schwab also provided accounting services for the funds in their omnibus account for all the fund shareholders to use.

The next step was equally brilliant. Schwab offered to waive the transaction fee for fund families that agreed to pay Schwab between 0.25 percent and 0.35 percent per year. The no-transaction fee (NTF) service was an even bigger hit with investors and fund families.

Initially, Schwab promised that fund families would not be allowed to pass the fee on to investors. The funds were receiving a windfall in two dimensions. The distribution channel was more cost-effective than anything else the no-load families had been able to generate for themselves. And, Schwab provided meaningful custodial services that relieved the funds of the costly burden of doing it themselves. In theory, no investor would ever pay a higher cost for a NTF fund than if she purchased it directly from the fund.

Out of the box, some fund families have found ways to pass on the additional costs. Some created entire new classes of shares with the fees buried in either a generous management fee or a separate 12(b)-1 fee. Others have slowly increased their expense ratios to compensate. In practice, all investors of the NTF funds are having to pay for the service whether they use it or not.

For Schwab, the service generates an incredible cash flow, an annuity that can be expected to continue forever. However, notwithstanding the success of the program in attracting assets, Schwab claims that it is not yet horribly profitable. Why? The NTF service may attract a high percentage of small accounts that generate frequent trades—the worst of all possible worlds for brokerage firms.

Schwab's fee to the fund families is a very high percentage of total expense ratios for many funds. For a few, including many index funds, the fee exceeds the total expense ratio. Many simply cannot afford to pay. Those funds risk being denied shelf space (or at least prime shelf space) at Schwab's store.

Of course, the success of the NTF program has spawned numerous competitors. Fidelity, Waterhouse, and other discount brokers have jumped on the bandwagon. However, Schwab's fees to the funds have become the industry standard. Due to the structure of the program, no competitor could pass on a lower fee to investors even if they wanted to, and there is little to entice them in that direction. The discount brokerage/NTF program is rapidly becoming the investor's vehicle of choice.

Today, no no-load mutual fund family can afford to ignore the programs. Unfortunately, the NTF programs are a strong factor in cost creep. No-transaction fee funds have on average 50 percent higher expense ratios than other no-load funds.

A STRATEGY TO HAVE YOUR CAKE AND EAT IT TOO

Smart investors can develop a strategy to have their cake and eat it too. A knee-jerk decision to use only NTF funds can be penny-wise and pound-foolish. It just takes a few seconds to calculate the trade-off between the annual, embedded, hidden NTF fee and a one-time transaction fee. Investors will quickly discover that they are often far better off paying the transaction fee. In some cases (large purchases) they can recover the transaction fee in less than a year. For instance, a $100,000 purchase might generate about a $30 transaction fee, while an NTF fund might cost in excess of $350 per year in additional fees inside the fund.

We have adopted a policy of placing the buy and hold core positions in index funds because of their very low annual expense ratios and low trading costs. Here it definitely makes sense to pay the transaction fee. Smaller positions in NTF funds are used as the rebalancing mechanism, for periodic small purchases for clients making repeat deposits, or to generate a stream of income via redemption for our retirees. The resulting blended portfolio has a very low annual expense ratio and almost never pays a transaction fee after the initial purchases.

THE ROLE OF INDEPENDENT DIRECTORS

We might be tempted to wonder where the independent directors are while these cost increases are being passed on to unsuspecting investors. By law, each fund must retain independent outside directors to represent the interests of investors. We would expect them to fight to the death for the rights of shareholders. Recognizing that cost is the enemy of the investor, our directors should resist increases to their dying breath. In practice, mutual fund independent directors lack any discernible backbone and appear to be born with rubber stamps attached to their hands.

Directorships are one of the ultimate plums of American society. Presumably only leading citizens who have made their mark are asked to serve. Board membership immediately places you among the powerful and the elite. In some ways it may be preferable to a seat in the United States Senate. Prestige and honor are great, compensation is generally nominal, and service is not considered burdensome or overly taxing. In return for dispensing a little wisdom, directors usually fly first class, stay in five-star hotels or resorts, and enjoy rubbing shoulders with other members of the elite.

Only a hard-core cynic would suspect that directors could be influenced by a mere $10,000 to $20,000 honorarium. But suppose a fund family appointed these same directors to twenty or thirty separate fund boards at once? Now we are talking about some serious pocket money. Perhaps in this context even a truly great director might find a request for an increase in management fee within the realm of the reasonable.

I find it truly puzzling why outside directors on hundreds of fund boards can mindlessly approve imposition of new 12(b)-1 fees. These fees are perfectly legal. And funds with 12(b)-1 fees may still have low to reasonable expense ratios. They allow funds to charge present investors so that the fund can go out and attract other investors. It's easy to see how a 12(b)-1 fee helps fund management. The extra charge allows them to go out and attract more investors and generate even more fees. But it's impossible to justify it on behalf of existing investors. What possible benefit could investors accrue? Yet outside directors supposedly represent existing investors.

The most charitable assessment possible on the role of outside directors is that they have been spectacularly ineffective in representing the shareholders they are charged to protect. The watchdogs are little better than lapdogs.

While we may not applaud 12(b)-1 fees and we may not enjoy overall expense creep, at least these items are fully disclosed. The facts are right there for all of us to see. We are free to avoid funds with high fees and, if we don't, we have no cause to complain. The fault is ours. There are many low-cost funds and families from which to choose.

DEALS CUT IN THE DARK

Other areas are inadequately disclosed, less understood, and occupy a gray area. The NASDAQ (National Association of Securities Dealers Automated Quotation System) market, by its very nature, encourages grayness. The NASDAQ market is really a group of dealers loosely tied together by a computer network.

Each dealer publishes a bid and ask price for stocks in which he makes a market. Dealers buy at the bid and sell at the ask price. The difference is known as the spread. Spread represents profit to the dealer. Spread, of course, is also trading cost to the investor.

Spreads tend to be higher on small, seldom-traded stocks and bonds and lower on larger, frequently traded issues. A number of academic studies have found that the spread on NASDAQ trades is higher than would be the case if a stock with the same size and volume was traded on a listed exchange.

In theory, with a number of market makers for a stock or bond, competition will force the spread to a minimum. In practice, there appears to be little such pressure on prices. Once a spread becomes accepted and if all the market makers hold the line, then all of them will have higher profits. It is not necessary for all of the market makers to get together in a smoke-filled room for a loose conspiracy to emerge. Cases of retribution, harassment, and abuse directed against market makers who cut the spread have been extensively documented.

As you might expect, when these practices make *The Wall Street Journal*, the NASD studies the problem. Predictably, swift and certain justice has not been the general rule as dealers examine their own and very profitable business practices.

SOFT DOLLARS

Before May Day, commissions were fixed and prices were bundled. All brokerage firms were full-service. Because there was no price competition, brokerage houses competed with each other on research and other services. Heavy traders and large accounts could supposedly count on superior research and early warnings of pending events. In addition, a practice of reimbursing clients for other research that the clients conducted on their own developed. The payments brokerage houses made to clients became known as soft dollars.

While commissions are now fully negotiable, the practice of soft dollars remains and has been expanded. Today, brokerage firms are reimbursing large clients with computers, furniture, research, and other goodies in return for high-volume trading. The problem with this practice as it applies to mutual funds, investment advisors, or other fiduciaries is that soft dollars accrue to the investment manager, while a larger discount on commissions would accrue to the investors. One must suspect that the client investor ends up with higher brokerage costs, and the manager has a reduced incentive to minimize such costs. Soft dollar practices are a clear conflict of interest for investment managers. Inadequate disclosure makes it impossible for the investor to properly access the impact of costs on his portfolio. Investors who believe that they are paying a manager or fund to do research might be surprised to find that the fund or manager is double-dipping.

PAYING FOR ORDER FLOW

Closely related to the soft dollar practice is paying for order flow. Especially in the NASDAQ market, large accounts or frequent investors can expect payments from brokerage houses for order flow. If payment for order flow went to the investment account, it would simply represent a discount on commissions and benefit the investor. However, these payments go directly to the manager. This practice eliminates much of the incentive for managers to search out and demand the best possible execution. Again, lack of disclosure from brokerage houses makes it difficult or impossible for investors to accurately determine the impact on the portfolio. Since October 2, 1995, the practice of payments for order flow must be disclosed; nevertheless, it often continues to be a hidden cost for the investor.

Often firms justify the practice as resulting in prices no worse than the best-quoted price. But this argument is self-serving and simply doesn't hold water. First, why shouldn't the payment be credited to the investment account? Where in this cozy little arrangement is the incentive for the investment managers to kill for the very best price and execution on behalf of their clients?

Lest you begin to believe that this is an occasional aberration rather than business as usual, consider the case of Charles Schwab's attempt to end order flow at their fully owned, market-maker subsidiary. Schwab announced an improved order system where not only would Schwab check all market makers for the best published prices, but they would also do a thorough search of all standing but unexecuted orders for an even better price. By making this extra effort, Schwab could guarantee buyers and sellers the very best possible prices and execute many trades inside the spread. In return for improved prices, Schwab proposed to end the practice of order flow payments made by their subsidiary. When Schwab made their proposal in October 1995, it was greeted by wide praise in the media and even public favorable comment by the SEC.

It was not to be, however. Schwab was faced with a client revolt and the threat of loss of massive business. They were forced to withdraw the proposal in December 1995. Brokerage houses and investment managers expressed their clear preference to continue to receive under-the-table kickbacks rather than the best possible price for their clients.

DIRECTED TRADES AND FEE SHARING

Large broker-dealers can exercise considerable power over the outside-load mutual funds that they distribute. In return for shelf space in their store, they routinely ask for (and get) a share of the fund's management fee and increased sales allowances, or require the fund families to kick in for other marketing expenses. These expenses will be reflected in the fund's expense ratio. Of course, this practice contributes directly to expense creep. Funds that have low internal expenses can least afford to pay and will be relatively disadvantaged in maintaining or establishing a sales network.

Broker-dealers or brokerage houses can require that outside mutual funds direct a portion of their trades through the facilities of the broker-dealer. An arrangement like this reduces the fund's ability to negotiate the very best possible execution or commission structure for their investors. Directed-trade agreements are not disclosed.

Funds that resist these tactics find their access to salespeople reduced, their sales agreements terminated, or the commissions paid to the sales-people reduced. Large broker dealers have begun to exercise their power over distribution networks in rather brutal, direct terms.

A few years ago, one of the nation's largest broker-dealers requested increased sales allowances from all the outside funds they did business with. To their credit, American Funds refused to participate. American Funds have very favorable expense ratios, excellent marketing materials, a very fine reputation for integrity, and solid performance. The dispute broke out in public at the broker-dealer's national sales convention. American Funds, who had contributed over $30,000 to be a sponsor of the convention, was publicly identified as refusing to support the economics of the broker-dealer. In addition, American Funds was forced to endure a public request the president of the broker-dealer made to the sales force asking the salespeople to consider this refusal when recommending funds to their clients. The commissions to the salespeople would be cut on American Funds products to compensate the broker-dealer for American Funds' refusal to cooperate. Henceforth, the sales force would be caught between the fund reputation and proven performance of American Funds products and a direct cost to their own pocketbooks. To their credit, the sales force continues to recommend a high number of American Funds' products. But few fund families have the economic clout (and backbone) to stand up to the big broker-dealers.

PREFERENCE BIDDING

Where mutual funds or investment managers are associated with market makers, another interesting possibility for undisclosed profit emerges. Fund managers can funnel trades to a related market maker even where that market maker is not advertising the best price. The associated market maker gets first crack at all trades. If the market maker finds that it can accomplish a trade profitably at the best-published price, it can execute the trade. Under preference bidding, the associated market maker receives a steady flow of profitable trades without even having to advertise the best price to the market.

Make no mistake about it. Making a market is a very profitable business. The associated market maker can rack up profits several times greater than the management fee of the fund or investment manager. And the investor is never the wiser. The practices of directing trades to associated market makers and preference bidding are not disclosed. Of course, the profits the associated market maker makes on the trades are never disclosed. The additional cost is impossible to measure with any accuracy. We can say that competition for best possible execution is not encouraged under either practice.

ECONOMIC AND MORAL IMPLICATIONS

These types of practices are at best unsavory. While not illegal, they are a violation of trust. Whether they pay commissions, or fees, investors have a right to expect that their representative, fund manager, or investment advisor is acting wholly on their behalf. Today, it is foolish to blithely make that assumption. As we have seen, it is not realistic to expect a self-regulatory organization to vigorously champion the investor's cause.

Efficient markets are the central core of our economy. Integrity of the markets is not a concern of just a few "pointy heads" in academia.

Efficient markets foster the optimum distribution of goods and services and result in the maximum wealth creation for the entire society. Few things are more important to all of us.

In perfect markets, both buyers and sellers have all known facts available to them. Neither has an advantage. It follows that full disclosure is the appropriate standard.

As investors we may have little interest in standing on our soapboxes and pointing fingers. Leaving aside a delicious sense of moral outrage, an important issue remains. In the absence of full disclosure, when deals are cut in the dark we are deprived of necessary information we need to make our decisions. The result is higher costs, inefficient institutions, and less wealth creation for the entire society.

REGULATORY REFORM

It may not be possible to completely avoid all forms of abuse. But the investor is far from powerless. Investors can and should agitate for regulatory reform. This course of action is slow but sure. Our markets are among the cleanest on earth. Each year they improve, and the progress is irreversible. Even SROs must react to an outraged public. After all, it's good for their business. Remember also that your congressman or senator can respond to your concerns. There is nothing like a call from a congressman's office to get the full, immediate, and undivided attention of even an entrenched bureaucrat.

VOTE WITH YOUR FEET

While we wait for the regulators to discover ethics, investors still carry a very big stick. Never forget Wall Street wants your money! Nothing gets through to them like a loss or gain in market share. Wall Street has seen regulators come and go and is prepared to ride out a little negative publicity. But movement of a few billion from high-cost funds to lower-cost funds like Vanguard will send a direct powerful message. It's simple. Don't buy or hold funds with high expense ratios or high turnover. You can improve your own bottom line while forcing reform. Do what is right for you, what serves your own best interest, and Wall Street will come around. Adopt the attitude that Wall Street is there to support you, not the other way around. Reward friends, punish enemies. Demand better, and it will be supplied. Capitalism is pretty neat stuff.

Sunlight: The Best Disinfectant

This next step takes slightly more effort: Inquire about the business practices of your funds, managers, or investment advisors. You have a perfect right to know what fiduciary standards they employ. After all, it's your money. And it's their job to keep you happy. Demand full disclosure of their business practices and any potential conflicts of interest. You should expect that they act in your best interest alone. Accept nothing less. Reward funds, advisors, and managers who practice ethically. If not, punish them by moving your funds. Acting on your own and pursuing your own best interest can enforce higher standards on the institutions that serve you.

Playing the Hand We Are Dealt

Not being much of a philosopher myself, I refuse to speculate endlessly on whether the glass is half-empty or half-full. From my vantage point the glass is mostly full. As pragmatists and informed investors we don't have the luxury of withdrawing in a fit of moral self-righteousness. Rather, our task is to inform ourselves and then choose the best from an amazing number of great tools. That action is simultaneously the best for us and the most effective agent for reform.

Coming up: A discussion of alternatives to mutual funds.

TWENTY-ONE

FUND
ALTERNATIVES

No-load mutual funds are about the most ideal building blocks for a globally diversified asset allocation plan you'll ever find. The combination of instant, broad diversification, liquidity, and low cost makes them the thinking investor's medium of choice. However, no-load funds are not the only possible way to achieve these goals, so let's look at a few alternatives.

CLOSED-END FUNDS

Closed-end funds are closely related to the more common open-end fund. Open-end funds continuously offer new shares to the public and provide liquidity via redemption of shares at net asset value. Closed-end mutual funds do not redeem shares directly from the public the way open-end funds do. Liquidity to the investor comes through the sale of shares to another investor on an exchange or over-the-counter.

New closed-end funds are almost always sold at a public offering price that includes a generous sales allowance or commission. As you recall, often these products are touted as being sold without commission. Technically correct, perhaps, but morally questionable. Usually the initial investor is really only buying ninety-six cents or less of stock for each dollar. So nobody should be surprised that after the initial offering is sold out and the fund begins to trade on a market, the price falls to the real net asset value. Why anyone would buy an initial offering is beyond me. However, the brokers receive several times as much commission—whoops, I mean offering allowance—for initial offerings as they would for an after-market trade. So they generally sell out.

More often than not, the price continues to fall. It's not unusual to see the price stabilize at about 80 percent to 85 percent of the net asset value. If you like to torture economists, just ask them why this happens. This effect is so persistent and widespread that opponents of the efficient market theory often cite it. One likely cause is the effect of hidden tax liabilities within the portfolio. Yet this only explains a small part of the difference. The problem has resisted rational solution and tends to make economists a little nuts.

Occasionally, optimism for a particular fund drives the market price far above net asset value. Only the greater fool theory can explain this apparently irrational pricing. Some investors track trading patterns and attempt to buy at historical low points and sell when the spread narrows. Of course the spread may never narrow. It may even get worse. The stock market has no memory, doesn't think it owes you anything, and makes no attempt to recoup your price.

Closed-end bond funds often trade at steep discounts. It's hard to resist the temptation to buy a dollar's worth of bonds for eighty cents or eighty-five cents. Investors looking for income can receive a handsome increase in yield by taking advantage of the discounts when they occur. This strategy is certainly worth looking into. While it may not eliminate all the problems with long-term bonds, it certainly can pad the income stream.

Closed-end funds are often proposed as a good solution to the problem of highly illiquid markets. For instance, in India the settlement of stock transactions can take weeks or even months. Other nations may have restrictions on the flow of capital out of the country. An open-end fund might have trouble liquidating shares in a small market to meet redemptions. A closed-end fund doesn't have that problem. So the closed-end fund offers us access to a market that we might not otherwise be able to enter. It solves the liquidity problem through another mechanism.

What we often observe is that a closed-end fund begins to trade on the domestic market more like a domestic stock than the foreign market it's supposed to represent. For example, if U.S. investors turn negative, they may first decide to dump their foreign holdings. The price of an Indian fund may suffer regardless of what is happening in India. The difference between net asset value in India and market price in New York may diverge sharply. Normal arbitrage cannot straighten out this strange result. So you may not get all the diversification effect you expect from the market.

A partial cure for this price disparity is to have a limited life for the closed-end fund. At the end of the limited life, either the stocks are all sold or the shares are transferred in kind to the holders. Neither is a perfect solution. One comes at the price of some pretty dramatic tax events. The other unloads the problem of selling the shares on to the investor, who presumably bought the fund to avoid those costs and aggravations. Many investors will buy limited life shares at a discount and wait for fund termination. However, they still run the risk that, at termination date, net asset value will have fallen below what they paid.

I would never buy a new offering. The chances are high that I can buy it at a steep discount somewhere down the road. I would never pay a premium in the aftermarket. And if I woke up one day to find that a fund I owned was trading at a good premium, I might be severely tempted to sell it to that greater fool and buy another one at a discount someplace else.

UNIT INVESTMENT TRUSTS

Unit investment trusts (UITs) are very much like closed-end funds, except that rather than try to manage a portfolio of stocks or bonds, they just buy a pool of assets and hold them. This approach reduces management costs to close to zero, but some very minor custodian and administrative costs remain. UITs are most often seen with bonds or municipal bonds. Investors receive interest, and their pro rata share of proceeds as bonds either mature or are called. Investors must not fool themselves into believing that a UIT can magically lock in a dividend. Our experience over the last twenty years of falling rates has been that calls quickly eroded the portfolios. Like their cousins the closed-end funds, prices can diverge rather far from net asset value, and some investors enjoy trading as prices fluctuate.

In summary, both closed-end funds and UITs can be a useful tool as part of a properly designed investment plan. Like everything else, they have their own risks and rewards.

REAL ESTATE INVESTMENT TRUSTS

Real estate investment trusts (REITs) are corporations that have elected special tax treatment. As long as their business is real estate and they distribute almost all of their income each year, they are not taxed at the corporate level. Once formed, REITs stock can be sold as any other stock, either over-the-counter or on an exchange. Many REITs own diversified properties all over the country. Investors who wish to hold real estate may find this a handy way to own a quality portfolio, have instant liquidity, and avoid the aggravation of being a landlord.

The trend of converting real estate to securities via the REIT structure is accelerating. As the real estate partnership/insurance/banking/savings and loan debacle of the 1980s winds down, major institutions view REITs as a way to unload distressed properties and to convert their headaches into liquid assets.

How well REITs track the performance of real estate triggers a lively debate. Do REITs perform along with the real estate fundamentals or act more like a stock? One opinion holds that Wall Street has never appreciated real estate and hasn't the foggiest notion of how to properly price REITs.

The opposition holds that individual parcels of real estate are often irrationally priced and that the local individual real estate market is hopelessly inefficient. This inefficiency occurs due to the scarcity of transactions and the inability to properly compare unique parcels of land and buildings. This school holds that when real estate is converted to actively traded securities, the market can do a far better job of sorting out real value than can the localized individual transactions.

If you like REITs, you should love real estate mutual funds that hold only REITs and other real estate–related stocks. Real estate often holds an almost mystical attraction for many investors. They see it as a unique asset, a great store of value, a refuge from the vagaries of the stock market, and an infallible inflation hedge. Many real estate funds are attractive because of their high yield, so they may become a bond substitute to some investors. In practice, REITs seem to have a high correlation to small company stocks and high sensitivity to interest rates. If so, real estate funds don't offer much in the way of a diversification benefit. We wouldn't expect them to be a great refuge in a market downturn. Recent experience tends to bear that out. They did well in a good market during 1993, but tanked along with other interest-sensitive offerings in 1994.

That year's dismal performance came in the face of rising expectations for real estate. The industry was just beginning to dig out from the excesses of the 1980s. Occupancy and rental rates were up, and construction was beginning to make a comeback. A fly in the ointment was the threat of further interest rate hikes that would cut the availability of financing for both new and existing buildings. This would have a negative impact on the number and price of buildings that trade. Real estate funds were hard hit by the rise in interest rates that year. If it looked like a bond or smelled like a bond, it was properly punished.

Real estate funds act a lot like bonds, a lot like small company stocks, and perhaps not enough like buildings. In a down market, I wouldn't expect them to be the best-performing asset class. Whether they add enough in the way of diversification to justify adding them to a properly balanced portfolio is an ongoing question. If you like the idea of REITs, perhaps you should carve out a portion of your small or medium cap domestic growth allocation to make room for them.

WRAP FEE ACCOUNTS

As investors began to resist the traditional churn-and-burn brokerage tactics, Main Street began to turn to mutual funds in a serious way. Independent mutual funds addressed many of the investor's concerns on cost, conflict of interest, and management. Worse yet, no-load funds were grabbing an increasing market share. The handwriting was on the wall: Traditional brokerage of individual shares was in danger of extinction. In an effort to protect some of their high-margin prestige business, Wall Street responded with the wrap fee account. Voilà! It was a public relations miracle. The commission-crazed broker magically turned into the impartial professional. The new title of financial consultant completed the transformation.

At first glance, wrap fees appear to correct many of the most glaring abuses. A closer look exposes just another PR bandage, a new set of proprietary products with even higher fees, poorer performance, and higher profit margins than proprietary mutual funds. The conflicts of interest aren't gone. They are just better hidden.

Like vanity license plates, wrap fees are often marketed to affluent investors who want more than a mere mutual fund can deliver. Wrap fees continue the mystique of individual investment management, private deals, and individual issues. In fact, wrap fee accounts may be great for the ego, but they're bad economics. Due to the substantially higher costs associated with the programs, they can be expected to deliver less than other alternatives.

The wrap fee supposedly covers the entire spectrum of services including the broker's compensation, thus eliminating any temptation to churn the account, and provides for a higher level of management expertise.

Clients are allowed a limited choice among in-house or house-approved managers. While clients own individual issues in their accounts, investment decisions are rarely personalized. The manager makes block trades, and a computer distributes shares between client accounts.

Each manager is expected to trade through only the introducing brokerage house. Hidden profits on trades in bonds or stocks where the house makes a market remain with the brokerage house. Many observers have opined that these undisclosed gains from trading are high enough that the brokerage houses could very profitably offer the wrap fee accounts for no charge.

For the sake of discussion, let's discount all these problems. A fatal flaw still remains for an investor who wishes to have an appropriate asset allocation plan. Unless you have true megabucks, you are just not going to be able to participate in many desirable markets and segments of markets by using wrap fee managers. Suppose you had a $1 million account, and wished to place 10 percent of it in the tiger economies of Southeast Asia. Where are you going to find a competent manager with expertise in the region willing to take an account for $100,000? It's not going to happen. And even if it did, how is that manager going to properly diversify your $100,000 over ten to fifteen economies using individual issues? At the end of the year, how are you going to rebalance the account, or liquidate a few percent to provide income for yourself? The practical reality is that it cannot be done efficiently. Cost is prohibitive, competent management highly unlikely, and diversification impossible.

VARIABLE ANNUITIES

It's just about impossible to build a case for annuities that makes economic sense. The most widely sold variable annuities have total annual expenses close to 3 percent. Contrary to most sales literature, the taxation of annuities is not favorable when compared to a reasonably tax efficient mutual fund.

To fairly compare an annuity and a mutual fund, the after-tax (post withdrawal) values must be considered for each. After all, it's what you can spend after the taxes are paid that matters. What we find is that the tax treatment on distribution is so bad that, even if the annuity wrapper were free, you wouldn't want it. By turning what should be a long-term capital gain into ordinary income, annuities wipe out any advantage of deferral. Ordinary income tax rates are almost twice what long-term gain rates are.

It gets worse. Annuities carry a 10 percent penalty tax on early withdrawals (prior to age fifty-nine and a half), usually charge a surrender fee during the early years of the contract, and are one of the few assets you can hold that don't receive a "step up in basis" at death. That means that your beneficiaries will get to pay income tax on any appreciation. That tax is forgiven at death for appreciated stocks and other assets except pension plans and traditional IRAs. When it comes to annuities, just say no.

EXCHANGE TRADED FUNDS

The explosion of product offerings in the exchange traded fund (ETF) universe offers investors viable alternatives to the traditional index mutual fund. While the total product available today falls short of $100 billion, or less than some of the largest single mutual funds, the growth curve is staggering. The ETF has been embraced by both institutions and individual investors and has unique characteristics that make it attractive to both markets. Certainly ETFs will be a potent force in future markets.

While there are significant differences between ETFs and index mutual funds, both offer passive investing and low-cost, tax-efficient, pure market exposure that replicates closely a widely followed index. In short, either are excellent choices for an investor seeking to build an effective asset allocation plan.

Index Fund Features

To recap, an index fund is a traditional open-ended mutual fund that seeks to replicate the performance of a selected index. Purchases and sales take place directly between investors and the fund. Pricing is fixed for both transactions at the close of business each trading day when the net asset value (NAV) is determined. Because all transactions occur between the fund and individual investor, the fund must maintain a portion of its assets in cash to provide for liquidity. Redemptions may cause tax implications to remaining investors.

ETF Features

By comparison, an ETF is created or redeemed in large lots by institutional investors. After creation, the shares trade between investors like a stock. So transactions between investors do not affect the fund. This relieves the fund from the obligation to hold as much cash and bypasses some possible tax problems for remaining investors. While much is made of these two advantages in ETF marketing material, in practice these issues are insignificant for established funds.

Because ETF shares trade freely and continuously, the market determines prices, and investors can buy or sell at any time that the markets are open. ETFs can be sold short and are exempt from the up-tick rule. Those provisions are important to traders and speculators but of little interest to long-term investors.

As previously mentioned, ETFs are priced continuously by the market so there is a potential for trading to take place at other than the net asset value. However, because large institutions can create or redeem ETFs at any time, these larger institutions take advantage of any significant mispricing through a simultaneous purchase and sale transaction called arbitrage. Arbitrage offers a small but risk-free profit to the institution, while forcing prices to remain close to their net asset value.

The Bottom Line

ETFs and index funds are so much alike that for many uses they are almost interchangeable. For long-term investors the most significant considerations may be expenses and acquisition costs. As these costs vary from firm to firm and plan to plan, investors will have to make an assessment of their unique situation.

In general, because ETFs have fewer customer support costs, they can offer lower expense ratios than an index fund. (This isn't always the case, so check the fund's prospectus.)

On the other hand, many index mutual funds can be acquired without commission or other cost. However, the commission costs to acquire ETFs can be significant. For instance, an investor making small repeat pur-chases of ETFs may incur enormous transaction costs relative to a direct purchase from a no-load mutual fund family. She might not recapture these costs through lower fees in any foreseeable time frame.

CONCLUSION

There is more than one way to skin a cat. To build an effective asset allocation plan we need building blocks with low cost, wide diversification, and a tightly targeted investment style. Closed-end funds, REITs, and UITs may be attractive alternatives to no-load funds for some investors, especially if purchased at attractive discounts. Wrap fee accounts are particularly attractive to the brokers who sell them.

In a perfect world, I could tell you that no-load funds and all those who operate them are pure as the driven snow. Alas, mutual funds are not entirely exempt from the less laudable practices of Wall Street. There remain important issues for regulators and investors to consider. I'll review both the business practices and ethical landscape of the Street. Then I'll suggest ways that you can help further perfect the system.

TWENTY-TWO

TENDING YOUR GARDEN

No gardener in his right mind expects to plant seeds and then walk away. Without reasonable maintenance, even the best gardens will slowly turn to weeds or be overrun by bugs and critters. Your portfolio also needs periodic tending in order to realize its maximum potential. This maintenance need not be burdensome in order to be effective, but it must be done with some regularity.

By now, you have examined your financial situation, objectives, and risk tolerance. You have used this information to design an appropriate asset allocation plan, and you have selected funds for each asset class. Your next step in executing your plan is to select the custodian.

FINDING THE RIGHT HOME FOR YOUR ASSETS

Whether you are using a financial advisor or are going it alone, there are lots of good and economical choices. For our purposes the two main candidates are no-load mutual fund families and discount brokerage houses. Another possible candidate is an independent trust company.

The first obvious consideration is to only use institutions of impregnable financial solvency. You don't need the additional risk that some rinky-dink outfit will go toes-up on you. There are too many great choices to use.

KEEPING IT SIMPLE

If you are just starting out with your investment plan, you can keep things simple by just using one family of no-load funds. Keeping things simple increases the probability that you will actually do the maintenance. If you are anything like me, as things get more complex, there exists a greater tendency to put things off. Using one fund family will give you many conveniences like telephone switching, consolidated monthly statements, and an annual consolidated tax statement. For instance, for retail investors Vanguard Funds have all the tools necessary to build a first-class, globally diversified, low-cost asset allocation plan within their family. They will even provide you with information showing you how to index just about the whole world's tradable economies. While personal preferences may vary, I can't imagine a better starting point. Whatever your decision, avoid funds with high turnover, high expenses, high minimum investment amounts, or annual account charges.

At some point as your account grows, you may wish to venture outside the walls of a single family of funds. (After all, even Vanguard doesn't have every fund you might care to own.) You may reach that point somewhere between $25,000 and $250,000 or even higher. You can still keep things simple by using the facilities of one of the discount brokerage houses like Fidelity, Waterhouse, or Charles Schwab. The discount brokerages open up hundreds of funds within the convenience of a single account. Of course, you will have to pay nominal transaction charges for the low-cost funds, but you will have access to entire families of NTF funds that you can use as required.

You can avoid any initial purchase charges on existing funds you wish to keep in your portfolio by transferring title to your discount brokerage account. This process may take a few weeks while the transfer clears, but should result in considerable cost savings. It has the further advantage of keeping you fully invested during the transfer process. A transfer of existing funds will not result in any adverse tax consequence that a sale and repurchase might trigger. The brokerage house will supply you with transfer forms that will go a long way toward making the whole process painless. Now that we have found a safe home for our assets, it's time to purchase our funds.

Get a Grip

A few simple tools will make it easy to manage our portfolio as we go along. First, build a simple spreadsheet that assigns a percentage for each asset class and fund in your asset allocation plan. You want to be able to plug in the total value of the account and have the spreadsheet calculate both the desired asset class and individual fund values for you. But, for now, we will just use it to place our initial orders.

Place your orders and wait for the confirmations to arrive. When they roll in, check them against your orders and keep them for your records. You should also receive a prospectus for each fund you purchased. Most people don't find this exciting reading. However, you should make the effort to look it over. (Actually, you should have read it before you purchased.)

At a minimum, always check and save all your confirmations and monthly statements. Once a year you should get a consolidated tax statement. It goes without saying that you will wish to keep the tax statement. Don't be too surprised if the first tax statement is followed by a letter from your brokerage apologizing for an error that they claim not to have been able to anticipate. (Sometimes they will blame unspecified computer problems.) This letter will shortly be followed by a corrected statement. I have even seen the process repeated. With all the hundreds of funds reporting tax information to the brokerage houses, it would be very unusual if somewhere along the line someone didn't make a mistake. If you are the kind of person who files his taxes on January 2, you will find this annoying. If you are like me, you will just find it amusing. Relax. It always gets sorted out.

Take a Break

You have accomplished a lot. Mellow out for a while. You have done the very best you can. Now you will have to rely on the market forces to do what they have always done. Unless history abruptly reverses itself, your superior portfolio will deliver very satisfying results over the long haul. Many of you will find this a very hard step indeed. Resist the temptation to tinker endlessly and to second-guess yourself. Turn off *Wall Street Week*, cancel your subscription to *Money* magazine, and refuse to be sucked into predictions of interest rate changes or market corrections. Spend that time you would have wasted by taking someone you love to the beach, or reading a great book. Get a life!

Not more than once a quarter, but not less than once a year, you should take time to evaluate your progress. The evaluation does not have to be complex or burdensome, but it will involve several distinct steps.

As a normal human being, you will first zero right in on the bottom line. You would be very strange indeed if you were not interested in whether you made or lost money. However, this is not important information. We know in advance that in about 30 percent to 40 percent of the quarters or years we evaluate, an equity portfolio might have lost money. The success or failure of our plan does not depend on any particular year or quarter. We will allow ourselves a brief distracting moment to feel either good or bad depending on the bottom line, then move on to the important part of the evaluation process.

As a first step, pull out the spreadsheet you constructed, and plug in your new capital value. See if your assets still are close to the asset allocation goal. If not, it may be time to reallocate back to your goal.

Reallocation accomplishes two objectives. First, it keeps our original risk profile. We know that some of our assets will grow faster than others over a long period of time. If we did nothing, then the mix of assets would change after a while. When the mix changes, the risk changes. The resulting portfolio will neither be optimum, nor within our risk tolerance.

The second big thing that reallocation does for us is to force us to sell high and buy low. Depending on the mix of assets we hold, a periodic reallocation could add as much as one percent to our annual average performance. In the portfolios illustrated in Chapter 15, the benefit ranged from 0.00 percent to 0.93 percent. While we are not going to attempt to time markets, it makes intuitive sense that last year's fastest-growing market segment is not likely to be next year's. Last year's dog will not be a dog forever either. So the discipline of reallocation will generally add value to a portfolio. Remember, of course, that nothing is going to work every year, but that this tactic has proven itself consistently over the long haul.

Like everything else, there are trade-offs. Reallocation may involve a transaction cost and/or a tax cost. If you are using a mix of no-transaction-fee funds at a discount brokerage house, or trading within a single family of funds at a fund family, you may avoid a transaction cost. And, if your account is an IRA or other qualified plan, you do not need to be concerned with taxes.

How often should you rebalance? Most studies would indicate that about once a year is optimum. Another approach that may make sense is to rebalance if your asset allocation gets some predetermined amount off, such as 2 percent to 5 percent.

Build Your Own Benchmark

The next step in performance monitoring is to build your asset allocation plan portfolio using only indexes. This is your real baseline for comparison. It will help you to understand the total performance of the portfolio and put it in perspective. It's not enough to know whether you made or lost money, or even how much you made or lost to evaluate your performance relative to your strategy.

The final step to effectively monitor your performance is to compare each fund to its appropriate index to see if it is performing according to expectations. If not, there may be valid reasons. For instance, international funds that overweighted Japan had lower performance than the EAFE (Morgan Stanley Europe, Australia, and Far East) index for the last several years. You may find that a valid position going forward and not be too concerned about past performance relative to the index.

Avoid Endless Tinkering

Given what we know about the efficiency of markets, the burden of proof on managers to show that they can actually add value is becoming very heavy. You may not wish to subsidize poor performance for very long in the hopes that the manager can pull it out. During these performance reviews we must vigorously resist the temptation to replace a disappointing fund with last quarter's hero. Endless tinkering is unlikely to improve performance, and chasing last period's stellar achiever is a losing strategy. If you believe (against the mounting evidence) that management can add value, you must give your selected manager a little slack and time for his strategy to pay off. Of course, if you invest in an index fund, your concern about not producing very close to the index should be minimal. My preferred solution to disappointing management performance has been to replace them with index funds, rather than trying to pick another hero. Picking next year's heroes has turned out to be a tougher problem than I ever could have imagined.

THE BIG PICTURE

For the most part, fund evaluation and performance monitoring are tactical in nature. At some point we must step back and look at the big picture. How often should we evaluate strategy?

Of course, we all understand that we should examine our strategy if any event in our lives changes our financial situation, objectives, time horizon, or risk tolerance.

Barring any life event–driven change, there are only two times to change the asset allocation plan. Every once in a while new fundamental research shows us a way to build better portfolios. For instance, just a few years ago, the Fama-French study and the follow-up research pointed out the superior results that could be obtained by pursuing a small company and value strategy. This information was fundamental and important enough to justify a total redesign of existing portfolios. However, insights like these don't come along every week.

We don't want to be reacting to every half-baked theory that comes along. As a rule of thumb, I expect to encounter at least two half-baked theories each week. So it's important to try to distinguish between proven, tested, fundamental academic or industry research, and total bull. None of us needs to be the first to try out a new idea. Let others blaze the way. Remember that it takes a long time to make up for a dumb mistake. Prudent investors should stick to well-proven, well-trodden paths. Investing should be rewarding, not exciting.

While the mutual fund industry cranked out over 1,500 new funds alone last year, few new and different opportunities were offered to investors. Most funds are virtual clones of other existing funds. For instance, emerging market funds begin to look pretty much the same. With only minor variations, they invest in the same markets, countries, industries, and stocks. Most emerging countries boast a cement factory, power plant, telephone company, and several breweries. I have lost track of the number of emerging market funds that hold Siam Cement. So a new emerging market fund is most likely not going to add a strong diversification effect to an existing portfolio.

Thailand, Malaysia, Singapore, Hong Kong, Brazil, Mexico, and Argentina are well-represented. However, opportunities in India, Pakistan, Hungary, Russia, Poland, Turkey, South Africa, and Jordan are slim pickings. All other things being equal, a fund that concentrates investments in a few of these smaller, less-developed countries might offer a strong diversification effect. When they become generally available, an investor might want to consider carving out a portion of his existing emerging market portfolio to make room for the new offering.

In a like manner, many funds that claim to invest in small companies have holdings of rather large size. Thus, if a new micro cap fund were to appear, an investor might seriously want to investigate whether it deserves a portion of the small cap allocation.

Carving out a portion of an existing allocation to make room for a new market or a new approach to a market segment to increase diversification is an evolutionary approach. We haven't made a fundamental change to the plan, but we do expect to pick up a measurable benefit in either risk or return at the portfolio level. Investors will want to keep an eye out for new approaches that offer these possibilities. Again, normal prudence and due diligence must be exercised. New isn't necessarily better, and every fund should earn the right to its slot in your asset allocation plan.

LESS IS MORE

Good asset management practices are strategic and evolutionary, not stagnant. You must keep your long-term goals and objectives firmly in mind while allowing yourself the flexibility to evolve as new research provides better solutions to the risk management problem, or as new market opportunities present themselves. Discipline is the key to success for the long-term investor. He or she must not fall into the trap of managing holdings by newspaper headline, sound bites, mindless prediction, gut feelings, or the last time period's results.

Developing a successful investment strategy for the twenty-first century is a lot like gardening. Both activities require patience, discipline, and faith. Periodic reviews should be viewed as an opportunity for fine-tuning and occasional modest course corrections, not radical revisions and second-guessing.

How can investors conspire to so consistently lose a game that is strongly rigged in their favor? On average, individual investors get such miserable returns that it threatens our belief in the efficient market theory. If markets are efficient, how do we do so poorly? It really shouldn't be possible. What else is at work here? In Chapter 23, we will look into the heart of the average investor to see why he fails so often to meet his goals. It may be that few of us are as rational as we like to think. For investors, self-defeating behavior may be the biggest risk of all.

TWENTY THREE

INVESTOR, HEAL THYSELF!

Early in my flying career, I discovered that success or failure, life or death often heavily depended on resisting the overwhelming urge to do something incredibly stupid. When things begin to go wrong, the temptation to take shortcuts or abandon carefully thought-out procedures mounts. Stress leads to mistakes. Avoiding mistakes leads to a long and happy life. In other words, I quickly learned that my own behavior could be a primary threat to my longevity.

Preventing yourself from doing the wrong thing to relieve the stress of the moment is key to survival. More than one pilot has feathered the wrong prop, blown the wrong fire bottle, or shut down the wrong engine by jumping into a problem before he had carefully thought it through. Mistakes like that can quickly ruin your whole day.

The United States Air Force recognizes that under stress, hasty, ill-thought-out actions lead directly to disaster. Millions of dollars and thousands of hours of training time are aimed at helping pilots establish disciplined, rational, and logical thought processes when the pucker factor rises. The primary emergency procedure, which every crew member in the Strategic Air Command had to recite during oral exams, was: "Stop, think, collect your wits." In other words, get a grip!

Pilots command incredibly complex machines in threatening environments. Yet, few accidents are caused by aircraft or system failure alone. Inappropriate pilot action or pilot error remains a leading cause of aviation accidents.

Investors, like pilots, operate in a complex environment. The environment occasionally produces moments of stress, but in this case the environment is basically friendly. The primary cause of investor failure is the behavior of the investors themselves. Many of them are their own worst enemy. To put it bluntly, they haven't yet learned to resist the overwhelming urge to do stupid things with their money. Investors, like pilots, can benefit from disciplined, rational, and logical thought processes when the pucker factor rises.

WHAT'S GOING ON HERE?

An examination of investor returns provides some startling and depressing insight. Investors don't even come close to market returns. How can this be? If markets are efficient, then most investors should have very close to market returns. It should be very difficult to blunder in a game that is favorably rigged.

I have stated that the value of the average stockbroker's advice is worth far less than zero. The large brokerage houses are understandably concerned that this perception should not spread. They would like investors to believe that their advice adds value. A recent study by Dalbar Financial Services supports both positions. Their 1993 report "Quantitative Analysis of Investor Behavior" divided mutual fund investors into two categories: sales force–advised and nonadvised. Then the study examined the investment results for both equity and bond funds for a ten-year period (January 1984 to September 1993).

In equities, the sales force–advised clients came out ahead of the no-load, do-it-yourselfers by a wide margin. Advised clients had a total return of 90.21 percent while the do-it-yourselfers got only 70.23 percent. Dalbar observes: "The advantage is directly traceable to longer retention periods and reduced reaction to changes in market conditions." We could infer that sage advice from the brokerage forces led to sharply improved returns.

This stunning victory for the brokerage force forces pales when we notice that the market as measured by the S&P 500 returned 293 percent. Dalbar continues: "Trading in mutual funds reduces investment returns. The 'buy and hold' strategy outperforms the average investor by more than three to one after ten years." Investor returns in both equity and bond categories were directly related to hold time. Longer holds equaled higher returns.

Friends, this is not a question of slightly suboptimal performance. This is a total disaster! How are Americans going to educate their children, retire in comfort, or meet any other reasonable financial goal when the average total performance of their equity investments falls short of 30 percent of the market's?

Incidentally, during the study period inflation rose 43.12 percent, so the average American equity investor has very little to show for his ten years in the market. And investors racked up this dismal result during one of the ten best years the market has given us. For all the reasons we have previously explored, Americans can simply not afford this dreadful performance. (Investors in bond funds did no better compared to the bond market indexes. Their interest rate predictions and market timing served them just as poorly.)

In order to appreciate the full magnitude of this disaster, it's important to understand that the study did not consider the larger question of whether investors ought to be in bonds, stocks, or cash. It only considered the results investors got relative to the broad general market in which they committed funds.

Presumably many investors in cash or bonds ought to have been in equities, and as a result far underperformed their actual needs. Available evidence suggests that many Americans are reluctant to assume even the reasonable risks necessary to meet reasonable financial goals. Systematically investing in the wrong markets and then seriously underperforming those markets is a surefire recipe for catastrophe.

INVESTORS DO THE STRANGEST THINGS

Another section of the Dalbar study traces month-by-month net cash flows by equity mutual funds against the returns of the S&P 500. The pattern leaps off the page at you: Market goes up, investors pour money in. Market goes down, investors take money out. It's a classic example of buy high and sell low! The process is repeated again and again with mind-numbing regularity. Investors simply could not restrain themselves from churning their own accounts. Folks, if you haven't noticed yet, this is not the way to make money.

During the study, investors displayed an amazing ability to market time in reverse, as they floundered and flip-flopped without any apparent strategy. However, the worse an investor's returns were as a result of his inept market-timing attempts, the more likely the investor was to blame the funds rather than himself.

Dalbar concludes: "The more an investor buys and sells funds, the lower the potential return." And, "Investors should focus less on buying the right fund or funds, and more on modifying their own behavior." After twenty-three years of watching investors do the strangest things, I can add a hearty, "Amen."

Mutual fund performance itself cannot be blamed for this awful result. The funds may be expected to turn in a performance slightly less than the indexes because of their fees, trading expenses, and requirements to keep some cash liquid for normal redemptions. The average fund performs about where we would expect: about 2 percent below the broad market indexes.

There is a huge discrepancy between the fund's return and the return of the average investor in that fund. At a meeting I attended just a few years ago, Peter Lynch, retired manager of Fidelity's Magellan Fund, disclosed that a shocking percentage of his fund's investors actually lost money. Now, no fund in the entire history of the universe has been more successful than Magellan. However, Magellan has been volatile, and the swings have alternately attracted investors and then frightened them off—just at the wrong times. The only thing Magellan (or most equity fund) investors needed to do to achieve truly great returns was to stay invested. But, a surprising number of them just couldn't make themselves do the right thing.

Investor behavior is so perverse, and investor returns are so dismal, that a whole branch of economics is devoted to trying to find out what makes investors tick. Investors often project their recent experiences forward. One recent study of investors found that no matter what they tell you about thinking long-term, most investors' perceptions and expectations are heavily influenced by their experience of the last eleven-and-and-a-half months. If the markets have been doing poorly for the previous year, investors begin to believe that they will continue to do poorly forever. They begin to sell. If they have been doing well, investors become euphoric and begin to believe that this time it is "different." The higher the price of the market goes, the more they want to buy. You needn't be a rocket scientist to see how this leads to self-defeating behavior.

WHAT HAVE INVESTORS LEARNED?

We must wonder if investors have learned anything from their dismal experiences. The answer appears to be a resounding no. The average investor hasn't the foggiest notion that he even has a problem, so he is several long steps away from starting to think about solving it. Survey after survey finds widespread misunderstandings of even the most basic financial concepts. Even investors who rate themselves as highly sophisticated have trouble distinguishing between stocks, bonds, CDs, and mutual funds when asked very simple questions.

My personal experience confirms the survey results. I can't remember ever encountering a potential client who had any idea what his actual investment experience had been, or how his experience had compared to any broad market index. Not one of my professional or business owner clients could guess within 10 percent what his portfolio rate of return was. I have never had a client who has been able to describe his investment strategy. Most appear to have invested aimlessly in scattershot fashion, hoping that something will work for them.

KNOW THYSELF

Another root cause of poor investor performance is self-delusion about risk tolerance. Hundreds of psychologists have tried to design questionnaires to root out investors' real risk tolerance. Unfortunately, we don't often get the correct information until the market declines. Then we find out what the investor really meant.

For instance, when investment advisors ask a potential investor about their risk tolerance, the answer is often misleading. If asked if he could endure a 10 percent, 15 percent, or 20 percent decline in asset value, he will often answer yes. Even if the advisor tries to convey that the question is not a test of courage, investors may not want to appear timid. What the investor may mean, but would never say, is: "I'll be out of here!" At the first downturn, the investor is gone. This, of course, locks in a loss and prevents a normal market recovery from making the investor whole and putting him back on the profit side.

Investors have to determine in advance what their real risk tolerance is. Perhaps they should ask themselves how much decline they could endure and still stay with the program. Once an investor knows what his real risk tolerance is, she can adopt a strategy with a high probability of never exceeding the allowable loss.

KNOW THY MARKET

Unrealistic expectations about either potential short-term declines, or long-term positive gains, will often lead the investor astray. An investor who has accepted the range of reasonable possibilities for both is far less likely to shoot himself in the foot. Advisors must not oversell, and investors must not con themselves. The more you know about how markets are liable to act, the better prepared you are to keep a long-term horizon firmly in mind.

THE TUNA FISH FACTOR

Nick Murray is one of the brightest and most entertaining guys in my industry. You probably haven't heard of him, because he writes and speaks to financial advisors about how to motivate clients to do the right thing for themselves. Helping clients to overcome their fears and avoid self-defeating behavior is one of the biggest problems we have. Nick shared the great idea of comparing investor behavior to grocery shopper behavior in his monthly column in *Investment Advisor Magazine.*

Let's pretend that you, your family, and your cat eat a fair amount of tuna fish. As you know, tuna fish comes in cans and has a long shelf life. We are used to buying it in large cans for $1.50. One day we go to the market and see that it is on sale for a dollar a can. What do we do? Do we see ourselves as impoverished because we have some cans back home on the shelf? Do we run home, grab all our unused tuna fish, and then run back to the store to sell it back? Of course not! We buy lots of tuna fish to take advantage of the low price. We know that we will need tuna fish for a long time, and the sale offers us a great opportunity to stock up for future needs. We have made the mental jump that low prices are good.

Stocks have a long shelf life, and we should buy them to use a long time in the future. But the average investor seems to operate on the assumption that low price is bad. Instead of seeing temporary low price as an opportunity to buy something he will need in the future, he wants to dump what he has. Nick and I have a little trouble trying to figure this kind of logic out.

ZEN AND THE MARKET EXPERIENCE

America is a can-do country. Our heroes are action-oriented and full of the right stuff. Most successful people got that way by using their skills to make something happen. Business responds well to can-do, positive, and active management. If business turns down, there are lots of things a smart businesswoman can do: Make more phone calls, hire more sales-people, buy advertising, change the product, have a sale, fire the sales manager, buy the competition, increase commissions, or move to a better market. Success in business depends on active management.

Investing is a different kind of cat. It is a very passive activity, some-what Zen-like. Markets don't respond to our can-do attitude. We can't just whip them into shape. They have their own flow. We must attach our-selves to the world's markets and allow them to carry us to our goals.

More often than not, if you have a good strategy in place, the best single thing an investor can do during a disappointing season is nothing. Of course, this type of thinking can make a successful, can-do, action-oriented, gung-ho investor just a little crazy. During times of stress, negative performance, or no performance, he wants to do *something*. All kinds of self-defeating behaviors come to mind: Fire the advisor, liquidate the account, move to another brokerage, sell the funds, circle the wagons, and pull in your horns. The fund that looked so good during last year's bull market now looks like a turkey. An advisor who recommends standing pat obviously doesn't get it, must be some kind of a wimp, can't have the right stuff, is obviously a dull tool, and is trying to justify his poor performance. Any idiot can see things are falling apart all over, and we need action now.

RELATIVE PAIN

Investor impatience is compounded by a relative pain, relative time problem. Market downturns hurt a lot more than good times feel good. It is much more painful to see your portfolio lose one percent than pleasant to see it gain one percent. And it feels longer. Two years of back-to-back declines, underperformance, or even just no performance can feel like a lifetime. And, as we have seen, even a superior portfolio will go through occasional extended periods of disappointment.

THE COCKTAIL PARTY FACTOR

To make things even worse, no matter how bad things may get for our investor, somewhere somebody is making money. Those people will certainly tell all within earshot. Most investors have a very selective memory. We all seek approval, and we all would like to be considered astute, sophisticated, and successful. During social gatherings or casual conversations it's not unusual to stress the positive and repress the negative. So the investment winners in our portfolios tend to get talked about more than the losers. Investors with disappointing recent performance will say nothing. After all, who wants to broadcast failure? So, the winners brag, and the losers keep mum. Soon, it may seem to our poor investor like everybody with an IQ over room temperature is making money except her.

So the temptation to second-guess herself grows and grows. If only she and her advisor had been more astute, she would be making money too. Perhaps it's time to try something else like all those other smart investors are doing.

Once this kind of cycle starts it can deteriorate into a tail-chasing fiasco. At least dogs that chase their tails remain on level ground. Investors can dig themselves into a hole as they ratchet themselves ever downward chasing yesterday's heroes.

THE ANALYTIC INVESTOR

The hard-driving, results now–type investor is familiar to every investment advisor and counselor. But there are other investors who also become their own worst enemies. For instance, the overly analytic investor never gets started because he never has enough information to make a decision. No matter how much data he has, it's never enough. No matter how many options he considers, there might be a better one. In the end, he never does anything. Of course, from his perspective he has never made a mistake.

Unfortunately, investment data changes every minute. We never have all the data, and risk can never be eliminated. Research can suggest superior strategies, but never perfect ones. Investors who wait for perfect solutions may never get started. This behavior is fondly known within the profession as paralysis by analysis. In Chapter 11, we saw the cost of excessive delay. Time is the investor's great friend and shouldn't be frittered away. Investors need to get it together and get going. Otherwise, they are never going to get anywhere. By their very nature, investment markets carry risk. By now, you are familiar with the traditional definitions of risk. However, we must consider if perhaps investors may pose the biggest risks to themselves.

MORE ADVICE FROM MOM

When I was very young, I got my first two-wheeler. It took a while to get up the courage to actually get on it and ride. However, shortly after my first successful ride, I learned to ride "no hands." Shortly after that I decided to try standing on the bicycle's seat while coasting downhill. My mother observed my efforts and commented that I was being just a little too cute for my own good. This comment was very shortly followed by a spectacular crash.

Left to their own devices, many investors get a little too cute for their own good.

The world's markets offer an easy way for long-term investors to profit from the expansion of the world's economy. It's called buy and hold. An investor has to work pretty hard to mess up this simple formula. However, as we have seen, most do. As Pogo, the great comic strip character of my youth used to say: " We have met the enemy, and he is us!"

Buy and hold is a very dull strategy. It lacks pizzazz and doesn't inspire much admiration at cocktail parties. It has only one little advantage: It works, very profitably and very consistently.

YOUR INVESTMENTS ARE YOUR FUTURE

There is a lot riding on the decisions you make. As you make those decisions, don't trip yourself. Investors with no knowledge, no plan, no discipline, no benchmarks, and no clue have no chance. They would be only slightly worse off to take their money to the dog track or play lotto.

It's hard work to build and implement a superior portfolio. But not nearly as difficult as maintaining that portfolio through thick and thin so that you reach your financial goals. The temptation to do something truly stupid can seem almost overwhelming. Train yourself to resist it.

RUN A FIRE DRILL

It may be helpful to run fire drills with yourself. Think about what your reaction would be if you were to wake up tomorrow and find that your portfolio has gone down 25 percent. Would you panic and dump everything? Or, would you say to yourself: "Gee, Frank told me there would be years like this. Risk happens. Well, it's going to be OK." Would you still have the same attitude a year or two later? The more you think through the possibilities in advance, the more likely you are to make good decisions.

The investment process is like most other things in life. In the long run the difference between winners and losers boils down to knowledge, superior strategy, and discipline. Books like this, other research, or good advi-sers can provide knowledge and define superior strategies, but only you can supply the discipline.

Many investors lack the knowledge, time, and inclination to manage their own funds. If so, they would do well to hire a professional. However, the best investment manager in the world will do them no good if they lack the discipline to stay aboard. The equity train will always reach the investor's financial goals. Only the disciplined investor will still be on board.

It would be easy to snicker at the apparently clueless behavior of most investors. That is certainly not my point. Investors are not stupid people. Most are very successful in many other aspects of their lives and careers. Our schools, the media, and the financial services industry have all done an unforgivably bad job of educating Americans to make reasonable financial decisions. Much of what we know now about the behavior of markets is very recently acquired knowledge. But the word is not getting out.

For most investors, hiring the right advisor can lead to a dramatic increase in net results, and a matching increase in the probability that they will achieve their goals.

In Chapter 24, we will examine the selection, care, and feeding of the investment advisor.

TWENTY-FOUR

THE CULTIVATION, CARE, AND FEEDING OF INVESTMENT ADVISORS

Many of you will correctly decide that you haven't the time, talent, resources, or inclination to manage your own nest egg. We all suffer from information overload and time constraints.

For most investors it makes perfect sense to delegate this responsibility to a full-time professional. But choosing the right advisor may take a little thought. A lot is riding on the decision. After all, your investments are your future. First you must decide if you need assistance, then you should consider how to structure the relationship to your greatest advantage. As we will see, how you pay a planner may be more important than how much!

So, it's time to explore the cultivation, selection, care, and feeding of financial advisors.

INVESTORS AS FROGS

As you all know, frogs are cold-blooded creatures. Within a very wide range, they are insensitive to temperature changes. Like small fish, they often freeze in ponds during the winter only to thaw out not much the worse for wear in the spring. It is said that if you put a frog into a large pot and then very slowly heat the pot, the frog will swim around quite happily until he abruptly dies! (I don't want to get tons of hate mail. Please believe me, I have never tried this!)

Many investors act like our frog. They swim around quite happily, oblivious to their peril until it's too late. They delay investing, invest in the wrong markets, get awful returns, fail to set goals or monitor their progress, and treat the whole matter as if it will solve itself. As time runs out for them to meet their goals, or the temperature slowly increases around them, they paddle around their little pots humming: "Don't worry, be happy!"

Strangely enough, most investors think they are doing a very fine job for themselves. In countless surveys, a heavy majority of investors rate themselves as above average. In one recent study, over half of the respondents that so rated themselves incorrectly identified money market funds as having greater expected returns than stocks. And all these people worked for a giant, well-known national financial services firm!

Few can tell you what their rate of return has been, how that compares with the market indexes, what their investment philosophy is, what their investment costs have been, how much risk they are taking in their portfolio, or what asset allocation might be appropriate to meet their own unique financial goals. Nevertheless, most remain convinced that their investments are in capable, nay, brilliant hands.

Not counting my dog, Schatzie, who can call the market turns at least as well as any guest on "Wall Street Week," America is a land of at least 270 million fully qualified investment advisors. Each feels perfectly free to give advice, and conversely may accept advice from any other advisor he happens to sit next to on the bus.

Numerous independent studies show that most investors are getting disastrously bad results. Few are even aware of just how bad their results are; fewer still have a clue about how to repair the situation. Almost none have projected the impact of that miserable performance in terms of their future lifestyle.

A RIDDLE WRAPPED UP IN AN ENIGMA

Far too many investors are hard-wired to fail. Left to their own devices, they will self-destruct. I often wonder why so few investors seek out professional assistance. It would be hard to imagine a field where more people needed help, or where the impact of professional help could have a more positive impact for people.

Some investors don't believe that professional investment advice is necessary, some suffer from financial phobias, some don't know that professional help is available to them, and some don't know whom to trust.

Most Americans don't fly their own airplanes, change the oil in their cars, fix their own plumbing, do surgery on themselves or their families, file their own taxes, prosecute their own legal cases, or educate their children. They are perfectly happy to leave that to experts. Yet they feel perfectly competent to direct their entire financial future by themselves. Even worse, they put up with years of terrible results without reaching the obvious conclusion that they could use a little help. These investors exhibit varying degrees of self-destructive behavior, denial, overconfidence, and delusion.

For investors, the stakes are very high. Your investments are your future. With the exception of your health, and the choice of your mate, no other factor will determine the quality of your life as much as your success or failure to obtain reasonable investment results.

While I would encourage every American to learn as much as he can about economics, finance, and investing, most will be far better served to delegate this important task to a professional. Professionals have an edge: better knowledge, equipment, discipline, tactics and strategy. If results are what count, as measured by probability of meeting your important financial goals, most investors can't afford anything less.

THE FEE-ONLY ALTERNATIVE TO BUSINESS AS USUAL ON WALL STREET

As previously discussed, traditional Wall Street firms have failed to deliver credible, objective advice. Their commission-based compensation system irreparably taints the advice process with conflicts of interest and hidden agendas. But there is a viable alternative to the commission-

crazed, churn-and-burn stockbroker. The independent, fee-only registered investment advisor offers objective advice, superior service, and economical and effective execution.

The vast majority of these firms are relatively small, without the marketing clout of the giant institutions. So, they are not "top of mind" when
investors seek out advice. But they offer a key invaluable advantage: objective advice. Because a fee-only advisor derives all of his income from fully
disclosed fees paid directly by the client, conflicts of interest are virtually
eliminated. There remains no financial incentive that would prevent the
advisor from providing the very best advice for each individual. So, while
the advisor may not always be "right" in his counsel, there are no hidden
agendas, or conflicts of interest to cloud his vision or taint the relationship. And, after all, what good is advice if it's not objective?

The demand for impartial professional advice is enormous and growing. For instance, since 1989, assets with Schwab's Financial Advisor
Service have grown to approximately a quarter trillion dollars managed
by 5,600 independent registered investment advisors! Fidelity and
Waterhouse are also experiencing exponential growth in similar services,
with others entering the fray close on their heels. Clearly, Americans are
looking for unbiased professional advice and an intelligent alternative to
Wall Street's commissioned-induced conflicts of interest and voodoo-
based investment schemes.

So, the genie is out of the bottle, and having tasted freedom, he's not
going back in. Americans are voting with their feet, and migrating to the
better system they demanded. Great stuff, this capitalism!

RECENT INDUSTRY TRENDS

The growth of assets for fee-only advisors has not gone unnoticed by Wall
Street. Investors want objective advice, and increasingly distrust the commission-based distribution model. Most traditional brokerage houses
have responded with me-too, look-alike fee-based offerings designed to
appear more objective. These offerings include expanded wrap-fee programs or asset-based pricing.

In the same manner, many commission-based investment advisors are
transitioning to fee-based pricing using products supplied through their
broker-dealers.

From the broker-dealers' or brokerage house's, perspective, these new services satisfy both marketing objectives and the need to obtain a more predictable cash flow. In part they rely on a blurring of distinctions between "fee-based" and "fee-only" compensation.

A look under the hood of the fee-based programs reveals many of the same old conflicts of interest. Recommendations are restricted to either proprietary products or offerings where the house has an (often undisclosed) interest, share of management fees, or restrictions on where transaction will be placed. As you might expect, the programs are neither objective nor unbiased.

The discount brokerages have most recently further blurred the distinctions by positioning themselves to provide advice. Schwab, for instance, is busy "reinventing full-service brokerage." In the process, they are morphing themselves back into a slightly lower-cost institution that the bulk of their clients previously fled. At the same time, they betray, cannibalize, and threaten the truly independent advisors that rely on them to provide brokerage and custody services. Not surprisingly, their advice is similarly tainted by the need to advance the profit expectations of the sponsor.

INTERNET SERVICES

The rise of the Internet has provided investors with entirely new channels for information, advice, and transactions. Numerous sites deliver market information and data, fund performance and analysis, asset allocation and portfolio construction advice, discount brokerage and custody ser-vices, and comprehensive financial planning advice. Some of these sites are extensions of traditional providers (e.g., Schwab, Morningstar), and some are new entries expanding the menu of services not previously available (e.g., DirectAdvice, Financial Engines). The ability of the Net to offer affordable quality interactive tailored solutions and information to investors has reshaped the financial services landscape, remapping distribution and supply channels at a frantic pace.

There is a dark side to the information explosion on the Net. Information is not the same as knowledge or wisdom. As the day-trading phenomena illustrated, access to tons of data and low-cost convenient trading may simply empower investors to do foolish things. Bad advice proliferates ranging from simply inane to downright fraud. So investors must still evaluate the quality, integrity, and competence of the online advice and services.

THE REVOLUTION BEARS FRUIT

The revolution on Wall Street is just beginning to bear fruit for the long neglected "small" investor. While the rich have always relied on professional investment advisors, today investors of more modest means can also avail themselves to high-quality advice. Several happy advances have converged to make this all possible:

- No-load mutual funds are an excellent, low-cost, off-the-shelf building block to construct efficient portfolios.

- Deregulation has spawned new entrant discount brokerages, sharply forcing down costs for a wide variety of services.

- New "back office" technology offered by the discount brokerage houses allows efficient personalized account supervision by professional advisors for investors of modest means.

FINDING AN ADVISOR

Another problem investors face is whom to trust. Unfortunately, it would be hard to imagine a field where more people offer help who haven't the tiniest little qualification for the job. As we have observed, the advice of the average financial "professional" is worth far less than zero.

Even worse, no field of any importance is so poorly regulated. The requirements for entry into the field are close to zero. For valid reasons, not everyone is allowed to call himself a brain surgeon or practice the art. Yet almost anyone can call himself a financial advisor. And registration with the SEC or state carries no assurance of competence or integrity. All but hardcore felons can expect routine approval. No examination is required in most states, and no practice or performance standards are imposed.

An investor who sets out to find a competent financial advisor has had few reliable guidelines to assist him. The good news is that because there is such a large demand for competent, objective financial advice, the field is growing in both numbers and sophistication. It's going to take a little homework to separate the wheat from the chaff. But by now you already know enough to do the job.

A COMMONSENSE CHECKLIST

Let's look at a few requirements you might consider. The first three are "written in stone," and should not be waived under any circumstances.

FEE-ONLY

You can eliminate many of the potential problems you might encounter by simply avoiding the commission-based salesman. In one stroke, you eliminate the vast majority of conflicts of interest between yourself and your advisor. A clear separation between the advice function and the brokerage function is the best consumer protection you could have. Why set yourself up to become the victim of a commissioned-crazed broker?

Things aren't always what they may seem. Some brokers advertise themselves as "fee-based" planners and advisors. These advisors charge a fee for making recommendations, and then take commissions on the products they sell. This is the worst of all possible worlds. Paying fees to a commission-based salesman doesn't guarantee objectivity, or eliminate any conflicts of interest. It just lets him get paid twice.

Many brokerage houses and broker-dealers allow their salespeople to act as both registered representatives (RR) for the house, and registered investment advisors (RIA). These dual licensed RR/RIAs are required to be "supervised" by the broker-dealer or brokerage house. In return for their "supervision" the broker-dealer or brokerage house gets a cut of the fees, and can determine where business is placed. In practice, this can result in higher fees passed on to the investor, and the potential for conflict of interest is obvious.

"Fee-offset" compensation arrangements allow a dual registered RR/RIA to pick and choose both the amount and timing of his compensation. He can place some client assets in commission products, and some in no-load mutual funds, depending on how he feels that day. The commissions paid for the load funds are applied as a credit against the annual fee. Often this practice is justified by the supposedly higher quality of the commission-based product. But, I guarantee you, for every great load mutual fund you can find, I can get a better one with the same objective in a no-load fund. It's easy to see that fee-offset is great for the salesman, but it's harder for me to imagine how it can ever benefit the investor. The conflicts of interest haven't gone away, they just get hidden a little better under another layer of cost.

To be sure that your advisor is fee-only, steer clear of any that have a broker-dealer affiliation or maintain an NASD license.

THIRD-PARTY CUSTODIAN

Use the services of a large discount brokerage to hold your assets. That way, if there is a problem with your account, the house has a problem, not you. Schwab, Fidelity, and Waterhouse, for instance, will be there tomorrow and have the resources to straighten out any problem you might have with assets under their care. Insist on statements directly from the custodian in addition to any that come from your advisor. Of course, read and carefully check your statements. Remember: Trust but verify!

LIMITED POWER OF ATTORNEY

Never allow an advisor the power to withdraw from your account. Disbursements, other than agreed-upon fees, should always go to you at your home or bank account. A limited power of attorney allows your advisor to trade on your behalf without running the risk of having your hard-earned assets disappear. In the very unlikely event that funds are misdirected for any reason, then the brokerage house has a big problem, not you! To repeat, you will still want to read and check closely each statement you get.

PROFESSIONAL KNOWLEDGE

As far as I am concerned, the above requirements are no-brainers. Violate them at your peril. But while we have eliminated many bad things that might happen to your account, we still haven't determined competence. Fee-only is not a panacea. It is just a better way to structure the relationship between advisor and investor. Many advisors could meet all the above requirements without having brains in their little heads. So now the requirements necessarily get subjective.

If you have carefully read this book, you already know more about how markets work and how to profit from it better than 95 percent of the "professionals" in the financial services industry. While this may surprise you, I can assure you that it is true. Don't let the fancy suits, titles, and expensive office space fool you. Most of the industry still wants to do things the way our grandfathers did. And bad advice can often be more profitable—for them—than good advice.

As a minimum, I would demand a college degree, preferably in finance, economics, business, or related field. Don't get too hung up on the major. Most colleges and universities haven't been teaching Modern Portfolio Theory or related subjects for more than about five years. For instance, I just talked to a graduate finance major from a major university who had never heard of Modern Portfolio Theory. Finance is not the same as personal finance, and little attention is given to portfolio construction.

I wouldn't give any extra points to attorneys or CPAs. As most of them will cheerfully admit, contrary to popular belief, they don't have any special qualifications in finance.

PROFESSIONAL ASSOCIATIONS AND CONTINUING EDUCATION

Because the field is evolving so rapidly, and because few of us were even exposed to modern financial theories in college, independent professional continuing education is essential. One of the key words here is *independent*. I have learned from bitter experience that training by broker-dealers teaches you just what they want you to know to sell their products. Product sponsors may not exactly lie, but they sure do slant any information they pass out. The operative philosophy seems to be that if they can fill the representatives up with BS masquerading as education, the reps will hit the ground and sell. Until they catch on, the reps are as much victims as the firm's clients. Of course, some never catch on. It's easy to let them spoon-feed you. But until an advisor takes responsibility for his own education, his value will be somewhat south of zero to his clients.

In the financial planning field, two institutions stand out for their accomplishments in advancing the professionalism of the industry. Both the Chartered Life Underwriter (CLU) and Certified Financial Planner (CFP) courses give a broad general understanding of the financial planning process. The CLU course has a strong insurance industry foundation, while the CFP course favors investments. This information is invaluable in assisting the planner to properly identify the needs of the investor and place his situation in context. Both institutions are independent of any company or sponsor, and have as their goal the advancement of professional standards within their particular industry. Both institutions are accredited by national educational associations, and both now offer advanced degrees in financial planning. Both also benefit from the dedicated volunteer support of some of the finest professionals in their respective fields. And finally, both require and supply exceptionally high-quality continuing educational courses as a requirement for maintaining the certification.

In particular, the CFP continuing education courses have done as much as all other institutions together to spread the word about the amazing advances in modern finance, and bring these benefits to the American investor.

There are undoubtedly other independent high-quality continuing education sources. No matter how he does it, you should demand an advisor that has a heavy schedule of continuing education. What we learned in college a few years ago might as well be from the Stone Age, and company-sponsored "education" is more often than not just glorified brainwashing.

BEYOND THE BUZZ WORDS

It goes without saying that you should expect your advisor to have an in-depth knowledge of finance. If you have any doubt about his qualifications, question him about his philosophy. Some points to consider are: how he utilize Modern Portfolio Theory to reduce risk, how much foreign exposure he recommends, his ideas about emerging markets, how he views the growth vs. value debate, the firm view on market timing, how much diversification he thinks is essential, the limitations of CAP-M, what particular asset allocation plan he recommends to meet your needs, and how he measures correlation between asset classes.

If you suspect that the advisor's knowledge consists of only buzz words or cocktail party chatter, bail out. The important thing is that you realize that you have the right to ask, and that you not be intimidated. Listen to what the advisor has to say about his techniques and philosophy, but don't let the session degenerate into a "sales track." Keep asking until you are either totally comfortable or decide to move on. It's your money, and your future.

ASSETS UNDER MANAGEMENT

At its core, investment advice is a personal-services business. It must be tailored to your individual needs and circumstances. So, even with great technology, there is a limit to the number of clients that an advisor can effectively serve. The average investment advisor has about $4 million in assets under his management. At that size, either they are part-time, or brand-new. While you don't necessarily want the biggest firm you can find, it's hard to imagine a viable business with less than $30 million to $50 million. Good staff, software, equipment, and services are expensive.

On the other hand, the firm is too large when you don't have reasonable access to the principal that make the decisions on your accounts.

LENGTH OF TIME IN BUSINESS

You will find few firms that have actively managed assets for more than six or seven years. The profession didn't really open up until Schwab began trading no-load mutual funds and offered their back-office capabilities to advisors. But while the business is new, many practitioners have long experience in other areas of the financial services industry. Most advisors started their careers as either stockbrokers or registered representatives, then gratefully made the transition to fee-only advisors when the opportunities presented themselves. You will want to restrict your search to industry veterans. Let the new guys learn with somebody else's money.

BROCHURES AND ADV

All investment advisors are required to furnish potential and existing clients with either a "brochure" or a copy of the SEC registration form (ADV Part II), which outlines their education, qualifications, experience, investment methods, fees, and other pertinent information about their firms. You can learn a great deal about an advisor and his business by carefully studying this form. These forms are currently available online for all federally registered investment advisors.

While the ADV Part I is not required to be delivered to clients, it contains invaluable additional information about the firm, and you should demand to see it also.

MINIMUM ACCOUNT SIZE

Some advisors demand very large minimum-size accounts. Successful firms may find that they spread themselves too thin by serving numerous small accounts, so in order to provide the attention their clients expect, they limit the number of accounts. Obviously, you will want to restrict your search to advisors that can economically serve your account, and value your relationship. There may be a practical lower limit for account size. But many advisors will accept accounts of $50,000 or even lower.

LOCATION

With fax, telephone, e-mail, worldwide computer networks, the Internet, and FedEx, location isn't nearly as important as it used to be. Advisors are no longer restricted to working from Wall Street, and clients don't care where they are as long as they have access when they need it. If you are the kind of person that just has to have frequent face-to-face meetings, you can probably find a great advisor in your hometown. On the other hand, today you may have a very close relationship with an advisor "on your wave length" clear across the country.

RECOMMENDATIONS

It may be human nature to want recommendations from friends and/or present clients, but they aren't much use. For many good and valid reasons, investment advisors are prohibited by law from using testimonials from clients or celebrities. For one thing, your investment needs may be a great deal different from Madonna's. If Madonna were my client (she isn't), she might not appreciate it if I divulged that fact to the world, or had all my potential clients call her. Madonna may be a great entertainer and talent, but she may not know any more about finance than you do. Finally, if I were to give out a list, you don't think I would include any one who might say something negative about me, do you?

Your friends may recommend an advisor to you. If so, you will still want to check the advisor out yourself. Mimicking your peers is an easy way out, but no substitute for a little homework. On the other hand, a bad reputation certainly should set off alarm bells.

REFERRAL SERVICES

Organizations like the CFP Society maintain referral services for the public. These may be a good place to start; however, not all highly qualified members of an organization may choose to use the referral service. Many successful firms are not actively seeking new clients, or only accept referrals from existing clients.

REGULATORY AGENCIES

Small investment advisors are regulated by the states, while large investment advisors are regulated by the SEC. The somewhat arbitrary dividing line is $30 million of assets under management. You should check out the regulatory history of your advisor with the appropriate agency.

An isolated incident may not be significant, but multiple complaints or problems are a pretty strong wake-up call. If in doubt, check it out. A quick check with the regulators can be a good first screen to eliminate the bad actors.

WHAT TO EXPECT

A successful relationship should start out with realistic expectations. So, let's list the things that investment advisors can't do before we get into what they actually do

Investment advisors can't:

- Time the market.
- Pick individual stocks.
- Protect against loss.
- Guarantee anything.
- Refer you to anyone who can do any of the above.

Given this somewhat negative list, you might be forgiven if you wondered if investment advisors can add value to the investment process, and, if so, what exactly their role ought to be. Having devoted considerable time and effort to the question of whether management can add value through market timing or stock selection, perhaps I have reached the point where I shall be hoisted upon my own petard.

The following is what investment advisors can do.

EDUCATE, COUNSEL, AND CONSULT

Investment advisors deal with a lot of very successful, bright people. But these people need guidance in our particular field. They aren't going to walk in the door with a clear understanding of their goals, financial situation, risk tolerance, and time horizon. They probably haven't a fully formed investment philosophy. Most don't have a working knowledge of Modern Portfolio Theory, or the many limitations of the Capital Asset Pricing Model. They may think market timing is a great way to prevent losses, or they may want to bet the farm on a single start-up software company. They may even think that anything other than T-Bills is for deranged minds only.

So, investment advisors are part educators, part psychologists, and part consultants. One thing is for sure: There is no hope until the client understands where he is, where he wants to go, and what his options are to get there. Unless the client has realistic expectations, and believes in the program, he is doomed to pursue rainbows endlessly. Nobody expects bright successful people to mindlessly sign on to a major investment program without all the facts, and without a clear understanding of the options.

As we have seen, even the most superior portfolio will encounter turbulence from time to time. And the environment is one of constant temptation and noise. The media provides us with many competing siren songs. So the initial education process must be constantly reinforced or else the client will soon return to his old self-destructive ways.

DESIGN AND IMPLEMENT

Once the parameters are understood by both parties, it's time for the advisor to design the asset allocation plan that offers the highest probability of long-term success. Generally, the solution should be framed that meets all the client needs with a comfortable margin for error with the least risk possible. The emphasis should be on meeting needs rather than beating markets or some other mythical yardstick.

CONTAIN COSTS

As a fiduciary of the investor's funds, one of the prime responsibilities of an investment advisor is to rigorously control total costs. While they provide an extremely valuable service, it certainly isn't an infinitely valuable service. The world's markets can only be expected to deliver so much. Every cent of investment cost must reduce that total return. While investment advisors charge fees, much of this cost can be offset in other areas. For instance, investment advisors should negotiate discounts on transactions fees, utilize low-cost funds wherever available, provide access to funds that retail investors generally cannot purchase for themselves, and strive to reduce the tax impact of their strategies.

Independent advisors generally have far fewer expenses built into their operation than the major Wall Street firms. The typical brokerage operation involves layers and layers of staff endlessly circulating memos to each other while housed in acres and acres of high-priced office space, dining at gourmet corporate dining rooms, with vacation perks based on sales of high-price proprietary product in luxury resorts. So you can't expect economy there. Because of the efficiency offered by modern technology, even very small accounts should be able to find high-quality advisors for fees of one percent of assets under management, while larger accounts should command discounts. Many investors will find that their total investment costs fall dramatically, although because they are fully disclosed, they may be aware of them for the first time.

OFFER MANAGEMENT, HOUSEKEEPING, AND SERVICE

Having determined goals, set strategy, and implemented your plan, there still remains a fair amount of grunge work. Performance reporting, portfolio rebalancing, consolidated statements, account supervision, and continuing research should all be done for you—so you can get a life. Of course, the consulting and communication process never ends. And you should expect reasonable access to the principals that make the decisions on your account whenever you need it. In addition, you should anticipate frequent reviews with your advisor to keep him apprised of your personal and financial situation, and get strategy updates.

Many fee-only advisors include consultations on estate planning, pension distributions, charitable gifting, college funding, asset protection, and other financial planning topics as part of their overall services.

The nature of the fee-only compensation structure requires the adviser to deliver consistently higher levels of service than his commission-based counterpart. Fee-only is pay-as-you-go. Advisors' contracts can be canceled with no penalty at any time. There are no strings holding dissatisfied clients. So advisors must keep clients for years before they are in the same position that a salesman is after his first sale. This requirement, in turn, means that advisors must only promise what they can deliver, rather than promise whatever is required to make the sale.

On the other hand, fee-only advisors who deliver the service they promise are free to go about doing the right thing for the client without the terrible pressure of having to sell something today. With conflicts of interest virtually eliminated, advisors and clients find themselves in a win-win-win relationship, a true partnership of shared interests.

THE BOTTOM LINE

Most investors cannot afford the advice they are giving themselves. Financial advis0rs can provide a valuable service that investors should at least seriously explore. Better strategy, better tactics, better tools, better execution, and better discipline can be expected to lead to better, more reliable performance long-term. The professional edge can yield big dividends. These dividends will be realized in terms of risk reduction, lower total costs, and a higher probability of actually attaining reasonable long-term financial goals.

Properly devised and executed, the consulting-design-implementation-supervision process will lead to substantially better performance than most Americans have been able to attain for themselves. If an advisor motivates a client to invest, steers him into the right markets and asset allocation plan to meet his needs, communicates reasonable expectations, and over time helps the client exercise the discipline required to ultimately meet his goals, his fee will be earned many times over.

TWENTY-FIVE

PULLING IT ALL TOGETHER: A SUMMARY

Than here is broad general agreement that America is about to launch an entire generation into retirement without sufficient financial resources to support them. These retirees can expect to live longer, retire earlier, and endure the thousand cuts of inflation longer than any of the generations that preceded them. There is also broad general agreement that America has one of the lowest savings rates in the world. Recently there has been some hopeful speculation that as the former yuppies and flower children actually feel the cold breath of retirement, savings rates will improve. So far this is just so much idle talk. Investors are loaded down with debt, and discretionary saving is, thus far, not an ingrained habit.

Meanwhile the tax code encourages conspicuous consumption and punishes thrift. Government, even if it wanted to, is not likely to be in a position to bail out the spendthrift. The demographics are just too discouraging.

Good News, Bad News

Little thought has yet been given to the idea that Americans must also invest more effectively. Survey the popular financial press or electronic media, and you will get the distinct impression that everything is just peachy. Investors are making great long-term decisions for themselves, and Wall Street is handing out sage advice. With just one more list of mutual funds that never lose from *Money* magazine, everything will turn out great!

Of course, the truth is not so comforting. Investors have been carefully trained and continuously conditioned to address the problem in the wrong way. While it's not exactly an Oliver Stone–type thing, there is a loose conspiracy to keep investors in the dark. Certainly, all the players never gather in a smoke-filled room to plot against investors. They don't need to. Apathy, greed, and ignorance all work quite naturally to keep investors locked in their mind-set. Almost all the players have an agenda adverse to the best interest of the investors. Wall Street wants investors to keep on buying expensive and profitable (for the house) proprietary products. The media is out to sell magazines, newspapers, or airtime; any useful information they might pass on in the process is almost an accidental byproduct. Fund companies and managers naturally resist the idea that they are not likely to add value through their vaunted skills in either market timing or individual stock selection.

So individual investors are being systematically sucked dry without being made aware of their viable alternatives. Like lambs being led off to slaughter, they innocently place their faith and future in exactly the wrong hands. As you can imagine, the social, political, and economic cost to America is enormous.

Lost in a sea of misinformation, investors float and drift hither and yon, reaping poor results. Using either no strategy or a fatally flawed approach, the overwhelming majority of investors place their meager and hard-earned savings in the wrong markets and then fail to even come close to a market return.

There Is Good News

However, all is far from lost. There has been a revolution on Wall Street. Investors need no longer submit to the tender mercies of Wall Street's barons. It's ironic, but investors already have available all the tools to turn the situation around. They just don't know it yet. Most large institutions have embraced the new colors, but the benefits have yet to filter down to the masses.

Ours has been a bloodless revolution, although we may expect some howling and rear-guard skirmishes from the barons. But the cost is small. First, investors must abandon their preconceived notions. Then they must take and use the gifts that modern finance has given to them.

ACTION ON SEVERAL FRONTS

New economic and financial theories have totally changed the investor's paradigm. No-load mutual funds have appeared with just the right building blocks to execute the improved strategies. Deregulation has added new institutions and discount brokerages with dramatically lowered costs. Modern communications has liberated investors from the requirement to physically inhabit Wall Street.

New technology places sophisticated and powerful management tools on the investor's desktop. A new breed of fee-only investment advisor can utilize all of these resources to deliver economical, unbiased, professional advice to the investor's doorstep.

Before investors can act effectively, they must transcend their misconceptions and vanquish the conventional wisdom. Until they purge a lifetime of accumulated misinformation from their heads, there isn't going to be room in there for anything worthwhile.

Academic theory and institutional experience have a lot to tell us, most especially that investing is a multidimensional process. For starters, investors must consider risk, return, time horizon, and correlation before they can construct an appropriate investment allocation plan for themselves.

RETURN ON INVESTMENT

Only equities offer investors a real rate of return sufficient to meet their reasonable long-term goals. With a little examination, most investors will conclude that fixed income and savings-type asset classes may be nothing more than a safe way to lose money, because their after-tax, inflation-adjusted return may be negative.

RISK

Risk is the only reason that every investor wouldn't prefer equities for their long-term investments. One of the most appropriate ways to measure risk is to use the variation around an expected rate of return. Higher variation is generally associated with higher returns in the investment world. Investment professionals often measure volatility using standard deviation.

Risk can never be avoided. For long-term investors, failure to assume reasonable risk may guarantee that they will never achieve reasonable financial objectives. In other words, the biggest risk may be being out of the market.

Many investors have an exaggerated fear of risk and may believe that risk equates to a probable total loss of principal. This misunderstanding may prevent them from making rational choices for their accumulation needs. Of course, investment risk is only short-term variation. Fortunately for investors, market risk falls over time. So risky assets may be very appropriate for even very conservative investors with a long-term time horizon.

Diversification is the primary investor protection. Default or business failure risk is almost a nonissue in a properly diversified portfolio. It is just about the only free lunch available in the investment business. Contrary to popular conception, diversification does not reduce expected return, only the variability of that return. Failure to diversify properly is an unforgivable investment mistake. Viewed from a slightly different perspective, the market never rewards investors for taking risks that could be diversified away.

CORRELATION

Some types of diversification are better for investors than others. Harry Markowitz demonstrated that by combining risky assets that do not move in lockstep as the market goes through its cycle, risk at the portfolio level can be reduced below the average of its parts. This observation made in 1952 led to entirely different and more rational approaches to investment management. Markowitz's work was the basis for Modern Portfolio Theory (MPT). Almost forty years later he was rewarded with the Nobel prize in economics. MPT revolutionized the way we think about investing.

By examining each investment for its contribution to the portfolio rather than just for its individual risk and reward, investors can fashion portfolios that fall above the traditional risk-reward line. That is to say, within limits, and over longer periods, MPT can increase rates of return and reduce risk at the same time.

TIME HORIZON

Investors cannot design an appropriate plan for themselves without understanding their time horizon. Risky assets are inappropriate for short time horizons. An investor that finds himself forced to sell a variable asset at a loss to cover a known or foreseeable commitment has committed a major blunder. On the other hand, because risk decreases with longer time horizons, and because risky assets carry an expected rate of return sufficient to realize realistic financial goals, investors should pack in risky assets as their time horizon increases.

Time horizon has little to do with an investor's age. Rather it should be measured until the expected liquidation of the investment. The concept that older investors must necessarily have lower risk tolerance is a diabolical idea that must be stamped out. In particular, retirement time horizon must be measured at least to the life expectancy of the investor. Only a simpleton believes along with *The Wall Street Journal* that investors can determine the appropriate percentage weighting of stocks in their portfolio by subtracting their age from one hundred. This is a surefire prescription for eating dog food in advanced age.

EFFICIENT MARKETS

Embedded into MPT is the concept that markets are reasonably efficient. Investors hate risk and so will demand higher rates of return to compensate them for risky assets. Stock prices are driven down for risky assets until the expected rate of return provides the necessary return to buyers. Investors will demand a rate of return that equals a risk-free rate of return, plus a market risk premium, plus a premium for the unique risk associated with the investment. Both buyers and sellers reach their opinion of the proper value of stock by studying all available data on the current condition and future prospects of the investment.

Knowledge and information travel so rapidly that neither buyers nor sellers will have an advantage. Few would argue that information is perfect, but prices end up being set efficiently enough that there may not be much point in trying to outguess the market. Too many hundreds of thousands of buyers and sellers have access to the same data in real time for any one of them consistently to realize an advantage.

Support for the efficient market theory comes from a variety of sources. In a groundbreaking study, Brinson, Hood, and Beebower found that in ninety-one of the largest pension plans in the country the overwhelming determinant of performance was the investment policy decision. In the study, the trio defined investment policy as the percentage of holdings in cash, bonds, and stocks. That simple decision accounted for 94 percent of the plan's performance, leaving less than 6 percent for both market timing and individual stock selection. Attempts to either market time or select individual stocks on average cost the plans. The obvious lesson is that investors should focus their attention on the factors that have the highest impact on return and avoid nonproductive and costly diversions with market timing and individual stock selection.

A study of mutual fund performance illustrates the futility of trying to beat the markets. On average funds underperform the market in which they operate by about their expense ratios. Four of five funds will fail to meet or beat an appropriate index. Beating an index for a particular time period tells us almost nothing about the prospects for a fund to outperform during a subsequent time period. While many institutions with vast resources have studied mutual fund performance, none have been able to reliably distinguish between luck and skill, or find a formula that will predict future above-average performance. Picking honor roll funds, funds with lots of stars, or funds heavily loaded with up arrows in down periods has proven to be a costly and self-defeating exercise.

There is an easy way and a hard way to do almost everything. Traditional attempts to add value through management are perhaps impossibly hard. Today, the weight of the evidence indicates that managers are unable to add value through either market timing or individual stock selection. In fact, attempts to actively manage equity portfolios have reliably increased both cost and risk (variability of returns) while lowering average returns.

HARNESS THE POWER OF ASSET CLASS INVESTING

However, there is an easier, lower-cost, lower-risk way to attack the problem. Asset class investing offers long-term investors superior returns and a much higher probability of achieving their goals. Simply put, investors can buy the whole market, or attractive portions of markets, through indexes. Rather than indulge in the fruitless exercise of attempting to beat the market, investors can harness or capture the incredible power of the world's markets. By combining these markets according to their risk, return, and correlation to each other (i.e., MPT), investors can form superior portfolios.

Asset class investing relies on neither market timing nor individual stock selection. It makes no predictions and requires no supernatural insight. For long-term success to be assured, disciplined investors need only assume that the value of the world's economy will continue to grow. This seems a reasonable bet for a capitalist to take, and 4,000 years of recorded history gives us some comfort.

Asset class investing has been embraced enthusiastically by institutions. In just a few years, about 37 percent of the institutional marketplace has adopted this approach. However, less than 2 percent of individuals utilize this no-nonsense, highly effective, low-cost, low-risk technique.

Investors who wish to increase their chance of success will find that no-load mutual funds offer almost the perfect building block for asset allocation investing. At their best, mutual funds offer instant wide diversification within a target market at very attractive low cost. However, with almost 11,000 nonmoney market mutual funds available in the United States alone, selection is a problem. As a rule of thumb, avoid any fund with either a front- or back-end load. Shoot for funds with very low expense ratios. Eliminate any funds that will not stay fully invested and that do not restrict themselves to a market or well-defined segment of a market (avoid style drift).

DEREGULATION: THE BEGINNING OF REVOLUTION

After May Day, Wall Street will never be the same again. The implications to investors are both positive and enormous. Previously, cost competition on Wall Street was illegal, and Wall Street provided the only game in town. Wall Street did what any good monopolist would do: It screwed the public with high prices and poor service.

Initially, deregulation resulted in higher costs for individual investors, but the arrival of new entrants tilted the balance of power in the individual's favor. Discount brokerages and no-load mutual funds slashed prices and improved service for investors of very modest means. But, when they combined forces in Schwab's mutual fund marketplace, small investors suddenly had all the tools to craft portfolios of remarkable sophistication without the help of Wall Street's robber barons. The runaway success of Schwab's program attracted more competition and will keep the pressure on the financial services industry for even further improvements. This is just another example of competition and capitalism delivering for you.

WALL STREET'S REAR-GUARD ACTION

Wall Street's barons can be expected to put on a spirited rear-guard defense of their valuable turf. No one is expecting their imminent demise. But they are clearly feeling the pressure to clean up their act, provide better service, and lower costs. They have an enormous disadvantage in both structure and cost. How much they can fiddle with a flawed compensation system remains to be seen. Conflicts of interest inherent in the commission-based sales system corrupt the entire process. The sales force is poorly trained to implement advanced strategies and the profit margins on those strategies are not sufficient to cover the tremendous built-in overhead of a giant brokerage firm. Thus far, no serious attempt has been made to pass on the cost savings generated by modern technology. Rather, Wall Street's bloated establishment has sopped up the savings. When the public wakes up, the Street is a natural candidate for vigorous downsizing.

Wall Street's big advantage in the retail market is marketing prowess. Generations of advertising have established a formidable brand name and identity. This position is constantly reinforced by enviable advertising and public relations budgets that ensure that Wall Street's barons are high in your consciousness when you consider investing. On the other hand, Wall Street's abuses have been so well-publicized, widely known, and shocking that few investors really like or trust the Street's used stock peddlers. As investors become more aware of their alternatives, they can be expected to defect in mass. Only market share loss is liable to get the Street's attention.

Voting with your feet will ensure the successful conclusion of the revolution. Doing what is in your own best interest will force reform.

A New Breed of Financial Advisor

Deregulation, along with advances in technology, has spawned an entire new breed of professional advisor. Fee-only advisors can now operate from any place with a plug-in phone line, bringing low-cost, independent, objective, professional advice of high quality and sophistication right to the investor's neighborhood. The clear separation of the sales or brokerage function from the advice function eliminates conflicts of interest and puts the advisor on the same side of the table with the client. Wall Street's abuses have been so frequent, and the advantages of fee-only compensation so obvious, that the demand for the new advisors has fueled explosive growth. While fee-only is a far better way to deliver service and advice, it doesn't guarantee competence or even honesty. Investors must still do their due diligence when selecting an advisor.

All that remains is for the individual investor to take advantage of the gifts he has been given. Everywhere the investor looks, things are better and growing better still. But the investor must look. The brokerage industry, the fund companies, and the media all have no deep commitment to providing fundamental education for the investor. Bad advice is far more profitable than good advice for nearly all the players. Wall Street's profits are simply not linked in any way to investor profits. As long as turnover is high, the Street wins either way. With almost 10,000 mutual funds clamoring for shelf space and public attention, hype is the order of the day in fund advertising. And, as long as Americans will buy dangerous drivel posing as serious financial commentary, the media will happily provide it.

America is a land of shocking financial illiteracy. Few investors have any kind of long-term plan at all; few recognize the dimensions of the problem facing them, yet most are supremely confident of their abilities. Most indulge in self-destructive financial behavior and lack even basic discipline. Predictably the results of this muddle are dismal. Projecting these results forward generates visions of almost unimaginable financial hardship as the boomers march off to retirement without the financial assets to sustain them.

JUST DO IT!

Most boomers still have time to avoid a financial disaster. But they had better begin to budget some serious investments along with their BMWs, hit the books, and do their financial homework. Investors must formulate meaningful investment plans, learn investment discipline, and reform their own behavior. This book and others on my reading list will give you the background you need to start. But start you must. Time is running out, and if you miss the benefits of the financial revolution you have nobody to blame but yourself.

Investors without the time, inclination, or resources to administer their investment program should consider delegating the duty to a qualified financial advisor. The vast majority of investors simply cannot afford the free advice they have been giving themselves. Investing is a serious business, and it is not likely that investors will stumble upon reasonably efficient portfolios by themselves.

MARX HAD IT WRONG

Marx just couldn't imagine that the workers could end up owning the system. Capitalism is the revolution of the twenty-first century and beyond. The market itself is the greatest wealth-generating mechanism the world has ever seen. A properly diversified portfolio of the world's equities will harness the tremendous power of the growth in the global economy for you. Riding that wave rather than fighting it is the ultimate investment strategy for the informed investor.

THE JONESES' RETIREMENT INCOME PORTFOLIO

YEAR-BY-YEAR RESULTS COMPARED TO THE LARGE COMPANY INDEX AND ONE-MONTH CDs

Returns Percentages, Jan 1975 – Dec 2002, Annual

	Large Co.	Port 5	CD
1975	37.21	33.42	6.63
1976	23.85	19.04	5.27
1977	-7.18	19.35	5.55
1978	6.57	22.07	8.14
1979	18.42	13.51	11.45
1980	32.41	20.35	13.59
1981	-4.91	8.7	17.27
1982	21.41	15.14	13.05
1983	22.51	23.46	9.37
1984	6.27	8.68	10.88
1985	32.17	31.16	8.3
1986	18.47	24.98	6.86
1987	5.23	16.55	6.57
1988	16.81	18.1	7.34
1989	31.49	16.99	9.17
1990	-3.17	-7.45	8.16
1991	30.12	18.34	5.97
1992	7.31	4.15	3.4
1993	9.61	17.71	2.66
1994	1.29	3.92	3.69
1995	37.08	15.56	5.38
1996	22.62	9.78	4.95
1997	33.07	7.52	5.36
1998	28.67	7.92	5.33
1999	20.78	13.7	4.94
2000	-9.25	1.38	6.19
2001	-12.07	1.36	4.24
2002	-22.23	-4.49	1.78

	Large Co.	Port. 5	CD
Ann. Ret.	13.24	13.19	7.14
Std. Deviation	16.47	9.77	3.52
Avg. Ret.	14.45	13.6	7.2

APPENDIX 2

THE JONESES' INCOME AND PORTFOLIO VALUES

Income From CDs: 1975-2002

RETURNS
Jan 1975 - Dec 2002
Annual

	Large Co.	Port 5	CD
1975	37.21	33.42	6.63
1976	23.85	19.04	5.27
1977	-7.18	19.35	5.55
1978	6.57	22.07	8.14
1979	18.42	13.51	11.45
1980	32.41	20.35	13.59
1981	-4.91	8.7	17.27
1982	21.41	15.14	13.05
1983	22.51	23.46	9.37
1984	6.27	8.68	10.88
1985	32.17	31.16	8.3
1986	18.47	24.98	6.86
1987	5.23	16.55	6.57
1988	16.81	18.1	7.34
1989	31.49	16.99	9.17
1990	-3.17	-7.45	8.16
1991	30.12	18.34	5.97
1992	7.31	4.15	3.4
1993	9.61	17.71	2.66
1994	1.29	3.92	3.69
1995	37.08	15.56	5.38
1996	22.62	9.78	4.95
1997	33.07	7.52	5.36
1998	28.67	7.92	5.33
1999	20.78	13.7	4.94
2000	-9.25	1.38	6.19
2001	-12.07	1.36	4.24
2002	-22.23	-4.49	1.78

	Large Co.	Port. 5	CD
Ann. Ret.	13.24	13.19	7.14
Std. Deviation	16.47	9.77	3.52
Avg. Ret.	14.45	13.6	7.2

Returns, Jan 1975–Dec 2002, Annual

	Port 5					CD	
	Return	Growth	Portfolio Value	Income (6%)	End Value	Return	Income
1975	33.42	$334,200.00	$1,334,200.00	$80,052.00	$1,254,148.00	6.63	$66,300.00
1976	19.04	$238,789.78	$1,492,937.78	$89,576.27	$1,403,361.51	5.27	$52,700.00
1977	19.35	$271,550.45	$1,674,911.97	$100,494.72	$1,574,417.25	5.55	$55,500.00
1978	22.07	$347,473.89	$1,921,891.13	$115,313.47	$1,806,577.67	8.14	$81,400.00
1979	13.51	$244,068.64	$2,050,646.31	$123,038.78	$1,927,607.53	11.45	$114,500.00
1980	20.35	$392,268.13	$2,319,875.66	$139,192.54	$2,180,683.12	13.59	$135,900.00
1981	8.7	$189,719.43	$2,370,402.55	$142,224.15	$2,228,178.40	17.27	$172,700.00
1982	15.14	$337,346.21	$2,565,524.61	$153,931.48	$2,411,593.13	13.05	$130,500.00
1983	23.46	$565,759.75	$2,977,352.88	$178,641.17	$2,798,711.71	9.37	$93,700.00
1984	8.68	$242,928.18	$3,041,639.89	$182,498.39	$2,859,141.49	10.88	$108,800.00
1985	31.16	$890,908.49	$3,750,049.98	$225,003.00	$3,525,046.98	8.3	$83,000.00
1986	24.98	$880,556.74	$4,405,603.72	$264,336.22	$4,141,267.50	6.86	$68,600.00
1987	16.55	$685,379.77	$4,826,647.27	$289,598.84	$4,537,048.43	6.57	$65,700.00
1988	18.1	$821,205.77	$5,358,254.20	$321,495.25	$5,036,758.95	7.34	$73,400.00
1989	16.99	$855,745.34	$5,892,504.29	$353,550.26	$5,538,954.03	9.17	$91,700.00
1990	-7.45	($412,652.08)	$5,126,301.96	$307,578.12	$4,818,723.84	8.16	$81,600.00
1991	18.34	$883,753.95	$5,702,477.79	$342,148.67	$5,360,329.13	5.97	$59,700.00
1992	4.15	$222,453.66	$5,582,782.78	$334,966.97	$5,247,815.82	3.4	$34,000.00
1993	17.71	$929,388.18	$6,177,204.00	$370,632.24	$5,806,571.76	2.66	$26,600.00
1994	3.92	$227,617.61	$6,034,189.37	$362,051.36	$5,672,138.01	3.69	$36,900.00
1995	15.56	$882,584.67	$6,554,722.68	$393,283.36	$6,161,439.32	5.38	$53,800.00
1996	9.78	$602,588.77	$6,764,028.09	$405,841.69	$6,358,186.40	4.95	$49,500.00
1997	7.52	$478,135.62	$6,836,322.02	$410,179.32	$6,426,142.70	5.36	$53,600.00
1998	7.92	$508,950.50	$6,935,093.20	$416,105.59	$6,518,987.61	5.33	$53,300.00
1999	13.7	$893,101.30	$7,412,088.91	$444,725.33	$6,967,363.58	4.94	$49,400.00
2000	1.38	$96,149.62	$7,063,513.19	$423,810.79	$6,639,702.40	6.19	$61,900.00
2001	1.36	$90,299.95	$6,730,002.35	$403,800.14	$6,326,202.21	4.24	$42,400.00
2002	-4.49	($284,046.48)	$6,042,155.73	$362,529.34	$5,679,626.39	1.78	$17,800.00
Total Income				$7,736,599.46	$5,679,626.39		$2,014,900.00

	Port 5	CD
Ann. Ret.	13.19	7.14
Std. Deviation	9.77	3.52
Avg. Ret.	13.6	7.2

ADJUSTING THE PORTFOLIO FOR INDIVIDUAL PREFERENCES

ANNUAL RETURNS AND SUMMARY DATA: 1975–2002

Returns, Jan 1975-Dec 2002, Annual.

	100/0	80/20	60/40	40/60	20/80	0/100
1975	51.58	42.75	33.91	25.08	16.24	7.41
1976	26.17	22.2	18.23	14.26	10.29	6.32
1977	26.38	22.1	17.82	13.54	9.26	4.98
1978	32.66	27.4	22.13	16.86	11.6	6.33
1979	15.25	14.07	12.9	11.72	10.54	9.37
1980	27.56	24.05	20.53	17.02	13.5	9.99
1981	4.9	6.82	8.75	10.68	12.61	14.53
1982	13.55	14.3	15.04	15.79	16.54	17.28
1983	33.41	28.51	23.62	18.72	13.82	8.92
1984	6.12	7.45	8.78	10.11	11.45	12.78
1985	44.73	37.87	31.02	24.16	17.31	10.45
1986	35.12	29.73	24.33	18.94	13.55	8.15
1987	21.62	18.45	15.28	12.1	8.93	5.76
1988	26.56	22.46	18.37	14.28	10.19	6.1
1989	21.94	19.53	17.12	14.72	12.31	9.91
1990	-17.55	-12.25	-6.95	-1.65	3.65	8.94
1991	24.09	21.02	17.95	14.87	11.8	8.73
1992	2.66	3.07	3.49	3.9	4.32	4.74
1993	27.13	22.44	17.75	13.06	8.37	3.68
1994	5.01	4.51	4	3.5	2.99	2.48
1995	19.93	17.53	15.13	12.73	10.32	7.92
1996	12.7	11.26	9.82	8.38	6.93	5.49
1997	6.91	6.72	6.52	6.33	6.13	5.93
1998	9.24	8.58	7.91	7.24	6.58	5.91
1999	19.88	16.71	13.54	10.38	7.21	4.04
2000	-1.45	0.3	2.06	3.82	5.58	7.33
2001	-3.27	-1.16	0.95	3.06	5.17	7.28
2002	-9.86	-7.21	-4.56	-1.91	0.74	3.39

DIMENSIONAL FUND ADVISORS INC.

FOR STANDARDIZED DATA CONFORMING TO SEC GUIDELINES SEE STANDARDIZED CHART.

APPENDIX 4

SAMPLE INVESTMENT POLICY STATEMENT

BALANCED PORTFOLIO

Registered Investment Advisor

3250 Mary Street, Suite 207
Coconut Grove, FL 33133
(305) 443-3339 / (800) 508-8500
Fax (305) 443-3064
E-mail: frank@InvestorSolutions.com
www.InvestorSolutions.com

INVESTMENT POLICY DISCUSSION

Prepared by Investor Solutions, Inc., Registered Investment Advisor

WHAT IS AN INVESTMENT POLICY?

An investment policy outlines and prescribes a prudent and acceptable investment philosophy and sets out the investment management procedures and long-term goals for the investor.

THE NEED FOR A WRITTEN POLICY

Requirements to which company retirement plans were subject originally created the need for written investment policies, as described below. We have found the process so useful for companies that we have expanded the concept and now make use of written investment policies for all investment management clients, including individuals.

With the enactment of ERISA in 1974, plan fiduciaries became liable for breaches in prudence and diversification standards. ERISA 402(b)(1) states, "Every employee benefit plan shall provide a procedure for establishing and carrying out a funding policy and method consistent with the objectives of the plan and requirements of this title."

A written investment policy allows our clients, whether they be individual or plan fiduciaries, to clearly establish the prudence and diversification standards which they want the investment process to maintain. Plan sponsors must develop a written policy whether they take an active role in the investment of pension assets, delegate the task to outside investment managers, or provide the participants with the right to direct their own accounts. Likewise for individuals. The net effect of the written policy is to increase the likelihood that the plan will be able to meet the financial needs of their investor and, if applicable, the plan beneficiaries through the development of specific objectives.

INVESTMENT MANAGER PERFORMANCE EVALUATION

Measuring the time-weighted return is not enough; the risk of each investment portfolio should also be considered. A portfolio that slightly underperforms the S&P 500 but carries only half the overall risk is superior on a risk-adjusted basis to a portfolio that slightly outperforms the S&P 500 but carries a full amount of market risk. Deciding when to replace a portfolio manager is often subjective as much as objective. Just because a manager had a down year or two is not a valid reason for replacement. This document lays out the procedures to be followed in order to create a system for making such decisions.

INTRODUCTION

The purpose of this Investment Policy Statement (IPS) is to establish a clear understanding between you ("Investor") and **Investor Solutions, Inc.**, Registered Investment Advisor ("Advisor") as to the investment objectives and policies applicable to the Investor's investment portfolio. This Investment Policy Statement will:

- Establish reasonable expectations, objectives, and guidelines in the investment of the Portfolio's assets.

- Set forth an investment structure detailing permitted asset classes and expected allocation among asset classes.

- Encourage effective communication between Registered Investment Advisor and the Investor.

- Create the framework for a well-diversified asset mix that can be expected to generate acceptable long-term returns at a level of risk suitable to the Investor.

This IPS is not a contract. This IPS is intended to be a summary of an investment philosophy that provides guidance for the Investor and **Investor Solutions, Inc.**, Registered Investment Advisor.

OVERVIEW OF THE CURRENT SITUATION

Investor has sought the assistance of **Investor Solutions, Inc.**, Registered Investment Advisor for the management of his investment accounts.

INVESTMENT OBJECTIVE: BALANCED

Investor's investment objective is **Balanced**. This objective is appropriate for investors:

- With a long-term time horizon, and/or

- Who are comfortable with some market risk, but desire a portfolio with substantially reduced volatility than the S&P 500, and/or

- Who can tolerate only occasional and modest short-term losses in their portfolio, and/or

- Who anticipate making substantial lump sum withdrawals (10–40% of total portfolio) within five years, and/or

- Who currently or shortly will rely on their investment income for most or all of their needs, and/or

- Require a liberal income (in excess of 6% per year), and/or

■ Would like both their income and capital to continue to grow to hedge inflation.

The investment-specific objectives for these assets shall be to achieve an average annual rate of return of the Consumer Price Index plus 5% for the aggregate investments under this Investment Policy Statement evaluated over a period of at least five years.

TIME HORIZON

Investor has a long-term investment horizon, may have need for current income, and may expect to take distributions for the foreseeable future. He is willing and financially able to tolerate substantial short-term fluctuations in the value of his account in return for higher than average investment returns.

For the purposes of planning, the time horizon for investments is to be in excess of ten years. Capital values do fluctuate over shorter periods, and the Investor should recognize that the possibility of capital loss does exist. However, historical asset class return data suggest that the risk of principal loss over a holding period of at least three to five years can be minimized with the long-term investment mix employed under this IPS.

RISK TOLERANCE

The Investor views himself as a below-average risk taker with regard to these investment assets. At the same time, because the Investor recognizes that seeking higher returns involves higher volatility, the Investor has indicated a willingness to tolerate occasional modest declines in the value of his portfolio.

The Portfolio will be managed in a manner that seeks to minimize principal fluctuations over the established horizon and is consistent with the stated objectives. Financial research has demonstrated that risk is best minimized by holding assets over time and through diversification of assets, including international investments.

ECONOMIC OUTLOOK

The Advisor is modestly positive about the global economy over the longer term, but does not rely on economic forecasts. He believes inflation will persist, and poses a long-term threat to accumulated wealth.

ASSET ALLOCATION

Academic research suggests that the decision to allocate total assets among various asset classes will far outweigh security selection and other decisions in impact upon portfolio performance. After reviewing the long-term performance and risk characteristics of various asset classes and balancing the risks and rewards of market behavior, the following asset classes were selected to achieve the objectives of the Investor's Portfolio:

ASSET ALLOCATION

Asset Category		Target Allocation
Equity		
Domestic Equity		
Large Value		9%
Large		6%
Small Value		9%
Small		6%
	Subtotal	30.0%
Foreign Equity		
Int'l Large Value		7.5%
Int'l Large		6%
Int'l Small Value		7.5%
Int'l Small		6%
Emerging Markets		3%
	Subtotal	30.0%
Fixed Income		
Bond Funds		40.0%
	Total	**100.0%**

Balanced

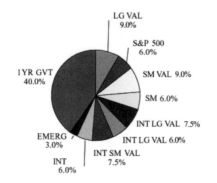

No guarantees can be given about future performance, and this IPS shall not be construed as offering such a guarantee. Asset class performance is estimated from unmanaged index data, and does not reflect management fees, transaction costs, or the effects of taxes. It should be recognized that the Portfolio may invest in both passively and actively managed mutual funds, that the actual weightings of these mutual funds can and will vary and, as a result, actual returns can be higher or lower than those presented below.

For illustrative purposes, *solely*, a portfolio of assets (exclusive of any funds which may be managed elsewhere) combined in a manner consistent with the normalized weightings suggested above and using standardized figures for each represented asset class based on historical norms and adjusted for today's environment suggests that 95% of the time, performance results can be reasonably projected as follows:

APPROXIMATED FUTURE RETURNS

For Investor's Allocation Based on Asset Class Categories

	One Year	Five Years	Ten Years	Twenty Years
Maximum for Period	30.20	19.43	17.01	15.33
Estimated Average	11.87	11.47	11.42	11.40
Minimum for Period	-4.73	3.86	6.00	7.55

All return calculations herein include price appreciation/depreciation, income distributions, and capital gains distributions. Calculations do not include the impact of management fees, transaction costs, or taxes. Above figures based on 95% statistical likelihood.

Assumptions Used to Calculate Expected Returns

Asset Class	Expected Return	Standard Deviation
Large Stocks (US) (S&P 500)	12.91%	16.28%
Small Stocks (US)	10.19%	26.27%
Large Stocks Value (US)	15.08%	16.17%
Small Stocks Value (US)	15.97%	21.97%
Foreign Stocks Large	14.08%	26.17%
Foreign Stocks Small	15.30%	30.05%
Foreign Stocks Value Large *	18.74%	21.55%
Foreign Stocks Small Value	15.30%	30.05%
Emerging Markets **	9.19%	32.63%
Bonds (US 1 Year Govt)	7.75%	3.29%

Portfolio geometric mean returns were projected on a pre-tax basis, and reflect historical data from 1/1/70 to 12/31/00.
* 1/1/75 to 12/31/00
** 1/1/85 to 12/31/00

REBALANCING PROCEDURES

From time to time, market conditions may cause the Portfolio's investment in various asset classes to vary from the established allocation. To remain consistent with the asset allocation guidelines established by this IPS, each asset class in which the Portfolio invests shall be reviewed on a quarterly basis by Investor Solutions, Inc., Registered Investment Advisor and rebalanced back to the recommended weighting if the actual weighting varies by 5% or more from the recommended weighting (e.g., from 10% to between 7% and 13% of total assets).

MARKET TIMING

No creditable research exists that would indicate that either risk can be reduced or returns increased through attempts to time the market. The Advisor believes that both risk and return are best controlled through diversification of assets and an appropriate asset allocation plan. Accordingly, Advisor expects to remain fully invested in the appropriate allocation plan at all times.

In the event that the Investor's risk tolerance, objectives, financial situation, or goals change, Investor will notify the Advisor in a timely manner so that the investment plan may be changed to reflect the new circumstances.

ADJUSTMENT IN THE TARGET ALLOCATION

The approved asset allocation displayed previously indicates both an initial target allocation and a range for each broad investment category. From time to time, basedon changing economic research and the various relative investment opportunities as perceived by **Investor Solutions, Inc.**, it may be desirable to make changes in the target allocation. **Investor Solutions, Inc.**, may determine such changes it believes will more effectively accomplish the Investor's objectives. However, no changes will result in the Investor being placed at higher risk than the agreed-upon plan. Subsequent investment will reflect the updated allocation, about which Investor Solutions, Inc., Registered Investment Advisor will keep you fully informed.

FREQUENCY OF REVIEW

The Investor recognizes that all investments go through cycles and therefore there will be periods of time in which the investment objectives are not met. Recognizing that no allocation is perfect all the time and that good years help to make up for bad ones, the Investor acknowledges the principle that asset allocation plans must be given an opportunity to make up for poor periods and that unless there are extenuating circumstances, patience will often prove appropriate when performance has been disappointing.

On an overall portfolio basis, the Investor establishes a goal of achieving the stated investment return objectives over a five-year period of time. A shorter time frame would contradict the principle that markets should generally be given the opportunity to overcome poor performance with subsequent excellent performance.

LIQUIDITY

The Investor has determined that liquidity may be required to meet his income and/or foreseeable distribution needs. Advisor will maintain sufficient short-term bonds and money market funds to satisfy these needs.

MARKETABILITY OF ASSETS

It is Advisor's policy that all funds shall be kept in fully liquid, readily marketable assets at all times. No unlisted securities, limited partnerships, restricted issues, or certificate of deposits with extended maturities shall be held.

DIVERSIFICATION

Investment of the funds shall be limited to no-load mutual funds, unit investment trusts, real estate investment trusts, no-load variable annuities, closed-end mutual funds and other diversified marketable securities in the following categories:

A. Permitted Investment Categories

1. Cash and cash equivalents, including money market funds

2. Bonds (corporate, U.S. government, or foreign high-quality or government)

3. Domestic Stocks

4. Foreign Stocks

5. Emerging Market Stocks

B. Excluded Categories for Investment

1. Options

2. Futures

3. Commodities contracts

4. Precious Metals

In addition, investments in limited partnerships and other vehicles which do not have readily available objective valuations shall not be permitted.

C. Minimum Number of Investment Categories

At all times there must be a minimum of five investment categories represented among the plan assets. There shall be no maximum limit to the number of categories.

SELECTION CRITERION FOR INVESTMENTS

Overview

The Advisor's policy requires that all investments be accomplished through pooled investment vehicles such as no-load mutual funds, REITS, closed-end funds, and unit investment trusts. The Advisor believes that this policy will result in the lowest-cost, lowest-risk, and most effective portfolios attainable for each selected asset class.

A. Passive Management

Where such funds exist, a majority of each asset class shall be comprised of institutional quality passively managed no-load mu tual funds. Such funds can be expected to accurately, economically, and effectively capture the market performance of the targeted allocation.

B. Active Management

Where utilized, actively managed mutual funds shall be chosen using the following criteria:

- The investment style and discipline of the proposed manager
- How well each proposed investment complements other assets in the portfolio
- Cost relative to other funds with like objectives, and investment styles.
- Diversification
- Consistency of investment style
- Past performance, considered relative to other investments having the same investment objective. Consideration shall be given to both performance rankings over various time frames and consistency of performance

C. Additional Investments, If Any

Any investment not conforming to the above criteria shall be individually approved by the Investor.

TAX POLICY

The Advisor's policy will be to minimize tax implications for clients subject to tax wherever possible. However, Advisor believes that maximum total after-tax performance is preferable to a tax avoidance policy.

DUTIES AND RESPONSIBILITIES

Investor Solutions, Inc., is a Registered Investment Advisor and shall act as the investment advisor to the Investor until the Investor decides otherwise.

Investor Solutions, Inc., shall be responsible for:

1. Designing and implementing an appropriate asset allocation plan tailored to the Investor's unique objectives, time horizon, and risk tolerance

2. Selection of an appropriate custodian to safeguard Investor's assets

3. Advising the Investor about selection and allocation of asset categories

4. Identifying specific assets and investment managers within each asset category

5. Monitoring the performance of all selected assets

6. Accomplishing changes to any of the above

7. Periodically reviewing the suitability of the asset allocation plan for the Investor

8. Being available to meet with the Investor at least twice each year, and being available at such other times within reason as the Investor requests

9. Preparing and presenting appropriate reports at least quarterly

Investor Solutions, Inc., will not take title or custody over any assets. All assets will reside in the custody of independent brokerage houses, and title remains with the investor.

Investor Solutions, Inc., accepts fiduciary responsibility for and will exercise discretionary control over all of the Investor's assets entrusted to its care.

THE INVESTOR

The Investor shall provide **Investor Solutions, Inc.,** with all relevant information on financial condition, net worth, and risk tolerances and shall notify **Investor Solutions, Inc.,** promptly of any changes to this information. The Investor should read and understand the information contained in the prospectus of each investment in the Portfolio.

ADOPTION

Adopted by the below signed Investor at _____ this _____ day of _____, 200__.

_____

_____

_____

RECOMMENDED BOOK LIST

Peter L. Bernstein. *Against the Gods: The Remarkable Story of Risk.* New York: John Wiley & Sons, 1998.

Peter L. Bernstein. *Capital Ideas: The Improbable Origins of Modern Wall Street.* New York: Free Press, 1993.

William J. Bernstein. *The Intelligent Asset Allocator: How to Build Your Portfolio to Maximize Returns and Minimize Risk.* New York: McGraw-Hill Professional Publishing, 2000.

John C. Bogle. *Bogle on Mutual Funds: New Perspectives for the Intelligent Investor.* New York: Dell, 1994.

John C. Bogle and Peter L. Bernstein. *Common Sense on Mutual Funds: New Imperatives for the Intelligent Investor.* New York: John Wiley & Sons, 2000.

Charles D. Ellis. *Winning the Loser's Game: Timeless Strategies for Successful Investing.* New York: McGraw-Hill Professional Publishing, 1998.

Roger C. Gibson. *Asset Allocation: Balancing Financial Risk.* New York: McGraw-Hill Professional Publishing, 2000.

Charles MacKay and Andrew Tobias. *Extraordinary Popular Delusions & the Madness of Crowds.* New York: Crown Publishing, 1995.

Burton Gordon Malkiel. *A Random Walk Down Wall Street.* New York: W.W. Norton & Company 2000.

Jeremy J. Siegel and Peter L. Bernstein. *Stocks for the Long Run.* New York: New York: McGraw-Hill Professional Publishing, 1998.

Larry E. Swedroe. *The Only Guide to a Winning Investment Strategy You'll Ever Need: Index Mutual Funds and Beyond—The Way Smart Money Invests Today.* New York: E.P. Dutton, 1998.

Larry E. Swedroe. *What Wall Street Doesn't Want You to Know: How You Can Build Real Wealth Investing in Index Funds.* New York: St. Martin's Press, 2000.

INDEX